GREAT WAR

WEST SUSSEX

Remembering 1914–18

EDITED BY

MARTIN HAYES AND EMMA WHITE

IN ASSOCIATION WITH

WEST SUSSEX COUNTY COUNCIL

Opposite: *'Sussex-by-the-Sea' poster by Charles Stadden,
supplied and on sale at West Sussex Record Office.*

First published 2014

The History Press
The Mill, Brimscombe Port
Stroud, Gloucestershire, GL5 2QG
www.thehistorypress.co.uk

British Library Cataloguing in Publication Data.
A catalogue record for this book is available from the British Library.

ISBN 978 0 7509 6065 6

Typesetting and origination by The History Press
Printed in Great Britain

SUSSEX BY THE SEA

Now is the time for marching
Now let your hearts be gay
Hark to the merry bugles
Sounding along our way
So let your voices ring, my boys,
And take the time from me
And I'll sing you a song, as we march along,
Of Sussex by the sea.

For we're the men from Sussex
Sussex by the sea,
We plough and sow and reap and mow,
And useful men are we:
And when you go from Sussex,
Whoever you may be,
You may tell them all that we stand or fall
For Sussex by the sea.

Oh, Sussex Sussex by the sea
Good old Sussex by the sea
You may tell them all that we stand or fall
For Sussex by the sea.

Light is the love of a soldier
Thats what the ladies say
Lightly he goes a wooing
Lightly he rides away,
In love and war, we always are
As fair as fair can be,
And a soldier boy is the ladies joy
In Sussex by the sea.

CHORUS ~ REFRAIN

Far o'er the seas we wander
Wide through the world we roam,
Far from the kind hearts yonder
Far from our dear old home,
But never shall we forget my boys
And true we'll every be
To the girls so kind that we left behind
In Sussex by the sea.

CHORUS ~ REFRAIN

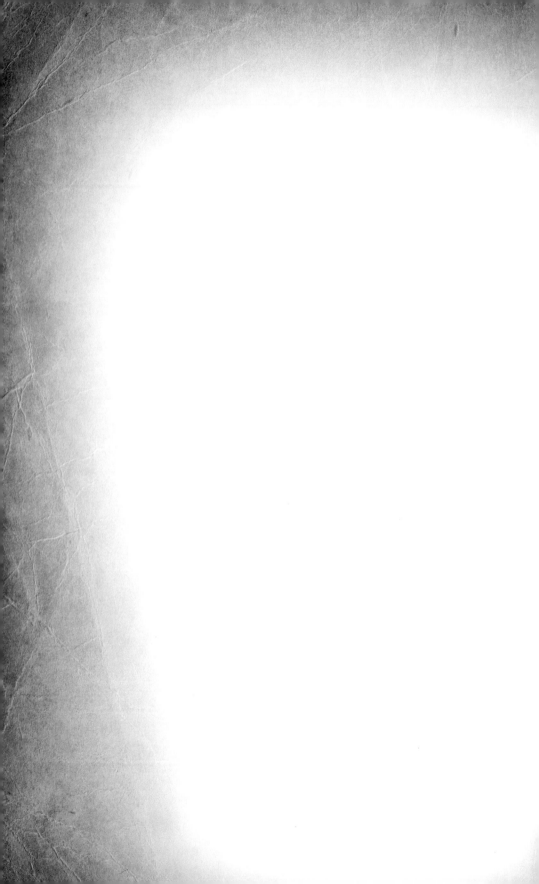

CONTENTS

PREFACE

The First World War was one of the most cataclysmic events of the twentieth century. A devastating conflict that claimed almost a million British lives, it also had profound political, social and economic consequences. The centenary of its outbreak in 1914 has produced much debate on how best to acknowledge the anniversary. Two issues are of overriding importance: our duty to remember and respect the service and self-sacrifice of people during those years, and that we ensure awareness and knowledge are preserved and cherished for the future.

We are proud in West Sussex to play our part in acknowledging the debt we owe to the generation of 1914–18 through an extensive programme of commemorative events across the county. At its centre is a wide-ranging project, generously supported by the Heritage Lottery Fund, which has seen the County Library Service and County Record Office working with over 150 heritage volunteers.

This book is an outcome of that project, drawing on the specialist expertise of a number of authors and also on the wealth of information brought to light by the digitisation and indexing of local newspapers. The result is a story never previously told in such breadth and detail, the story of a county's contribution to the war effort, both on the battlefield and on the home front. Our hope is that it will honour the memory of those who served at home and overseas and add to our understanding of the war as it affected the people of West Sussex.

Louise Goldsmith, Leader; Amanda Jupp, Chairman;
West Sussex County Council

FOREWORD

The centenary of the outbreak of the First World War is a good time to take stock of what we know about that dreadful conflict. In the case of Britain, in some respects we have a far more nuanced picture than we had only a few years ago. For example, the idea of widespread war fever in August 1914 has been debunked. Depending on age, gender, class, and where they lived, individuals' responses to the sudden coming of war varied greatly. Similarly, the notion of widespread disillusionment with the war has been challenged by historians. A more accurate picture is of the vast majority of the population on home front and battlefronts committed to fighting a total war, grimly determined to see it through to victory. Although this attitude was encouraged by a judicious mixture of social and political reform and propaganda, such external influences did not create it. Rather, it reinforced a core belief that there was something worse than the war, and that something was defeat at the hands of Germany.

While the national picture of the United Kingdom in the First World War is clear enough, what is all too often lacking is the local detail that gives texture to the portrait. That is why books like this one are so valuable. This series of case studies of West Sussex presents a fascinating and multifaceted view of an English county at war. Covering subjects as diverse as recruitment, billeting, the Royal Sussex Regiment on the battlefronts and the experience of civilians on the home front, this is exactly the sort of micro-history we need. The extensive use of local newspapers as a source is a strong feature of many of the contributions. Especially at the beginning of the war, the press suffered from little censorship and is thus an extremely important source.

This book is a significant piece in the mosaic which, when combined with the various other local histories, will give us a more balanced understanding of the British experience of the First World War. *Great War Britain: West Sussex* is a fine achievement and could stand as a model for collaborative local histories of this type. I congratulate everyone involved in it, and commend it warmly to a wide readership.

Professor Gary Sheffield
University of Wolverhampton

INTRODUCTION

The centenary of the outbreak of the First World War in 1914 has given us the opportunity nationally to commemorate one of the most devastating events in modern history and locally to assess its significance and impact for the people of the towns and villages of our county.

The cost in terms of casualties, the sheer scale of the sacrifice, was catastrophic, with over 16 million dead and 20 million wounded across the world. In Britain few communities escaped unscathed and most family histories today bear its mark. It was a conflict that had profound and long-lasting consequences, casting its shadow over world affairs in the interwar years, and yet responsible too for more positive developments in such diverse areas as women's rights, medicine and aviation. The war, through its very immensity, its embodiment of service and selflessness, its juxtaposition of horror and courage, has imbedded itself in our national identity, enshrined in the literature of the great writers of those years and ennobled by the unheralded deeds of men and women both on the battlefield and the home front. At this anniversary, it charges us with the privilege of honouring the lost generation of 1914–18 and the duty of ensuring that remembrance is respectfully and securely passed on to new generations.

This commemorative history seeks to outline the part played in the war by the people of West Sussex and by those who fought in the county regiment, the Royal Sussex Regiment. It is a record of service and sacrifice, both on the home front and overseas on the Western Front and in other theatres of war.

It is a most unusual publication. It is the product of over 180 West Sussex people (see Acknowledgements), one outcome of a multifaceted community-based project, inspired by the centenary and dedicated to the distinguished role of a regiment and to the heroic efforts of a county on the home front.

We are very grateful to the Heritage Lottery Fund, whose substantial grant enabled the project to happen. The magnificent response of locals to an appeal in 2012 led to 154 people coming forward. Most were trained as volunteers to index, research or digitise local documents, whilst others donated or lent material relating to the war. The results of their work were the capture of 19,000 pages of archival material, over 10,000 newspaper articles, references to 14,000 servicemen and others, and the writing of over 90 case studies of people and topics. The advice, support and training provided by archive staff at West Sussex Record Office, and the access they gave to newspapers and original documents, was another key factor in the success of the project.

Advances in digital technology, and the Heritage Lottery Fund grant, enabled the high-resolution scanning of ten local newspapers, 1914–1925, to produce searchable text on DVDs. These newspapers can be used now for all types of research, to find individual people, events and topics at the press of a button. The DVDs are held at various large town libraries and complete sets are at Crawley Library, Worthing Library and West Sussex Record Office. Over 200 key articles can also be viewed on the new website Great War West Sussex 1914–18 (www.westsussexpast.org.uk).

To write the book, twelve authors were recruited from academic, archive, public library, publishing and research backgrounds. The author biographies acknowledge that all are well qualified; some are leading experts in their fields, whilst all have a fascination with the First World War period and interest in military or social history.

The opportunity presented by digitising and indexing over 10,000 local newspaper articles is probably unique and enabled the authors to access a body of information which would have taken a single researcher several years to unearth. Much hitherto undiscovered material was revealed, which has enriched the story, particularly with personal accounts and local evidence. This, together with new research, substantially contributed to the compilation of this book.

The book covers the modern administrative county of West Sussex. This is a larger geographical area than was the case in 1914. Included are communities then in East Sussex but subsequently transferred to West Sussex on local government reorganisation in 1974; specifically Burgess Hill and villages to the south, East Grinstead and the area west to Crawley, Haywards Heath and places to the north, south and west.

The subject matter of the book broadly embraces both the military and the social aspects of the war as they affected the county. In a book of this size, for this particular series, it is not possible to cover every conceivable topic. For example, law and order, local societies, and transport systems, might all be subjects for future books. The war's impact on local authority education remains to be studied, whilst the important contribution of public schools has been largely covered by previous publications. We hope this book will encourage further research.

It has been estimated that over 50,000 Sussex men took part in the fighting, most signed up for the army, and many went into the Royal Sussex Regiment (see Chapter One). The many complex influences and pressures on those who volunteered, and later those conscripted, are fully explored. Their service overseas has been described in regimental histories but this book draws on source material previously untapped by historians, including uncatalogued regimental archives and articles and letters hidden away in county and town newspapers. This book pays tribute to their endurance, courage, sacrifice and suffering.

On the home front, the war effort in West Sussex has been researched in detail, producing remarkable stories and surprising outcomes. The county hosted many thousands of servicemen, initially billeted in local homes and later housed in huge military camps. Early in the conflict came blackouts to counter air raids, special constables were enrolled and most towns and villages formed civil guards (Volunteer Training Corps, a kind of 'Dad's Army') to protect themselves. West Sussex even saw a top secret project to counter the submarine threat. Initiatives such as 'make do and mend', recycling, rationing of food, coal, gas, petrol etc., and the Women's Land Army, all originated in the Great War.

Existing hospitals, numerous convalescent homes and non-medical buildings were transformed to care for several thousand wounded during the course of the war with surprising recovery rates. The scaling up of industry, the conversion of many local companies' production to arms etc. manufacture, and the mobilisation of women into the workforce, also happened in this period. Increased food production, helped by the largely rural county, was hugely important in staving off the malnutrition suffered in Germany. Local churches were a unifying force for the local population and played their part in maintaining morale. The success of local people in raising money (at least £1 million, worth £55 million today), arms production, comforts and goods supply and food production, were all key elements in supporting our victory.

The issues faced by the servicemen who returned, and the plight of bereaved families, are also explored. We learn how they coped, or not, with mental and physical disabilities, and how they suffered financial problems, reduced incomes, low pensions, unemployment and some surprising public hostility. The book describes how memorials emerged to those who did not return. At first temporary shrines appeared, followed by plaques and windows in churches, works of art, and the well-known, substantial stone memorials and buildings, all fitting tributes to those who laid down their lives.

This book is one aspect of our commemorative project. Throughout the centenary period, from 2014 to 2018, a substantial programme of events is planned to take place at public libraries, West Sussex Record Office in Chichester and in community venues, including advice panels and roadshows, talks, travelling displays and book promotions. The Great War is a milestone in world history. It is also a deeply moving subject. All involved in this project and this publication have been affected, but rewarded too, by the work they have done.

We hope that the main legacy of the project, the website and the book will be to prompt young people to gain a better understanding, and greater appreciation, of the suffering and sacrifice made by many thousands from our county, at home and abroad. Those people, particularly the 'lost generation' of young men and their unfortunate families, should never be forgotten.

Martin Hayes, County Local Studies Librarian, WSCC Library Service
Alan Readman, former County Archivist, West Sussex Record Office

AUTHORS

Dr Caroline Adams has a BA (Hons) in history from the University of York, an MA in landscape and regional history from the University of Leeds, and a PhD in sixteenth-century local history from the University of Chichester. She has a professional archives diploma from the University of Liverpool and is a member of the Archives and Records Association. Until July 2014, she was senior archivist at West Sussex Record Office, and is now a freelance archivist and historian. She is a co-author of collaborative publications with the library service, various journal articles, and has edited *Who Are You?: Family History Resources in West Sussex Record Office* and *Recipes from the Archives.*

Justin Burns has a BA (Hons) in economic and social history from the University of Bristol and an MSc with distinction in information and library studies from the University of Wales, Aberystwyth. He has a diploma in strategic management, awarded by the University of Chichester and is a member of the Chartered Institute of Personnel and Development. Justin is a chartered librarian, has worked for West Sussex County Council Library Service since 1997 and manages Worthing Library.

Martin Dale is a West Sussex-based local history researcher and writer with a particular interest in the military history of the county. He published his first book, exploring the names on Pulborough's various war memorials, in 2012 and more recently has written a case study on West Sussex coastal defences and Zeppelin raids for the West Sussex & the Great War project. Currently he is writing a series of books to act as a Roll of Honour during this First World War centenary period and researching a book on Second World War air raids on West Sussex.

Dr John Godfrey has degrees in politics, law, historical geography and military history. The research for his DPhil at the University of Sussex related to land ownership and farming on the South Downs between 1840 and 1940. He currently researches and writes on aspects of the social, landscape and military history of Sussex in the nineteenth and twentieth centuries. Dr Godfrey is chairman of the Sussex Heritage Trust, a trustee of the Weald and Downland Open Air Museum and the South Downs Society, and a deputy lieutenant of West Sussex. He is a member of the council of the National Trust and a visiting lecturer in the Department of War Studies, King's College London.

Prof. Keith Grieves is the author of *Sussex in the First World War* (Sussex Record Society, 2004) and has a research interest in the social and cultural history of Britain in the era of the First World War. His published articles on Sussex in the Great War include the recruitment of 'Lowther's Lambs', village war memorial debates, the development of village halls and the 4th Battalion, Royal Sussex Regiment at Gallipoli. He has degrees from Bognor Regis College of Education and the University of Manchester and taught at Worthing Sixth Form College before going to Kingston University in 1990 to teach history and education.

Martin Hayes has a BA (Hons) in history from Queen Mary College, University of London, and is a chartered librarian (DipLib). He has been county local studies librarian at West Sussex County Council Library Service since 1986 and has project managed seven Heritage Lottery-funded projects 2002–14. He is a co-author or editor of the following books: eighteen *Local History Mini-Guides to Research* (WSCC, 1995–2007), *Scientists and Inventors in West Sussex* (WSCC, 1996), *Sussex Seams: A Collection of Travel Writing* (Alan Sutton/CHIE) and *Crawley's History, a Guide for Residents and Researchers* (WSCC, 2008).

Martin Mace has a BSc (Hons) in geology from Royal Holloway, University of London. He has been involved in writing and publishing military history for more than twenty-five years. He began his career with local history, writing a book on the Second World War anti-invasion defences in West Sussex. He is the author or co-author of more than thirty-five books on subjects from the Battle of Hastings to the Special Operations Executive. Having launched *Britain at War* magazine, he has been its editor since the first issue in May 2007.

Alan Readman has a BA (Hons) in economic history from Sheffield University and a diploma in archive administration from University College London. He was an archivist at Lincolnshire Archives Office and West Sussex Record Office, retiring from the latter as county archivist in 2013. He is co-author of *D-Day West Sussex* (WSCC, 1994) and *Cinema West Sussex* (Phillimore, 1996). He has written and lectured widely on local and family history and on the Royal Sussex Regiment, whose archives he has catalogued in *The Royal Sussex Regiment: A Catalogue of Records* (WSCC, 1985).

Prof. Brian Short is emeritus professor of historical geography at the University of Sussex, where he lectured from 1974 until his retirement in 2009. Beginning with his PhD thesis on the agriculture of the High Weald of Sussex and Kent (1973), his research interests have remained focused on rural society and agriculture, primarily in the nineteenth and twentieth centuries. He is the author of over seventy publications, including many on the rural history of South East England. His forthcoming (November 2014) book *Battle of the Fields*, concerns the activities of the War Agricultural Committees in the Second World War.

Katherine Slay is on the staff at the West Sussex Record Office, where she works as part of the Collections Management Team, supporting access to archives. Her involvement in local history has included recording monumental inscriptions and war memorials in Chichester. Her listing of the 7,000+ names of the Great War Royal Sussex Regiment casualties in Chichester Cathedral was completed in 2001. She has also edited the diaries of her great-great-great-grandfather, a Bedfordshire Quaker, and is currently writing a life of her great-grandfather who died at Gallipoli in 1915. Her most recent publication is *Graylingwell War Hospital, 1915–1919* (2013).

Tim Stanton has a BA in history from Royal Holloway College, University of London, and an MA in information studies from the University of Brighton. He is a chartered librarian (MCLIP) and has worked as a librarian with West Sussex County Council Library Service since 2000. He has been an information librarian at Crawley Library since 2007. Tim was a co-author of *Crawley's History, a Guide for Residents and Researchers* (WSCC, 2008). He has been a military history researcher for some years and has delivered numerous local history talks on people and topics related to West Sussex and both world wars.

Emma White has a BA (Hons) in history from Queen Mary College, University of London, and is originally from Kent. She has worked previously in both Croydon and Bromley Borough Archives and has recently graduated with an MA in British First World War Studies at the University of Birmingham. Emma is currently the heritage project manager for West Sussex County Council Library Service, managing the West Sussex & the Great War project. She is studying for a PhD in the use of dogs in the First World War at the University of Chichester.

Acknowledgements

The authors and West Sussex County Council (WSCC) would like to thank most sincerely:

The Heritage Lottery Fund for funding the project which enabled this book to be researched.

Our project volunteers for indexing, research, digitisation, donations, loans, picture research and other tasks: Bob Adams, Richard Amery, Owen Atfield, Christine Ball, Ivan Ball, Jaqui Ball, John Barnes, Patricia Barns, Andy Bartram, Roger Bateman, Elizabeth Berry, Kathie Bignell, Lynda Booth, Terry Bousted, Sarah Brennan, Richard Bryant, Catherine Buller, Lesley Card, Norma Carter, Robert Carter, Christine Cawte, Diana Chatwin, Richard Clifton, Brenda Collins, Irene Colwell, John Commins, Peter Cox, Sheila Crighton, Martin Dale, Mike Dancy, Megan Davies, Christine Deadman, Graham Dewsall, Stephanie Druce, Monica Edmonds, Graham Edwards, Sandra Edwards, George Elliott, Ian Evans, Elizabeth Everett, Jade Ewers, Richard Feest, Tracy Fells, Henry Finch, Sue Fisher-Pascall, Hugh Fiske, Brenda Forrester, Dr Luc François, Maria Fryday, Kim Geall, Heather Gibbs, Peter Gibson, Andrew Gilbert, Sheila Glue, Judy Goodall, Ian Goodwin-Reeves, Janet Green, Wendy Greene, Reg Grigg, Rodney Gunner, Mandy Hall, Bernard Harrison, Christopher Harrison, John Henderson, Margaret Holloway, Caroline Holmes, Peter Holmes, Dr Jo Horwood, Nicky Hudson, Peter Jeffery, Pamela Johnson, Geoffrey Godden, Linda Kane, Ron Kerridge, Eleanor Kilby, Jean Kirk, Steve Lancaster, Graham Langridge, Leigh Lawson, Pamela Lee, Angela Levy, John Lewis, Malcolm Linfield, Helen Litten,

Chris Loader, Chloe Lodge, Alan Lygo-Baker, Pam Lyle, Nicola McDowell, Brian McLuskie, Marion McQuaide, Simon Machin, Sue Mackerell, Paul Mackerell, Deborah Malins, Sally Manning, Joanne Marychurch, Bill Matthews, Carolyn Mason, June Meachen, Peter Melody, Olive Miles, Ed Miller, Carolyn Mynott, Karen Nesbitt, Lauren Nightingale, Carole Paternoster, Jim Payne, Nigel Peake, Rosemary Pearson, Jennifer Penny, Stephen Porter, Rebecca Price, Tricia Priestly, Eddie Pullen, Stuart Pullen, Irene Read, Helen Richardson, Peter Ruffle, Pat Saunders, Dudley Sawer, Paul Schofield, Joshua Seaman, Victoria Seaman, Alan Seymour, Hilary Sherwin-Smith, Robin Sherwin-Smith, Sally Shire, Barry Smith, John Smith, Becky Sohatski, Ann Spalding, Keith Stacey, Richard Standing, Catherine Steeden, Carol Sullivan, Harold Taylor, Geraint Thomas, James Turner, Julie Wade, Anna Waghorn, Nick Ward, Bob Waters, Julia Westgate, Gerald White, Elizabeth Wickstead, Deborah Wigmore, Alan Wilcox, David Willard, Ivor Williams, Sue Williams, Vee Willis, Sarah Wilson, John Winch and Tim Worley.

All WSCC Library staff for their support, and particularly Val Blower, Louise Cowdrey, Jane Dore, Helen Lewis, Beverley Kinahan, Sue McMahon, Janet Peters, Geoffrey Redman, Sadie Rule, Rebecca Savill, Victoria Seaman, Lyndsey Power and Sue Worrall, who were project volunteers.

West Sussex Record Office searchroom staff for all their help: Alex Barford, formerly searchroom assistant there, for her enthusiasm and help in identifying source material; Clare Snoad and David Milnes for digitising images; Wendy Walker, county archivist, for permission to quote from and reproduce documents.

Colonel Robin McNish, of The Royal Sussex Regimental Association for reading and commenting on the final draft of the chapters on the Royal Sussex Regiment.

The Royal Sussex Regimental Association for permission to quote from and reproduce documents in the regimental archives deposited at West Sussex Record Office in Chichester.

The many people who have donated records to the regimental archives of the Royal Sussex Regiment, helping to create one of the best archive collections of a county regiment and an outstanding memorial to the service and sacrifice of the generation of 1914–18.

Mrs Margaret Gowler for permission to quote from and reproduce documents of Ralph Ellis deposited at West Sussex Record Office. Mrs Susan Whitley for permission to quote from and reproduce records of Reginald Whitley deposited at West Sussex Record Office.

Margi Blunden and Mrs Lucy Edgeley (on behalf of the Blunden Estate) for permission to quote from documents and published works of Edmund Blunden.

Elizabeth Bridges, Christ's Hospital School Archives and Museum, Horsham, for access to *The Blue*, October 1917, with extract quoted by kind permission of Christ's Hospital Foundation.

The following museums for their help and/or for permission to use illustrations: Arundel, Cuckfield, East Grinstead, Horsham, Imperial War Museum, Marlipins (Shoreham-by-Sea) and Steyning.

East Sussex Record Office (The Keep) for access to Chailey Heritage Craft School records.

Many other people who assisted by doing research, offering information, reading and commenting on text and helped in other ways, including: Prof. J.D.G. Dunn, Dr A.W. Foster, John Grehan, Sue Light (Scarletfinders military nursing website), Greg Slay and Simon Worrall.

ABBREVIATIONS

ASAEF	Air Service of the American Expeditionary Force
BE	Bleriot Experimental (aircraft)
BEF	British Expeditionary Force
CAEC	County Agricultural Executive Committee
CQMS	Company Quarter-Master Sergeant
CSM	Company Sergeant Major
cwt	hundredweight (112lbs or about 50kg)
DORA	Defence of the Realm Act
DSO	Distinguished Service Order
ESCC	East Sussex County Council
FPD	Food Controller and Food Production Department
GOC	General Officer Commanding
lb(s)	pound(s) in weight (about 453g)
NRF	National Relief Fund
NT	Norman Thompson (aircraft manufacturer)
POW	Prisoner of war
RD	Rural District
RDC	Rural District Council
RE	Reconnaissance Experiment series (aircraft)
RFC	Royal Flying Corps
RSM	Regimental Sergeant Major
RSPCA	Royal Society for the Prevention of Cruelty to Animals
RSR	Royal Sussex Regiment
SSFA	Soldiers' and Sailors' Families' Association
UD	Urban District
UDC	Urban District Council

VAD	Voluntary Aid Detachment
VPCNS	Vegetable Products Committee for Naval Supply
VTC	Volunteer Training Corps
VWO	Voluntary Work Organisations
WAAC	Women's Army Auxiliary Corps
WAC	War Agricultural Committee
WI	Women's Institute
WSCC	West Sussex County Council
WSCCLS	West Sussex County Council Library Service
WSRO	West Sussex Record Office
YMCA	Young Men's Christian Association

Notes on the currency in use 1914–18

Please note that, in the text, any £ amount in brackets, after a £ sum, denotes its modern value, based on an increase of x57 in the Retail Price Index from 1916 to 2012*.

d penny or pence (pre-1971 currency)
s shilling(s) (pre-1971 currency)
twelve pennies (12d) make one shilling (1s)
twenty shillings (20s) make one pound (£1)

*Measuring Worth website
www.measuringworth.com

Prelude
to War

Extract from the *Mid-Sussex Times*, three weeks after the declaration of war:

Everybody and everything so quiet, so placid! One could hardly realise … that over in the 'cockpit of Europe', not very many miles away, gigantic armies were fighting out tremendous issues, and that thousands of precious lives were being battered away by shot and shell. Here in the peaceful Sussex villages people were pursuing their ordinary vocations … Yet in these tranquil parishes one did see some signs and hear some talk of our nation – indeed our Empire – being at war. In the rural post offices, in the shop windows and on hoardings were the appeals to patriotic manhood. Join Kitchener's Army! Join The Territorials! Join The National Reserve! One heard of the many brave sons of the Southdown country who had been called up for service, of the nippy Boy Scouts who were emulating them by guarding the railways, of the Red Cross nurses who were making provision for wounded warriors, and of a generous public contributing cheerfully to relief funds. You cannot have a great war nowadays without its effects being felt in even the tiniest village and hamlet, and the people who can do their everyday work as if times were normal, who can keep cool in a great crisis, and who can 'just hope on and go forward' are a credit to any country.

And so war came to West Sussex. This is the story of how the people of our county responded to both the call to arms, through the Royal Sussex Regiment, and to the often underestimated vital role played by local people, those on the home front.

Post office,
West Hoathly,
c.1910. (WSCCLS,
PC007336)

Saddlescombe and
the Sussex Downs,
c.1910. (WSCCLS,
PC006214)

1

MOBILISATION AND RECRUITMENT

By Dr John Godfrey

The British Army in 1914

Historically, Britain relied on the Royal Navy to maintain the security of the country and to defend its overseas interests, with the support of a small standing army of volunteers. However, largely as the result of the reforms instituted by Richard Haldane, the Liberal Secretary of State for War from 1905 to 1912, by 1914 the country was better prepared than it would otherwise have been to participate in a land war on the continent of Europe. In the summer of 1914, the British Army consisted of three distinct elements: the Regular Army, the Territorial Force and the Reserves. The Regular Army comprised some 250,000 men, the majority of whom were recruited and organised in county-based infantry regiments, each containing two battalions of approximately 1,000 men. One of these battalions would normally be deployed overseas, principally on colonial duties, and the other would be at home, available for deployment, including to Ireland, and providing drafts to reinforce the battalion overseas.[1]

In Sussex, the 1st Battalion, Royal Sussex Regiment (RSR) was deployed in India in 1914 and throughout the First World War, while the 2nd Battalion was accommodated at various locations in Sussex and beyond, in barracks and at camp. On the latter, Hugh Miller, in his account of the experiences of the regiment on the Western Front, writes that:

Bell-tented camps, set out in immaculately straight lines on grassy, dry, rolling tracts of the English countryside provided pleasant living quarters during that summer of 1914. Purpose-built rifle ranges and assault courses taxed the skill and fitness of the men, as did the long and frequent route marches, but there was no enemy, no true battleground terrain and no in-coming shells and bullets.[2]

The Regular Army was supported by the Territorial Force of part-time soldiers who, while partly trained, were not available for immediate deployment and, crucially, were not required to serve overseas. The administration of the Territorial Force was in the hands of County Associations, led by local landowners and other notables, who were responsible for recruiting, training and equipping all of the Territorial units originating in a particular county or city. In Sussex, the president and chairman of the County Association was the Lord Lieutenant, the Duke of Norfolk, of Arundel Castle, who took a close interest in military matters generally and the organisation of the Territorial Force in particular: indeed, the Norfolk Commission (1904), which he chaired, led to the creation of the Territorial Force from the former auxiliary units.[3] The 4th and 5th Battalions, RSR, were the county Territorial units, the 4th Battalion mainly recruiting in West Sussex and the 5th Battalion in East Sussex. The legislation creating the Territorial Force also established the Special Reserve, which was composed of men with no previous military experience who made themselves available for service in the Regular Army, in the event of mobilisation.[4] In addition, men who had previously served in the Regular Army formed the General Reserve and were eligible to be recalled to the Colours in the event of a general mobilisation.

These elements (the Regular Army, the Territorial Army and the Reserves) formed the first two components of what Peter Simkins refers to as the 'four armies' that fought in the Great War, the others being Kitchener's 'New Armies' (which arose from the Secretary of State's successive calls for volunteers from August 1914 onwards) and the fourth 'army' of conscripts resulting from the introduction of compulsory military service in 1916.[5] Simkins writes that, 'As the result of these initiatives,

Britain's Army in the First World War became the largest in the nation's history. Between August 1914 and November 1918, 5,704,416 men passed through its ranks' and he describes this increase in the size of the army as, 'The product of a gigantic act of national improvisation which had considerable repercussions throughout British society'.[6] The rest of this chapter examines, principally through a close study of relevant reports in local newspapers, the nature of these repercussions in West Sussex.

The Mobilisation of the Regular Army, the Territorials and the Reserves

The immediate and pressing military task facing the British Government on the declaration of war with Germany on 4 August 1914 was to quickly mobilise and deploy to northern France a British Expeditionary Force (BEF) to support the Belgian and French armies in resisting the German advance towards Paris. Bruce Gudmundsson describes the process of mobilisation as:

> … an extraordinary smooth one. Within a week the lion's share of this gargantuan exercise in administration and logistics had been completed, and many elements of the Expeditionary Force were already embarked on the ships that would take them to the Continent. Soon thereafter the great task was complete, and the Special Reserve took up its principal wartime duty of training the men … needed to keep the Expeditionary Force up to strength.[7]

Members of the 2nd Battalion, RSR, embarked for France on 12 August 1914. They were engaged in the mobile campaigning which preceded the entrenchment of the opposing armies and fought with distinction at the Battle of the Marne and later at the First Battle of Ypres, earning for the Royal Sussex the epithet 'the Iron Regiment'.[8] The mobilisation of the Regular Army proceeded in Sussex in parallel with the 'embodiment' of the Territorial Force. In Worthing, Captain H.E. Matthews, head of H (Worthing) Company, 4th Battalion, RSR, was reported on 19 August as having appealed for former members of H Company

Territorials, probably the 4th Battalion, RSR, in South Street, Chichester, en route for the railway station and France; 5 August 1914. (WSCCLS, P000657)

under the age of 35 to re-join their unit.[9] Within a week of war being declared, Territorials in Chichester 'complied with the order to mobilise by assembling at the old depot in East Row, and at half past three they marched to the railway station, there to entrain for duty at Newhaven'. Their special train picked up the remainder of the 4th Battalion, including contingents from Bognor, Eastergate, Arundel and Littlehampton en route, and 'on arrival at Newhaven, some of the men were quartered in the workhouse'.[10] Keith Grieves refers to 'the well-defined sense of territoriality' which characterised both the 4th Battalion, based in Horsham, and the 5th (Cinque Ports) Battalion, which had its headquarters in Hastings and relished its historic title.[11]

Reservists mustered in Chichester, Arundel and Littlehampton.

All day Wednesday Chichester was the scene of great animation. By every train there arrived in the city parties of Reservists of the Royal Sussex Regiment and many others came by road. In groups they made their way to the Barracks, and there they received their kit, preparatory to leaving to join the 2nd Battalion at Woking.[12]

Arundel Reservists assembled at the Town Hall in Maltravers Street. 'Major Maxwell, their commander, expressed his full satisfaction with the apparent enthusiasm and fitness of the men.'[13] The following day, seventy Littlehampton Reservists assembled at the drill hall. The *Littlehampton Observer* commented that, 'The men are keen on serving their country … and, to judge from the records and appearance of many of them, they would prove quite good enough to keep the Germans under'.[14]

With the mobilisation of the Regular Army, the Territorials and the Reserves in Sussex and the dispatch of a contingent of the RSR with the BEF to France, the first phase of the mobilisation of the army in Sussex was completed within weeks of the declaration of war. Attention now turned, nationally and locally, to the need to rapidly expand the number of recruits. This task fell to the new Secretary of State for War, Lord Kitchener of Khartoum, who took formal charge of the War Office on 6 August 1914 and immediately unveiled his radical expansion plans.

Kitchener's 'New Armies' in Sussex

Gudmundsson recounts that, 'The next morning, he [Kitchener] made public, in the form of announcements to the press, newspaper advertisements and posters, his intention to expand the Regular Army by 100,000 men, each of whom would be enlisted 'for a period of three years or until the war is concluded'.[15] The response by the authorities in Sussex was to form a new service battalion of the county regiment, which was to become the 7th (Service) Battalion, RSR. The national recruitment campaign, which featured the famous image of Kitchener, with bristling moustache and pointing finger, was complemented locally by the publication, in poster form and in local newspapers, of 'A Call to Arms!!', telling men that 'Your King and your Country need you urgently' and that a new regular battalion was being added to the county regiment. The poster challenged readers: 'Will you come forward or must recruits be obtained outside the County? We are confident you will help to uphold the honor [sic] of the County of Sussex.'

A CALL TO ARMS!!

KITCHENER'S ARMY.

Your King and Country need you urgently.

A NEW REGULAR BATTALION

is being added to your County Regiment,

CALLED THE

7TH SPECIAL SERVICE BATTALION

ROYAL SUSSEX REGIMENT,

Forming part of the 35th Brigade of Lord Kitchener's 2nd Army.

Will you Come Forward

Or must Recruits be obtained outside the County?

We are confident you will help to uphold the honor of the County of Sussex.

Men are urgently required to enlist in the above regular Battalion.

Men between the ages of 19 & 30 can enlist for the duration of the war.

Men must be medically fit; be 5ft. 3in. high and upwards; have chest measurement of 34 inches.

Ex Regular N.C.O's and men, and men belonging to the National Reserve can enlist for the above Battalion; conditions on application.

Married men or widowers with children will be accepted, and will draw separation allowances.

APPLY AT ONCE TO THE NEAREST RECRUITING OFFICE.

Owners of cars will greatly assist by driving intending recruits direct to the nearest recruiting office or to the Barracks at Chichester, where the above Battalion is being formed.

God Save the King.

RECRUITING OFFICES:

CHICHESTER—The Barracks.	LEWES—Drill Hall.	TUNBRIDGE WELLS—8, Neville Street.
HORSHAM—Drill Hall.	HAYWARDS HEATH—Drill Hall.	BRIGHTON—21, Windsor Road; 8, Coombs Terrace, Lewes Road.
WORTHING—Drill Hall.	HURSTPIERPOINT—Drill Hall.	HOVE—20, Church Road,
UCKFIELD—Drill Hall.	BEXHILL—Drill Hall.	HASTINGS –33, Brook Street.
RYE—Drill Hall.	BATTLE—Drill Hall.	EASTBOURNE—Ordnance Yard.
PETWORTH—Drill Hall.	CUCKFIELD—Drill Hall.	BOGNOR—Hambledon Chambers.
ARUNDEL—Drill Hall.	LITTLEHAMPTON—41, Gloucester Place	

Printed by T. G. Willis & Co., Printers & Stationers, 21, East Street, Chichester.

Recruiting poster, 7th Battalion, R.S.R. (WSRO, RSR MS 7/5)

Men aged 19–30 were invited to enlist for the duration of the war and the addresses were given of ten recruiting offices in barracks and drill halls across West Sussex.[16]

Local newspapers across the county featured the recruitment campaign and, in editorial coverage, expressed strong support for the new initiative. On 19 August 1914, the *Chichester Observer* reported that:

> Upwards of 1000 men are required for the [new] Battalion Royal Sussex Regiment (Kitchener's Army), and up to date only 120 men have been enlisted for it. Sussex men, aged 19 to 30 are urged to enlist. Recruits will be armed, clothed and equipped at the Barracks, Chichester, and will receive preliminary training ... If the war continues, this new Regiment will have every chance of seeing some fighting... The Duke of Norfolk, as Lord Lieutenant, has sent an appeal to the Mayor of Chichester for every effort to be made to secure recruits for Kitchener's Army.[17]

7th Battalion, RSR, at Chichester Station. (WSRO, RSR 16/15)

On 26 August, the *Littlehampton Observer* reported that an appeal had been made by Major W.L. Osborn, later to be colonel of the RSR, for Sussex men to come forward without delay to join the 7th Battalion.[18]

The local newspapers began publishing the numbers of men who had signed up in the various towns and villages, encouraging competition between them, applauding those who were doing well and highlighting others where the numbers were considered to be disappointing. Thus, Worthing was congratulated on producing 365 recruits by mid-August,[19] while the *Littlehampton Observer* reported that, 'The response to Lord Kitchener's appeal has not been so good in the country as in town districts, on account of the harvest, but this is now nearing completion'.[20] A feature of the recruitment campaign was the opportunity presented to men who lived or worked in the same place to volunteer together. Thus, on 2 September, the *Chichester Observer* reported that:

> Early in the morning about 30 employees from Messrs. Shippams' factory went to the barracks in a body. The firm had made them a generous offer of an allowance of 10s a week all the time they remained on active service. Most of them joined the 7th Battalion, which is being trained at Colchester.[21]

In all, some 100 men left Shippams to join the forces during the course of the war and their progress was carefully followed by the chairman, Mr Ernest Shippam. The men's letters to him are preserved in the West Sussex Record Office (WSRO)[22] and provide valuable evidence of their experiences of war, the strength they drew from their contact with workmates at the front, and their hopes of eventually resuming 'normal' life at home.[23]

The appeal for recruits was successful: the *West Sussex Gazette* reported on 10 September that 2,896 men had enlisted so far at the county depot in Chichester, 1,850 of whom had enlisted in county battalions. The 7th Battalion was full on the previous Friday and it had been decided to form an 8th and a 9th Battalion: there were enough men available to fill the 8th Battalion and a good start had been made on the 9th.[24] The success of the recruitment campaign was influenced by a series of well-attended public meetings held across West Sussex. They were organised by local honorary recruiting officers and patronised by notable citizens. In the towns, the leading figures were usually the majors or chairmen of Urban District Councils (UDCs), and in rural areas, the traditional landed gentry tended to take the lead, encouraged by the Lord Lieutenant and other members of the West Sussex-based aristocracy, such as the Duke of Richmond and Lord Leconfield. Often, there was a guest speaker, perhaps a Member of Parliament, not necessarily connected with West Sussex, or a military figure. Such meetings were reported at Worthing,[25] Littlehampton,[26] Storrington,[27] Chichester,[28] Bognor,[29] Cowfold,[30] Burgess Hill,[31] Horsham,[32] Faygate,[33] Pulborough,[34] East Grinstead,[35] and Crawley.[36] The themes developed by the speakers at these meetings included: Germany is the aggressor; might is not right; poor France and Belgium; German atrocities; it could happen here; the country is united; the Empire is behind us; our cause is just; England expects. Women were urged to shun 'shirkers' and 'idlers' who failed to volunteer, with Captain Matthews telling a Worthing audience that, 'He would like to hear the expression more freely used "No gun, no girl!".'[37]

Sergeant William Teunon and Lillian Lawson, Littlehampton, 1915. (Original owned by Leigh Lawson; WSCCLS, L001177)

The meetings were routinely combined with parades, flags, bands and the singing of patriotic songs, concluding with the National Anthem.

While all this activity was going on in Sussex, and throughout the country, Kitchener decided to launch a campaign to recruit another 100,000 men for the Regular Army. An announcement to this effect was made in the third week of August 1914. In Sussex, the decision was made to create three further battalions of the county regiment, which became the 11th, 12th and 13th Battalions. While the first round of recruiting had been directed by influential landowners, such as the Duke of Norfolk, the second wave was organised by a relative newcomer to the county, Colonel Claude Lowther, the owner of Herstmonceux Castle in East Sussex. Ably assisted by Colonel Harman Grisewood

of Bognor and the Hon. Neville Lytton of Crawley Down, Lowther set about creating a new fighting unit which became known collectively as the Southdown Brigade, or more familiarly, 'Lowther's Lambs', reflecting the Southdown name and the fact that the new battalions acquired a lamb called Peter as their brigade mascot. The brigade also had its own marching song, 'Lowther's Own', which was sung at a patriotic smoking concert at the Lambs Hotel, Eastbourne.[38]

The *West Sussex Gazette* reported on 10 September 1914 that:

> Lord Kitchener has authorised Mr. Claude Lowther MP to raise a corps of Sussex men for Kitchener's army. The corps will be composed of companies of men from the principal Sussex districts and will work, train, serve and fight together as a regular infantry unit. The Battalion will train at Cooden, near Bexhill.

The report quotes Colonel Lowther as saying that, 'Lord Kitchener recognises that men often prefer to serve side by side with friends and relatives rather than to be drafted into different regiments to serve with strangers'. Potential recruits in West Sussex were invited to contact Mr Grisewood at The Den, Bognor.[39]

Grisewood appeared on the stage at the Pier Theatre, Bognor, later that week to appeal for volunteers during the interval. He was enthusiastically applauded when he said he would like to see a large number of recruits from Chichester, Littlehampton and Arundel, 'who would be linked up so as to serve side by side with their neighbours'.[40] A day or two later, the Hon. Neville Lytton made an appeal for volunteers at a public meeting at Horsham and, according to the press report, 'several men gave in their names'.[41] Grieves writes that Lowther 'embraced the "Pals" principle of joining, training, fighting (and dying) together' and that, 'the battalions of "Lowther's Lambs" or Southdowners drew on associational landscape forms without endorsing customary social hierarchies and moral control'.[42] The Southdown Brigade had much in common with the 'Pals' battalions raised in some of the cities of northern England and is a good example of attachment to landscape and locality influencing the motivation of soldiers to enlist and then endure the conditions of modern warfare.[43]

Colonel Lowther and 11th Battalion officers at Cooden. (WSRO, RSR Acc 242 1)

As batches of recruits, to both the service battalions and the Southdown Brigade, left their home towns for training prior to deployment, they were seen off by local people with

*Soldiers on parade,
High Street,
Shoreham-by-Sea,
1916. (Marlipins
Museum, 89.549)*

bands and flags. Although the demand for recruits was apparently insatiable, as 1914 drew to a close, local papers in Sussex expressed some satisfaction in the number of men who had come forward to join the forces. Several papers published 'Rolls of Honour', recording the names and units of local men who had answered their country's call. That for East Grinstead, for example, listed the names of 327 men, 91 per cent of whom had joined the army, 7 per cent the Royal Navy and just 2 per cent the Royal Flying Corps (RFC).[44] However, as the nature of mechanised warfare and the fact that the war would not be over by Christmas became clear, the government was forced to consider for how long the country could rely on voluntary recruitment and when, not if, the introduction of conscription would have to be contemplated.

Conscription and its Consequences

Voluntary recruitment continued through 1915, but the introduction of a national registration scheme, carried out largely by local volunteers in West Sussex, heralded the implementation of the Group Scheme, introduced by Lord Derby as director of recruiting, which invited men who had not yet enlisted to indicate their willingness to be called up in due course, the timing to be dependent on each man's age and circumstances. However, the scheme did not produce the number of recruits needed to fill the gaps created by the number of casualties being sustained and, early in 1916, the government grasped the nettle and enacted the Military Service Act, which provided for the conscription of all unmarried men aged between 18 and 41. The Act also provided for the introduction of military service tribunals empowered to grant certificates of exemption on the grounds of national interest, hardship, ill-health or infirmity, and conscientious objection. Local authorities were required to set up local tribunals to hear cases in the first instance, with rights of appeal to a county and, ultimately, a national tribunal. From March 1916 onwards, local papers in West Sussex carried extensive reports of the proceedings of the local and county tribunals. These reports are particularly valuable as the original case papers were, on the orders of the government, destroyed after the war, with the records relating to just one English county (Middlesex) and the Lothian and Peebles area in Scotland being retained and now accessible to researchers at the National Archives.[45]

The majority of appeal cases reported in the West Sussex local papers relate to the first ground of appeal under the Military Service Act, namely that it is expedient in the national interest that the applicant should, instead of being employed in military service, be engaged in other work. Applications were either dismissed or a time-limited exemption granted, which might be subsequently renewed. Applications were sometimes made by individual employees, but more often by their employers on their behalf. Examples of successful applications include those of a Lavant shepherd who had single-handed responsibility for a large flock of 800 sheep,[46] a Thakeham master blacksmith and farrier under contract to the government to make 1,000 shoes for mules a fortnight,[47] and an Angmering thatcher who claimed that the work of thatching ricks for farmers was of national importance.[48] The significance of the contribution of thatchers to the war effort is borne out by a reference in the notebook of Mr W.J. Passmore of Applesham Farm: visiting Tottington Farm, Upper Beeding, for the War Agricultural Executive, he found 'nearly £400 damage had been done to rick through thatcher being called up'.[49]

Recruits for Lord Kitchener's Army leaving Shoreham-by-Sea, September 1914. (Marlipins Museum, 94.2463)

The names of men exempted under the Act were 'starred' in the National Register and they were issued with an armband which confirmed their status. There are reports of men who were regarded as improperly avoiding conscription ('absentees') being brought before the courts, fined and handed over to the military authorities. Cases included three young gypsies in Chichester[50] and an actor appearing at the Pier Theatre, Bognor.[51] Relatively few cases were reported of men applying for exemption on the grounds of conscientious objection. Only those applicants who were able to demonstrate a strong religious or moral objection to combatant duty and to withstand tough cross-examination by the tribunal, and in particular the military representative, were likely to succeed. Applications by a Cuckfield man, a former member of the Society of Friends[52] and an architectural woodcarver from Burgess Hill[53] were refused on the ground that the applications were not deemed to rest on religious or moral convictions. An East Dean hurdle maker, who held that it was contrary to Christ's teaching for him to fight and kill his fellow men[54] and an assistant master at Ardingly College, who had a conscientious objection to taking life,[55] were granted conditional exemption, subject to review.

It has been estimated that some 50–60,000 men from Sussex fought in the First World War,[56] the overwhelming majority in the army, mainly in the county regiment. The process whereby those men were identified and then encouraged, cajoled and, finally, coerced into joining the forces illustrates the fundamental changes which were taking place in British society during the second decade of the twentieth century, as traditional deference to landlord and employer gave way to more democratic and egalitarian attitudes. The process was already under way, as illustrated by the radical social agenda of the 1906 Liberal government, the rise of the labour movement and the struggle for women's rights, but the war hastened that process. Things would never be the same again, either in Sussex, or in the rest of Britain.

2

THE ROYAL SUSSEX REGIMENT

By Alan Readman

In 1914 the Royal Sussex Regiment (RSR) comprised six battalions. Of the Regulars, the 1st Battalion was in India, where it remained until December 1919. The 2nd Battalion was based at Woking but would spend the war on the Western Front. The 3rd (Special Reserve) Battalion, first at Dover and then Newhaven, trained drafts for the overseas units of the regiment. The three Territorial battalions, the 4th, 5th (Cinque Ports) and 6th (Cyclist) Battalions, stationed respectively at Horsham, Hastings and Brighton, were all destined to see active service abroad.

During the war, the regiment expanded to twenty battalions with the raising of service battalions for Lord Kitchener's 'New Army' and most of these served overseas.[57]

Badge of the Royal Sussex Regiment.

The Western Front

British and Commonwealth forces served in several theatres of war across the world but the relative scale of their influence has inevitably meant that the main focus of attention has fallen upon the Western Front.

The Western Front, selected locations in France and Belgium. (Adapted from G.D. Martineau, A History of The Royal Sussex Regiment, 1701-1953 (Royal Sussex Regimental Association, 1955, p. 162)

The First Months of War

The order to mobilise was issued on 4 August 1914. The 2nd Battalion, RSR, formed part of the 2nd Brigade, 1st Division, and was amongst the first of the British troops landed in France on 13 August.

In a letter to his mother in Arundel, Private Harold Morley described their arrival at Le Havre from which they entrained for the Franco-Belgian frontier:

> We must have travelled two or three hundred miles past Amiens and Arras, and got out at a small station named Wassigny. You would be surprised how well the French people treated us. We stopped at all large stations, and there were crowds of people on the platform, with loaves of bread, cigarettes, tobacco, milk, cider, eggs boiled, chocolate, and all kinds of ripe fruit. It was a glorious time for us.[58]

The first major action of the BEF was at Mons on 23 August. The overwhelming troop numbers and artillery strength of the Germans, coupled with the retreat of the French forces on their right, necessitated retirement. Though not involved in the battle, the 2nd Battalion experienced the long fighting withdrawal to the River Marne.

In his diary, Drummer George Whittington recounted their ordeal:

> It was so hot that the men were falling out and even dropping down in the road in dozens. We have had exceedingly long marches that our troops are nearly done up … We have had fair food but have been for at least five days without a dinner at all.[59]

Whittington was killed at the Battle of the Marne, on 10 September 1914, when the battalion suffered over 100 casualties in its first experience of severe fighting at Priez.

Private Charles Mitchell wrote to his father in East Grinstead about their part in the battle:

> We started away just before dawn from our camp, and I should think it was about an hour after dawn when we encountered the enemy. They were on the opposite side of a valley, and as we came over the brow of the hill they opened on us with a storm of rifle fire and shrapnel from about 900 yards. We had no cover whatever and we lay there for 20 minutes to half an hour. Then we got the order to retire back behind the ridges … You can guess it was just a wee bit warm.[60]

In those first weeks of the war, there was fluidity in the front and for a time the Germans were pushed back, halting on the heights above the River Aisne.

On 14 September, the Battle of the Aisne began, the Allied attack failing to consolidate initial gains against greater numbers of men and artillery. The 2nd Battalion was heavily engaged on high ground near Troyon.

Private Mitchell's letter gives his thoughts on the day:

> We again started before dawn and we soon found the enemy; then the rumpus started, and we had the hottest time I have ever had in my life … We drove the Germans back and held them there for eight days … General French complimented the regiment on the way it took the position and held it.[61]

Harold Morley gave a more blunt assessment: 'The battalion that morning walked right into a death trap. The German artillery were firing on us at a range of 450 yards. Shells were bursting over us like drops of rain.'[62] The battalion lost its commanding officer, second-in-command, adjutant and six other officers killed in a total of 213 casualties on that one day.

This engagement marked the beginning of the end of mobile fighting. The Western Front degenerated into a four-year-long stalemate, with infantry well-entrenched, backed by machine-gun fire and heavy artillery, and periodic efforts to restore movement to the line producing costly but fruitless attack and counterattack.

The 2nd Battalion remained on the Aisne until 15 October, moving round to positions covering the Belgian city of Ypres.

Its defence was seen as vital to protect the Channel ports and the British Army's supply lines.

In the First Battle of Ypres the Germans vastly outnumbered the British in men, machine guns and artillery, but their indecisiveness and the superiority of British rifle fire meant their assault failed to achieve a conclusive victory. Fighting continued until 22 November when the onset of winter curtailed further hostilities.

The 2nd Battalion, for its unyielding line, earned from captured prisoners the title of 'the Iron Regiment' but paid a heavy price; 405 casualties were sustained on 30–31 October alone.[63]

Aubers Ridge, 9 May 1915

After Ypres, to reinforce the depleted BEF, Regular brigades were augmented by Territorial units and the 2nd Battalion was joined by the 5th. Their first major action was on Sunday, 9 May. The objective was to capture the trenches and redoubts on the plain at the foot of Aubers Ridge and then occupy the high ground.

The offensive commenced at 5 a.m. with a heavy bombardment for thirty minutes. The infantry was told to expect little resistance but the artillery failed to destroy the enemy trenches or cut their wire. To reach the enemy lines the men had to cross flat terrain, raked by carefully sited machine guns.

Three companies of the 2nd Battalion led the left of the attack across the 300 yards of No Man's Land and, although their role was intended only as support, most of the first three companies of the 5th Battalion swarmed over the top to join them. 'Where the Iron Regiment go, we go too', was

'No end of brave things were done.' A letter from Colonel Langham describing the 5th Battalion's part in the Battle of Aubers Ridge. (Sussex Daily News, 21 May 1915, cutting in WSRO RSR Ms. 5/65, pp. 59-60)

SUSSEX AND THE WAR.

THE FAMOUS NINTH OF MAY.

High Praise for the 5th Battalion Royal Sussex.

LETTER FROM COLONEL LANGHAM.

AN APPEAL TO THE MEN OF ENGLAND.

Lieut.-Colonel Langham, commanding 5th Royal Sussex Regiment, has sent home a letter descriptive of the action on Sunday, 9th May, which gives a vivid pen picture of the terrible ordeal the 2nd and 5th Royal Sussex and other battalions had to undergo. He explains the dispositions for the attack on the strong German positions, the 2nd Sussex being on the left of the assaulting line, and the 5th Sussex in the second line, immediately in the rear of the 2nd Battalion. The latter got to within from 40 to 80 yards of the German lines; and of the 5th, "C" Company, less one platoon, "A" Company, less one platoon, and the whole of "B" Company went out in the second line. "Then the most murderous rifle, machine gun and shrapnel fire opened. . . . People say the fire at Mons and Ypres was nothing to it."

"No end of brave things were done, and our men were splendid, but helpless." Some of them were 300 yards out from the battalion's parapets, and retirement was as difficult as advance. Major Langham, Dodd, Perry, and Hobart got back wounded; Faxan and Dawes unwounded. Roy Fazan was killed, and it is feared, others. "The last I saw of Grant," says Colonel Langham, "he stood on our parapet giving the directions to "B" Company, and they went over like one man. Haigh and Napper were wounded behind the firing trench. I am afraid Napper may lose one eye, and Dodd his left hand; but surgeons nowadays do wonders."

"I got all mine together, re-organized them properly, had them numbered off, said a few words to them as to marching out of action like soldiers, and went off in fours. We had no stragglers, and at last got to our billets, a long way back. For this I have received some welcome commendation for the spirit of discipline shewn by us all. . . . I am sure we have not disgraced the old Sussex Regiment; and we were cheered by several strong parties of other regiments."

"THE LOSSES OF THE FIFTH."

"At present we have lost in killed, wounded, and missing, 11 officers and over 200 men, and I am afraid the missing (4 officers and 43 men) must all by now be considered as killed; though of course by a sort of miracle, some may turn up. I don't think any are taken prisoners, unless the Germans got some wounded men that night.

"The only thing to be thankful for is that they did not use their chlorine gas, but the wind was the wrong way. By the by, one of our fellows, named Glover (who is lent to the Communication troops as a motor cyclist), came to see me at ——. He had got into some of the gas, and was suffering from a sort of chronic bronchitis. His voice was hoarse, he could not lie down with comfort, and at night he woke up every half hour.

"I cannot see how and why, with barbarities like these to face, every man in England who can bear arms, and is not engaged in making things for the firing line, does not come forward, ready to do his bit."

the cry.[64] They met a withering rifle and machine-gun fire as well as shrapnel. On that morning each battalion lost some 200 killed, wounded or missing.

Captain Eric Fazan wrote a letter of sympathy to the mother of Captain Ferris Nelson Grant, killed in the battle:

> I saw him leading 'B' Company into action and it was splendid. My brother (who was killed) was his 2nd in Command and I am sure (that if he had to be killed) we would both ask for nothing better than that it should be in action following such a truly brave man.[65]

Grant had already been awarded a Military Cross and was killed leading a charge. Standing on the parapet, he hailed his men, 'England expects. You know the rest. Come on "B" Company!'[66]

In a letter home, Lieutenant-Colonel Frederick Langham described how, when the order came to retire, he led the remnant of the 5th Battalion from the battlefield:

> I got all mine together, reorganised them properly … said a few words to them as to marching out of action like soldiers, and went off in fours. We had no stragglers, and at last got to our billets, a long way back … I am sure we have not disgraced the old Sussex Regiment; and we were cheered by several strong parties of other regiments.[67]

When they met up again with the Regulars, they were greeted with shouts of 'Good old Fifth'. As a Territorial unit, this was the approval they would have valued most.

The battle was no less devastating for the 2nd Battalion. Regimental Sergeant Major W.F. Rainsford recorded the action in his diary:

> The enemy's line was a veritable hotbed of machine guns … Casualties began to stream back to the Dressing Station with stories that it was impossible to advance against such appalling machine gun fire. Lines of men got near the enemy's first trench only to be driven back to the centre of No Man's Land. Officers could be seen

rallying the men to a further advance. These small advances were carried out under a perfect hail of bullets and gun fire; great shells were seen to be bursting in the centre of bodies of men lying down in the open. In an hour it could be seen that the attack had failed.[68]

Casualties grievously affected communities and families. In Chichester it was noted that fifty-five of the battalion fatalities had enlisted in the city. At West Hoathly, Private William Comber, aged 42, left behind a widow and eight children.[69]

Battle of Loos

After Aubers Ridge, the 2nd Battalion continued in the front line and the Battle of Loos, beginning on 25 September 1915, drew them into the biggest Allied offensive of the year, one which saw the first use of poison gas by the British.

The attack was hampered by an inadequate Allied bombardment and fickle weather conditions, occasionally blowing gas back towards the British lines.

The battalion attacked in the vicinity of the Lone Tree, the single cherry tree standing in No Man's Land in front of Hulluch. Private F.A. Colvin recorded in his diary being met by clouds of chlorine gas and murderous rifle fire.[70] Sergeant Archibald Cleare from Chichester died from gas poisoning, the second son of ex RQMS William Cleare to be killed in the war.[71]

It was here that Sergeant Harry Wells won a Victoria Cross, one of four awarded to the regiment during the war. When his platoon officer had been killed, he took command, rallied the men, and, with great bravery, led them on towards the German wire, before he too was killed.[72]

The failure of Loos was exacerbated by High Command's misuse of New Army Divisions, untried and unfamiliar with war conditions, deployed barely three weeks after leaving England.

The 9th Battalion was one such service battalion to suffer. It had arrived in France on 1 September and lost

Sergeant Harry Wells, 2nd Battalion. Posthumously awarded the Victoria Cross for his bravery at Loos. (WSRO RSR Ms. Uncatalogued. VC papers of Sergeant Harry Wells)

19 officers and 362 other ranks during the battle. Private Sidney Munnion wrote of the attack in a letter to his brother in Ardingly. In the days preceding, they had marched over 50 miles to the line, with little food or water, and were then straight into action:

> Shells were dropping all the time, and machine guns, snipers, rifle fire, bombs and gas were going – it was awful! … Seeing the dead and wounded about is the worst part of it, especially the latter … My nerves seem gone, but we are a long way down country again, resting, so shall soon feel better.[73]

'Three of No 9 Platoon.' Sketches by Sergeant Ralph Ellis from his journal of the 7th Battalion, 1915–16. (WSRO Add. Ms. 25,004, f. 22r)

The Hohenzollern Redoubt, March 1916

North of Hulluch, in the Loos sector, was the Hohenzollern Redoubt where, in mid-October 1915, the 2nd Battalion was joined by the 7th.[74]

This was the scene of mine fighting, where tunnels were dug under enemy positions with the object of blowing up his trenches. The Germans exploded four large craters in No Man's Land and occupied the lips of them. Here, in March 1916, there was severe crater fighting, with heavy casualties. Ground was gained by the 7th Battalion and counterattacks repulsed. The battalion was officially commended and its commanding officer, Colonel Osborn, was awarded the DSO.

The journals of Sergeant Ralph Ellis of Arundel cover this phase of the 7th Battalion's war. His text is complemented by sketches of the men and drawings of countryside, shelled towns and villages, and the trenches. The following extract depicts a scene in the Field Ambulance Dressing Station at Vermelles, situated in a cellar beneath the remains of a brewery:

> There on the brick floor lies a figure, just where he is hit no one could say at a glance, so plastered is he with mud from head to foot. He has fallen face downwards into it and of his face as he lies there, only his fine white teeth are noticeable with the lips slightly drawn back, the remainder of the face is a smear of mud, no noise escapes those tightly clenched teeth, and there, not a yard away is a little mongrel dog who is straining – straining his body forward until without moving his stiffened legs, with tongue outstretched, he just manages to quietly lick the mud-covered face. There is so little to distinguish that quiet, prone figure from the earth, but that bit of a dog seems to know by instinct that here lies a man friend suffering and gives of his sympathy with human intuition and tenderness, the only one there who has time for such things.[75]

The Boar's Head and the Somme

The 2nd Battalion remained in the Loos sector until early July 1916, when the 1st Division was moved down to the Somme for what was planned as an Anglo-French offensive to breach the German lines and end the stalemate on the Western Front.

It would be joined by the Territorials of the 5th Battalion, by the 7th, 8th and 9th service battalions, and by the three Southdown Battalions. The county regiment was to take its full part in one of the bloodiest battles of the war.

Catastrophe was to strike even before the Battle of the Somme began. A diversionary attack was launched on German positions known as 'the Boar's Head' at Richebourg L'Avoue in the Pas de Calais in an attempt to delude the enemy into believing the offensive was to be there and not down on the Somme.

This was the first major action involving the 11th, 12th and 13th (Southdown) Battalions, Lowther's Lambs, which had landed in France at the beginning of March 1916.[76]

The attack, on Friday 30 June, met crippling machine-gun fire going through the wire and in the course of a morning they lost 17 officers and 349 other ranks killed and nearly three times that number wounded. The 13th Battalion was almost wiped out and the 12th cut by half. Again, as most of the casualties were Sussex men, local places and families were badly hit. Amongst the dead were three brothers from Worthing, Alfred, Charles and William Pannell, the last-named 12th Battalion and the others 13th.[77]

The scale of the losses was indicated in a letter sent home to Bognor by Sergeant James Isted:

> We were making an attack at dawn but we never took the German trenches, as they were waiting for us, and mowed us down as fast as we got there … I am afraid Sussex has been badly hit this time. My Company lost all its officers … Nearly all the Sergeants were killed or wounded. I was very lucky to get out of it alive. I believe there are a good many killed and wounded from Bognor.[78]

This day produced many acts of bravery but one in particular has etched itself into regimental history. Nelson Victor Carter joined the 12th Battalion and quickly rose through the ranks to company sergeant major. At the Boar's Head, under intense fire, he eliminated an enemy machine-gun post and repeatedly went over the parapet to rescue the wounded from No Man's Land. He was fatally wounded but his gallantry was recognised with the award of a Victoria Cross. A fund was set up in Eastbourne to support his widow and baby daughter and had raised £408 by July 1918.[79]

The Boar's Head delayed the Germans moving troops down to the Somme but otherwise was a disaster. Lowther's Lambs, only four months into overseas service, had been decimated, in just four and a half hours of battle.

The Somme Offensive began for the infantry on Saturday, 1 July 1916. The bombardment again failed to destroy the enemy's defensive emplacements or undermine its infantry in their deep dug-outs. At 7.30 a.m., an Allied army of 66,000 men climbed over the parapets to cross the few hundred yards of No Man's Land. At the end of the day, German artillery and small arms fire had accounted for 57,000 of them, of whom 19,000 were killed.

Hero of the Boar's Head. CSM Nelson Victor Carter, VC, 12th Battalion, killed in action on 30 June 1916. (WSRO RSR Ms. Uncatalogued. VC papers of CSM Nelson Victor Carter)

The Battle of the Somme lasted until mid-November and total British losses amounted to 400,000 killed, wounded or missing. Although the county regiment was not involved on that first day, eight of its battalions were drawn into subsequent stages of the battle.

Sergeant Charles Tulett, a Chichester man, served with the 7th Battalion and his memoirs offer a remarkable testimony of one man's experiences of the Somme, here describing the attack at Ovillers on 7 July:

> On the evening before the attack, I was detailed to go down to the transport to collect a draft of 16 men, mostly youngsters about 16 or 17 years of age. Of these, we had four in our platoon pitched straight into battle and over the top we went only to be met by artillery fire and a very heavy barrage of machine gun fire causing terrible casualties.
>
> I had gone about ten yards when a shell exploded quite close to me, burying me up to my shoulders, also killing many of those poor lads. Luckily some of the lads dug me out, very shaken and shocked … When we had gone a few more yards I had a bullet through my tin helmet, taking a small piece out of my ear …

> However, I still struggled on and most of the troops who were fortunate to do so had reached the German lines, but I now had come to some of the Kaiser's crack troops, Bavarian and Prussian Guards, engaged for a while in hand-to-hand fighting. I shot one but at that moment I received a bullet through my right wrist, causing me terrible pain, but managed to get to the trench, which was full of English and German men, but mostly German, dead.[80]

The 2nd Battalion arrived on the Somme on 9 July and a week later moved up to the front line, in readiness for an attack on the German line at Pozières. They were spotted moving to assembly positions and the attack met heavy fire. Soon in action again, near High Wood, they captured and held their objectives, despite strong counterattacks. Gains were achieved at such heavy cost that by the end of September, when the 1st Division left the area, the combined losses of the battalion on the Somme had risen to 44 officers and over 1,000 men.

Glowing tributes were paid by war correspondents to 'the heroic work of the gallant Sussex in the Big Push'. Philip Gibbs of the *Daily Chronicle* spoke fondly of them, these boys far from home thrust into a battle that, for many commentators, came to epitomise the folly and futility of the trench war:

> On the right were the Sussex men – fair-haired fellows from Burpham and Arundel, and little old villages lying snug in the South Downs, and quiet old Market Towns like Chichester – Lord! a world away from places like Pozières.[81]

The 8th Battalion early in its training was converted into a Pioneer battalion and served as such throughout the war. Their duties included trench digging, laying roads and tracks, and building dug-outs, dangerous occupations as their working parties, often in the front line, were regularly under sniper fire. They were also required to fight as infantry, the battalion suffering nearly 100 casualties in their first two days of the Somme battle.

The 9th was another service battalion moved to the Somme. Raised at Shoreham, it had already distinguished itself in battle. In February 1916 Lieutenant Eric Archibald McNair, aged 21, was awarded a Victoria Cross for his gallant defence of a crater at Hooge, near Ypres.[82] Private Mervyn Jupp won a Distinguished Conduct Medal for his gallantry in that action. He was quickly promoted to sergeant, though only 22, but was killed by a shell on the Somme on 31 August 1916. A moving letter of sympathy was sent to his mother, in Hassocks, by Harold Dudeney, the machine-gun officer of the battalion:

He was a splendid soldier in every way, and died fighting for his country, as so many of our poor brave fellows have done and are doing every day … He was one of the most unassuming and yet at the same time one of the most gallant fellows I have ever met, and although he has now been taken from us his memory will never fade. His loss has been keenly felt by the whole battalion, and personally I feel it *very much*. But how much more must you, his dear mother, and all his relatives feel it! May God be with you all and bless you and comfort you in your irreparable loss is my sincere prayer.[83]

Charles Tulett, 7th Battalion, home on leave, outside Shippam's factory in Chichester. (WSRO Slides Collection. 'Royal Sussex Regiment in Great War' presentation. Slide No. 50)

The three Southdown Battalions arrived on the Somme in mid-August. Their harrowing ordeal continued and at one time the 11th Battalion held trenches on the front for five weeks without relief. Private George Sydenham gave a graphic account of his experiences in a letter home to Haywards Heath:

I and three or four others went over the parapet together, with machine gun and rifle fire as thick as rain, to say nothing of the Huns' heavy shells, shrapnel, Krupps, whiz-bangs, etc bursting all around us. We were never intended to have to face such warfare.[84]

Even when behind the front, shellfire might plague the men, its incessant screaming at times shattering their nerves, as Lieutenant Ivan Margary, 7th Battalion, explained in his account of the support line trenches, early in October:

> Shells came over not in occasional bursts but in a steady stream. At least one, and more often three or four, were bursting every minute ... Men were constantly being buried in twos and threes, and almost as soon as one lot had been extricated, another lot would be buried somewhere else. Often it was several minutes before frantic digging could get them out again ... The constant violent concussions had a very curious effect upon us all. Even those who did not in the least complain of actual 'shell-shock' shook quite visibly, and some were almost unable to control the movements of their hands.[85]

As the campaign progressed, tactics were altered and in September tanks were introduced, but over boggy craters and shell-holes these were slow and susceptible to mechanical trouble. Ralph Ellis testified to the state of the distressed battlefield in his account of the 7th Battalion's war, here referring to a move back up to the front line near Agny in October:

> You cannot mistake the way, it is marked by the crumpled forms of those who first advanced with the tanks and those who since hurried along the track ... Heavy shells visit here at any old time, targets abound, the ground is burdened with our guns and supporting infantry dumped into bits of crumbling trenches ... No one lingers here except pain and death.[86]

The strategic impact of the battle has been widely debated. Contemporary politicians decried the casualties, particularly among the new volunteer army created by Lord Kitchener. For General Haig, however, the Somme marked a definite stage on the road to victory. Verdun had been relieved as a consequence and enemy forces on the Western Front worn down.

Passchendaele, 1917

After the Somme, the remnants of the Southdown Battalions moved to the Ypres sector, serving in and out of the trenches from December 1916 to January 1918.

An officer of the 11th Battalion then was Reginald Whitley of East Preston. He recalled an unofficial Christmas Day truce and how the Royal Sussex cheered as a German tenor stepped out into the open to sing Wagner's 'O Star of Eve'. They responded with 'Sussex-by-the-Sea', an 'unequal exchange' he thought.[87]

On 5-7 July 1917, hastily scribbled notes in his pocket diary give indication of an impending big push:

> No further notes to be written. GOC wound up about divulging plans. WAR with a capital W. All letters and diaries, personal kit to go back. Picnic brewing. Writing to [East] Preston with warnings. San Fairy Ann. Wot a luvly War. No further details available owing to intensive preparations for attack at Ypres.[88]

Lieutenant Reginald Whitley, 11th Battalion, wounded at the Third Battle of Ypres. (WSRO RSR Ms. Uncatalogued. Papers of Lieutenant Reginald Whitley)

There are no further entries until 31 July, the first day of the Third Battle of Ypres, or Passchendaele as it came to be known, after the village nearby. Early in the action he was struck down by contaminated metal from a flying bomb. A cryptic note records the moment: 'Knocked out at St. Julien, North of Ypres. Blighty!! Finis at 3.50 a.m. I am sorry!!'[89]

Third Wipers, as the Tommy called it, was fought in incessant rain and constant shelling. This was a desolate salient of canals, ditches and muddy swamps. The offensive, which lasted until November, resulted in gains for the Allies but was not the breakthrough Haig intended.

From the diary of Lieutenant Gerald Brunskill, 5th Battalion. Aerial view of the battlefield at Poelcappelle during the Passchendaele campaign, 1917. (WSRO RSR Ms. 5/93)

Herbert Banfield, 13th Battalion, described in his diary the moment they went over the top on the first day of the battle:

Tierney did not let us know we were going over then. I think he was wise. So when I saw the horizon ahead break into red flame I was surprised. Immediately the whole heaven was aglow with bursting shell, red and green rockets, showers of golden rain, and our ears were deafened with an avalanche of sound. Our senses were muddled. We were too bewildered to think.

We instinctively broke into a shuffling run. We struggled through shattered wire, following a white direction tape. Shells were bursting all around. We heeded them not. Our ears sang and sang again. Swish, swish, went the eighteen pounders over our heads. We hugged a row of shattered willows and crossed No Man's Land. We staggered through shell holes, round them and fell into them.[90]

The papers of Lieutenant-Colonel William Millward offer further insight. On the outbreak of war he enlisted as a private in the 11th Battalion, rising through the ranks by March 1917 to command it, a feat rare in the same battalion. His habit of giving the men catching practice with apples in off-duty moments appealed to his signals officer, the cricket-loving Edmund Blunden. In such simple but inspired ways were spirits raised and relations fostered between officers and men.

Blunden grew up in Kent but was educated at Christ's Hospital in Horsham. His book, *Undertones of War*, is acclaimed as a classic account of the trench war; compassionate prose accompanied by a selection of war poetry.

Amongst the Millward papers is a report by Blunden on Third Ypres:

Lieutenant-Colonel William Colsey Millward, DSO, who rose through the ranks to command the 11th Battalion. (WSRO RSR Acc. 3057)

... the first part of the attack was carried through so amazingly quickly that whatever blood lust we had been cultivating had no chance of making good. All the same some of our impressions may be interesting. We had hardly crawled out to our starting point when a roaring drone away back signified that one of our heavy batteries had opened and immediately a devil's concert of artillery and M.G. struck up. The Bosch had been pumping shells in during the assembly and now he barraged too, almost synchronising his fire with ours; we now began to sweat blood and my tongue seemed (like the Psalmist's) to cleave to the roof of my mouth. It was unnerving also to see the oil drums flaring on HIGH COMMAND, and round there the Bosch put over a number of star shells which helped to make No Man's Land as light as broad day for a minute ...[91]

55

'Over the Sacks.' First page of the report to Colonel Millward from his signals officer, Edmund Blunden, on the opening of the Third Battle of Ypres. Written in pencil on message paper. (WSRO RSR Acc. 3057)

A month earlier, Blunden had enjoyed a reunion with four contemporaries from Christ's Hospital, all serving with the regiment. They met at St Omer, 'The Feast of Five', Horace Amon, William Collyer, Ernest Tice, Arnold Vidler and Blunden. His friend Collyer, 13th Battalion, was killed in No Man's Land during the first minutes of the battle; Tice, 11th Battalion, a few hours later. He wrote of this shortly afterwards:

Through the gloomy smoke of war, and dull obliterations of all our old guiding marks, it is not within the fighting man's power to see the Delectable Mountains and the Happy Valleys to which we trust to come: yet your nobility and your excellent sacrifice, dear Tice and dear Collyer, now seem to be like the kindly light which leads us through the dark to inevitable good. Where you are, I am sure you know all is well.[92]

The Final Year of War

The fall of Russia enabled German strengthening of the Western Front, designed to achieve a breakthrough before the Americans could revitalise the Allied cause. The Spring Offensive on the Somme and the Marne in March-April 1918 brought with it devastating German artillery bombardment and overwhelming infantry-cavalry-tank attacks.

The Southdown Battalions were in the Hem sector, south of the Somme, when the attack began on 21 March. The 12th had virtually ceased to exist as a battalion but the 11th and 13th participated in the bitter fighting to stem the German advance.

Both battalions were decimated by heavy losses and the residue returned to the Ypres sector at the beginning of April. On the 9th, the 13th Battalion was in the line near Kemmel and faced another major German attack. What remained of the battalion was destroyed. Herbert Banfield described its last, desperate days in his diary:

> Continual retirement, involving much rearguard fighting, lack of food, loss of sleep and foot weariness till mind and body were absolutely exhausted, and then still to struggle on, filled in a round of ten days which seemed ten years.
>
> Then the order came for a counter attack. There were only scattered remnants of umpteen divisions. They went forward so wearily, so miserably. They fairly dragged their laggard limbs over the heavy ploughed land, sticky as gum, for it was raining hard. Too fed up to worry about shells. Bullets however close were unheeded. Death seemed welcome. We got up that ridge somehow, and were greeted, as we breasted the top, with a perfect hail of bullets.[93]

Other service battalions of the regiment had similarly heroic stories to tell of fortitude against the odds in the spring of 1918. The pioneers of the 8th Battalion, during the German push between Armentieres and Béthune, took their full share in the defensive fighting. One of its casualties was Private Harry Chant of Angmering, killed on 6 April by a bomb dropped from a low-flying aeroplane, a relatively unusual fate, the more tragic as it was witnessed by his brother, John, also serving with the battalion.[94]

In adversity, the 9th Battalion showed a fearless defiance and in his account Captain Harold Saxon MC stressed how Sussex pride played its part. Defending positions at Fervaque Farm, his company was eventually overwhelmed and the survivors captured:

> Even to me who knew them well and expected much of them, the spirit which the men showed to the end was a revelation ... No unit except our own seemed to offer any resistance or even to stay. They were surrounded

and gave up any expectation of relief – the mist gave a feeling of blind helplessness ... Yet they never for a moment considered there was any other job for them but to stay and fight ... To the end they held themselves better than the enemy, and to the end they jeered and dared them to come on.[95]

The Spring Offensive brought the 4th and 16th Battalions from Palestine to assist in the Allied counterattack. This began at Le Hamel on 4 July and culminated in a decisive victory at Amiens on 8 August. Forward movement was finally restored to the line and the Germans were pushed back into Belgium.

Nevertheless, the Allied victories in the 'Hundred Days' leading up to the Armistice were hard won, none more so than that achieved by the 2nd Battalion on 4 November in taking the Sambre-Oise Canal.

Led by Lieutenant-Colonel Dudley Graham Johnson, attached from the South Wales Borderers, the battalion crossed the canal by the lock south of Catillon. In his diary, he noted that they found the lock houses to be full of Germans and machine guns, added to which his men faced a hailstorm of shells. In its last action of the war, just seven days before the Armistice, the 2nd Battalion suffered 100 casualties, Colonel Johnson winning the Victoria Cross for his personal courage and leadership.[96]

The Armistice and Demobilisation

Charles Tulett was with the 7th Battalion on Armistice Day:

On leaving the trenches we passed through a small French village where there was a small group of elderly men and women who came running over to us, hugging and kissing us, with tears in their eyes, so pleased to think that it was all over, a very emotional occasion, one I shall never forget.[97]

They mustered in the village square for a thanksgiving service and the villagers wept with joy at the playing of 'La Marseillaise'.

Demobilisation began in mid-December, a gradual process completed in June 1919, when the final cadre arrived back in Chichester.[98]

The 2nd Battalion was also detained over the winter, with the British Army of the Rhine, holding the bridgeheads until the Peace Treaty was signed. The battalion War Diary records the celebrations encountered on the 'March to the Rhine'; here describing the welcome in one liberated Belgian village:

> At Chastres a procession of maidens and youths bearing banners, headed by a Cure and accompanied by a Concertina, presented a bouquet of flowers to the Commanding Officer and marched in at the head of the Battalion.[99]

On 17 December the battalion crossed the frontier into Germany with Colours flying and band playing.[100] After the Rhine, the cadre of the battalion, five officers and fifty-one men, arrived back in Chichester on 16 April 1919, four years and eight months after leaving for France.[101] Its nominal roll shows that over 6,000 men had passed through the battalion during the war. After allowing for casualties and transferees, only two men had been with the battalion at the beginning of the war and were still there at its end.[102]

Other Theatres of War

Gallipoli

Launching an attack on Gallipoli was intended to break the stalemate of the Western Front by destroying the power of Turkey and pulling German troops to the East.

The first invasion in April 1915 was not a success and a fresh initiative was planned. For this, the 4th Battalion landed at Suvla Bay at 11.45 p.m. on Sunday, 8 August 1915.

A letter from CQMS W.G. Willis of Chichester described the landing, the men dropping down into water up to their hips and wading to the shore in the darkness, a distance of 50 yards.[103]

Lance-Corporal Harold Proctor wrote to his mother in Bognor, with his experiences:

The Turks were ready to receive us, and no sooner than we got within range of their artillery they opened fire, and our warships opened fire on them. You never heard such a terrible noise in all your life. There were shells bursting and killing our chaps by the dozen. Eventually we managed to get on land and we had to face fire from their machine guns and rifles. I can tell you it is marvellous that everybody was not killed, for the bullets were flying past our heads like rain, and anybody else but British soldiers could never have managed it. Well, we got the order to fix bayonets and charge, and we made a rush. Every one of us went mad. They never waited for us, for they are rank cowards when it comes to the bayonets.[104]

Major Sydney Beale's appeal from Gallipoli for more men 'to fill the gaps in the ranks' of the 4th Battalion, 1915. (WSRO RSR Ms. 4/70)

MEN OF EAST GRINSTEAD!

YOU ARE WANTED

By your Chums in the Trenches, to fill the gaps in the ranks of the

4th BATT. ROYAL SUSSEX REGT.

Read this Extract from a letter written by Major BEALE, who is with the 4th Royal Sussex in Gallipoli :—

"It is more and more impressed on me here that one battalion at home is not enough to keep one battalion on this sort of service up to strength unless the home unit is constantly and steadily filled up with men as the drafts are sent. Our real need, therefore, is for more men, and it will be the same for some time to come. I am quite sure that the news that the battalion had been in action brought some recruits. Please try to make East Grinstead understand that the news of more recruits will be the signal for the battalion to be sent into action again. In our attack the men were splendid, a fact which, I am glad to say, is likely to be recognised in a public way soon. On two occasions parties of the enemy have tried to find our men asleep in the trenches, and both attacks were handsomely repulsed. In fact, on the last occasion we not only had dead Turks to show, but a patrol followed them up and brought in some more rifles and ammunition. The casualties, I am glad to say, have not been severe, considering the conditions of the fighting, but the wastage generally has been rather heavy and should be replaced without delay."

JOIN AT ONCE!

Printed, by permission of the Censor, by Henry W. Cullen, East Grinstead.

Private Harry Tuck of Worthing was killed in action on 9 August. He was barely 15 years of age. Described in a local newspaper as 'remarkably well developed for his age', he had persuaded recruiting officials he was of army age and joined the reserve unit of the 4th Battalion. He promised his mother he would not go abroad but when numbers were required to bring the active service contingent up to strength, he was among the first to volunteer. Under-age recruitment was not uncommon until the introduction of conscription in 1916 made it more difficult to falsify age.[105]

Sergeant Frank Newman of Haywards Heath was one of the battalion's casualties from dysentery which was severe enough to be invalided home. He attributed his illness to the flies, the smell and the lack of provisions, the latter occasioned by 'the mules having stampeded in bringing them up'.[106]

It was a gallant but desperate campaign, undermined by poor leadership, and evacuation became the only option, the 4th Battalion leaving in December to join the Egyptian Force. Like Dunkirk, it was hailed at home as some sort of victory but in reality the Dardanelles remained untaken at a cost of 250,000 Allied casualties.

Egypt and Palestine

Both the 4th Battalion and 16th (Sussex Yeomanry) Battalion were involved in the Egyptian Expeditionary Force and the advance into Palestine in 1916–18.

The British garrison in Egypt was strengthened for the protection of the Suez Canal. Fighting in the Sinai Peninsula in 1916 initially saw the Turks pushed back to Gaza and Beersheba. The first full-scale battles were at Gaza in March-April 1917 but heat, exhaustion and a lack of water contributed to the failure of the two separate British assaults.

A letter home to Haywards Heath, from Private B. Cook, outlined the 4th Battalion's experiences of the first battle. After a full day's marching, and an artillery bombardment, the infantry prepared to advance on the Turkish positions:

> How we got across that shell-swept plain God only knows, for shrapnel was bursting all around us … The sun was shining down on us pitilessly, and, worst of all, we were short of water, as it was impossible to get transport up, for as soon as the camels … advanced they were cut to pieces. At last we arrived … into a large gully, where we had a breather. Then came the order to fix bayonets and charge. With a mighty shout, over the top we went, into the front line through a perfect hail of bullets and shrapnel, which dealt out death and destruction all about … We put up as brave a fight as any Regiment ever did, but we had to retreat at last, for no living thing could hope to get through that inferno of shell-fire … I cannot praise the good old Sussex too highly.[107]

Under General Allenby's inspired leadership, renewed attacks on Beersheba and Gaza in October-November were successful, opening the way into the Holy Land.

The 16th Battalion took a leading role in the advance into Palestine. In his battalion history, Captain Herbert Ivor Powell-Edwards praised its achievements in the Battle of Sheria on 6 November 1917; advancing through a well-entrenched zone under incessant fire, capturing 350 prisoners and inflicting heavy casualties:

Victory Parade. The 4th Battalion march through Bethlehem, December 1917. (WSRO RSR PH 4/56)

The Battalion had covered itself with glory in an action which was essentially a 'soldier's battle' and in which artillery fire on our own side had been quite absent till the last moment ... They had out shot, out manoeuvred and out fought a stubborn and courageous enemy; company commanders, subalterns and NCOs had supported one another's actions most effectively and section leaders had shown themselves possessed of a dash, drive and initiative in action which were the admiration of the officers ...[108]

The elation of being part of a conquering army was savoured, the 4th Battalion being showered from balconies and windows with dry figs and oranges as it marched into Bethlehem on 10 December 1917, but though a notable success, the campaign had little material impact on the heart of the war in France and Flanders.[109]

India

Early in the war, most British troops in India were transferred to Europe and other theatres. One brigade of Regulars was kept back to protect the North West Frontier and this included the 1st Battalion.

It took part in operations against rebellious tribesmen and endured sickness occasioned by the extremes of heat. During the Third Afghan War in May-August 1919, its gallant defence of posts on Orange Patch Ridge was formally recognised by a change of name to Sussex Ridge. Its casualties during the war included forty-four fatalities.

During this time, drafts were despatched to reinforce units in Mesopotamia and it was from its officers on the North West

Camp of the 1st Battalion at Ali Masjid, Khyber Pass, Third Afghan War, 1919. (WSRO RSR PH 1/40)

Frontier that emerged one of the most fascinating characters of the war. Colonel Gerard Leachman had travelled extensively in Arabia and in 1915 was sent to Basra, where he organised an Intelligence Service against the Turks. He lived in the desert, dressed as an Arab, spoke the language and, in some eyes, his exploits bore comparison with those of Lawrence of Arabia.[110]

The remaining Regulars in India were supplemented by Territorials and in February 1916 the 1st Battalion was joined by the 2/6th Battalion. Its experiences are recorded in battalion journals, the *Royal Sussex Herald*, published fortnightly throughout the war.[111] In addition, several hundred photographs exist, products of the Kodak vest-pocket autographic camera, known as 'the soldier's camera'.[112]

Skirmishes against hostile tribesmen enlivened the routine of frontier patrols and garrison duties. In May 1917, the battalion joined the Waziristan Field Force and encountered its toughest fighting against the Mahsuds.[113] A memorial was erected in Lahore in November 1919 in memory of the four officers and fifty-six other ranks of the 2/6th who died in India during the war.

Northern Russia

The 11th Battalion returned home from France in June 1918. At Aldershot it was reorganised for service with the North Russian Relief Force, sent to support the British garrison at Murmansk and Archangel. The garrison was originally intended to protect the two ports from seizure by the Germans after the collapse of Russia in 1917 but was retained until the course of the Bolshevik Revolution had been resolved.

The battalion sailed from Leith in September 1918, to endure a winter that brought sub-zero temperatures, influenza and pneumonia. Following its ordeal on the Western Front, involvement in a civil war in the inhospitable lands of the Arctic Circle appeared poor reward.

The story is told in the diary of Sergeant William Chessum. They were kitted out on the advice of the Antarctic explorer, Sir Ernest Shackleton. Their home was the monastery at Pechenga. They admired the Northern Lights and learned to ski. Early in 1919, they were transported by reindeer and sleigh to

N.C.O.s AND MEN OF THE 11.TH BATT. ROYAL SUSSEX REGT

IN ARCTIC DRESS.

Kola, a garrison 10 miles inland from Murmansk. Here they guarded the railway and provided armed escorts on trains carrying supplies to the fighting forces up country.

They were not intended to take part in the fighting themselves, but when more reserves were needed they were moved to Kandalaksha, a small port on the Murman coast. Illness in such extreme climatic conditions claimed lives and in 1988 excavations of a former British military cemetery at Murmansk revealed the graves of eight men of the 11th Battalion. The battalion remained in Russian Lapland until August 1919.[114]

Photograph from the diary of Sergeant William Chessum, 11th Battalion, with the North Russian Relief Force in the Arctic Circle, 1919. (WSRO RSR Ms. 7/61)

Living in the Trenches

How did they cope with it all, that generation of young men, plucked from the towns and villages of Sussex and transported to the ghastliness of the Western Front?

Alongside the prospect of death or mutilation on the battle-field, there was the daily trial of survival amidst the desperate conditions of the trenches. Space was cramped, shared with rats and lice. With corpses and food scraps lying about, the rats grew fat and bold. Lice infested clothing, sometimes inducing trench fever, causing headaches, inflamed eyes and muscle pain. Trench foot could ravage a battalion, the potential for gangrene posing a real threat. In cold, wet, insanitary conditions, the rubbing of feet with grease was vital.

Lieutenant Ivan Margary, 7th Battalion, from East Grinstead, gave his impressions of trenches on the Arras battlefields in June 1917:

Ralph Ellis, whose journals of the 7th Battalion give a graphic insight into life on the Western Front. He was later commissioned with the Queen's (Royal West Surrey) Regiment. (WSRO Add. Ms. 25,001)

If one got a peep at the ground around the trenches, one saw it was dotted all over with little heaps, dead bodies. Some were buried close to the trench, even in its sides or floor, and occasionally a limb protruded. The smell was appalling ... During the days, which were hot and bright, the trenches swarmed with hosts of large green bluebottle flies which were most unpleasant. It was difficult even to eat one's food without a dozen or more trying to settle on the plate on one's lap.[115]

Letters, diaries and memoirs, and the columns of local newspapers, reveal something of how the infantryman adapted to life at the front and suggest a number of factors sustained morale in the trenches.

There were many who were supported in their darkest hours by their faith. They left England assured their duty was both to country and God. The Dean of Chichester urged 4th Battalion recruits to join the fight on behalf of 'the whole civilised world'.[116] The Church emphasised this was a righteous war against a godless enemy. At Fernhurst, Revd George Ranking compared the sufferings of his parishioners serving at the front with those of Calvary.[117] Army chaplains and organisations such as the Soldiers' Christian

Association, sought to sustain spiritual life at the front. Ranking went out there himself in March 1917 as a chaplain but was killed later that year.

It was a source of strength that their new experiences were endured alongside friends from home or at least fellows from the same familiar county. Sergeant Charles Tulett, 7th Battalion, spoke of the camaraderie of the trenches in his memoirs:

> The friendship and spirit was tremendous and it mattered not whether you were coming or going out of the line someone was always ready to hand you a cigarette or a drink of char and we can never forget the parcels from home. I can remember my parents sending me out a nice rabbit pie, but when it arrived it was in a very smashed state but I did the best I could and shared it around. It was most enjoyable and we had a jolly good laugh.[118]

Mutual support and comradeship derived too from the sense of brotherhood created by belonging to a county regiment with a proud history. The title 'Iron Regiment', so hard won at Ypres, inspired the men. Letters home constantly refer to the stoic qualities of the 'Old Sussex' in holding the line, or carrying on the attack, when others proved less resilient.

Comforts sent by family and friends or by committees of good ladies were gratefully received. For Christmas 1914, Catherine Buchanan of Lavington Park despatched over 1,000 boxes to men of the regiment in France, each containing chocolate, handkerchiefs, postcards, pencil, cigarettes, soap and socks, muffler or mittens.[119]

In letters home, their concerns were invariably less with great issues of war than with everyday matters of survival such as health, warmth and food, and with news of pals and family. For civilian soldiers, thoughts of home gave them an inner strength, a steadfast determination, to endure the fear and deprivation of a war of unknown duration. Censorship, in any case, limited the war news sent home but many letters seem to shield family from too close an awareness of the writer's new world.

CSM Nelson Victor Carter, 12th Battalion, wrote home to his wife and daughter from the Fleurbaix sector in March 1916:

Just a few lines to let you know that I am in the pink of condition and I hope that you are both the same. I have written to Jess, have you heard from him, is he out of Hospital yet. I may stand a chance of running up against Ernest out here. This is a lovely place, plenty of everything including Weather as well. I want you to send me out my sleeping helmet and a pad of writing paper and Envelopes. We have still go[t] old Bones and he looks after the food part of the Business … I am getting as fat as a little pig and as happy as a little dog with two tails …[120]

Towards those less needful of such protection, there are tantalising glimpses into the reality of trench war. Private George Baker, 13th Battalion, wrote to Ernest Shippam, his employer in Chichester: 'I have seen things that I would not write about. It makes me shudder when I recall it to my mind.'[121]

Constant exposure to such things bred a sense of self-preservation in the battle-hardened infantryman, as Baker confided:

When you kill a German who tries to stop you, and a second and a third one, you just give him a mechanical look to see if he is dead and then pass on. The usual severance of Death is lost on you. If you argue at all it is in this strain 'His life or mine' and the instinct of self-preservation prevails above all else. It is not callousness it is just War.[122]

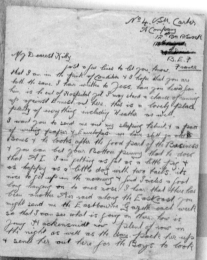

Leave was a precious release, yet could be times of mixed emotions, pleasurable in anticipation but not always in reality, and marred at the end by the torment of parting.

The courage of the soldier going back from leave was not easily shared. Writing in August 1916, a correspondent of the *Mid-Sussex Times* captured the emotion of departure:

'My Dearest Kitty.' Nelson Victor Carter's letter home to his wife, written shortly after arriving in France with the 12th Battalion in March 1916. (WSRO RSR Ms. 7/27)

A young man in khaki who had been home was 'off back'. He was happy and smiling. It was those on the platform who felt the going away … The old dad stood on one side, tight-lipped, and said nothing. A girl wept and dabbed her eyes with her handkerchief. Mother kept biting her lip. Her heart was very full. When she did speak it was to say, with tears in her eyes, 'You'll write, won't you?' … The whistle blew, and the guard waved his hand … The mother turned swiftly and her cheeks were wet with tears. Only the Man of Sorrows fully knew the depth of that mother's sorrow. And she is one of many![123]

Rest time behind the lines was relished. Ralph Ellis was one for whom the respite that punctuated front-line duty provided, in observation of life and nature, the sustenance to offset a little the ugliness of war. Here, he describes one such interlude, with the 7th Battalion in rest billets at Festubert in the winter of 1915/16:

These were vagabond days, too few in number when one could find time to wander out into the swampy, deserted meadows, overgrown with tall rushes and coarse grass, giving cover to coot and moor-hen, seeking to disturb the bittern I thought to be there and other interesting wild-fowl, then returning to a dimly lit billet, a blazing wood fire, and to revel in sleep, curled up snugly in blanket and great-coat.[124]

Charles Tulett recalled a period of relief away from the crater fighting in the Hohenzollern Redoubt:

The place was Béthune, a lovely spot, where we could buy plenty of edibles and wine, and the inhabitants were very kind and helpful to us. Our first days were spent in fitting out with clean clothing, bathing, inoculation, etc, also route marches to get boots and feet in order. In the evenings we had concerts … The Corps of Drums whenever possible would come and meet us from the trenches during relief. As soon as we were away it was so inspiring when the Band struck up all the marches and old songs, which we joined in and let rip at our hearts content, so glad to be away from it all, if only for a short while.[125]

Organised entertainment was valued as a means of maintaining morale. A letter from Lance-Corporal T. Turner, 8th Battalion, in February 1918, spoke of the regiment's own Concert Party:

> One of the most popular and well known parties who have toured France and Flanders are 'The Star Shells' composed entirely of men from the Pioneer Battalion of The Royal Sussex Regiment … They were formed just over twelve months ago … Our theatre at present is situated in close proximity to our firing line, and the boys call in to see us on their way back from the line after doing reliefs.[126]

Thoughts of home. Private James Henry Taylor Edwards, 4th Battalion, writes home to his mother in Chichester. (WSRO RSR MS. Uncatalogued. Papers of Private James Henry Taylor Edwards)

Letters home show the men raised their spirits with their own impromptu sing-songs at opportune moments and, in response to requests from the front, local newspapers organised the despatch of musical instruments to help 'liven things up'.[127]

One song in particular galvanised the Sussex boys. William Ward-Higgs of South Bersted wrote 'Sussex-by-the-Sea' in 1904 for a sister-in-law on her marriage to an officer of the 2nd Battalion. It became an inspirational marching song in the war.[128]

In his diary, RSM Rainsford spoke of the 2nd Battalion marching to the front line at Aubers Ridge singing the song 'lustily'.[129] Drummer Ballam, in a letter home to Horsham, reported that it was sung by the Royal Sussex in the trenches as they waited the signal to go over the top at the start of that battle.[130] Colonel Langham marched the remnants of his 5th Battalion out of the same action, singing the song. 'You can tell them all, that we stand or fall, for Sussex-by-the-Sea.'

Similarly, humour was a foil to the brutalisation of the trenches, diverting attention from the horrifying and playing its part in raising spirits and preserving sanity.

The cartoons of Bruce Bairnsfather featuring 'Old Bill', a curmudgeonly soldier with walrus moustache and balaclava, knee-deep in mud, under a torrent of shells, personified the image of war in the trenches as dogged endurance, resilient spirit and ironic humour. One Chichester lad wrote home from Flanders in October 1917: 'The rain and mud here is terrible now, just like the Bruce Bairnsfather cartoons.'[131] West Sussex can in part claim him as its own as he lived at Northchapel for a while.

Poetry was another artistic product of the war, often poignantly contrasting the idyll of home with the hell of the trenches. Great names adorn the literature of the war but others are unknown or long-forgotten.

One was the unidentified 'Field Officer' of the 4th Battalion, Royal Sussex, who published *A Soldier's Sonnets: Verses Grave and Gay* in 1916.[132] 'A Mother's Lament' confronts the loss of a son and evokes the pain of that most heart-rending moment: the knock at the door, the telegram boy and the dreaded news. These lines would echo the sentiments of so many mothers bereaved by the war:

"George", a great humourist, but to whom the terror of war was always present. Killed by a stray bullet at Hulluch. Sept. 1915.

'George, a great humourist.' A sketch, poignantly captioned, by Sergeant Ralph Ellis of a fellow soldier of the 7th Battalion, killed at the Battle of Loos. (WSRO Add. Ms. 25,002, f. 10v.)

> There was no other child to fill your empty bed,
> You were my all, my life, my only joy.
> And in the garden of my broken heart
> The flower was plucked, for you were dead.

The Aftermath

Casualties

A total of 7,302 names are inscribed on the memorial panels in the Regimental Chapel of St George in Chichester Cathedral. This figure comprises 390 officers and 6,912 other ranks killed during the war.

For the 2nd Battalion, with over 1,700 dead, there are nominal rolls and casualty lists that quantify exactly the scale of their losses, revealing not only those killed but also the vast numbers

The Royal Sussex Regiment Memorial Chapel in Chichester Cathedral, unveiled on 11 November 1921, showing on the right some of the panels naming the fallen of the First World War. (WSRO PH 17,404)

of wounded and hospitalised. Some were burdened by their wounds and disabilities, physical and mental, until their death fifty or sixty years later.[133]

For the long-term casualties, and for the widows left behind, there was the ongoing problem of making ends meet in a society yet to invest in a welfare state. Some widows quickly remarried but the war drastically reduced the availability of potential bread-winners. Public subscription, such as that which sustained the Carter family, played a part. The Royal Sussex Regimental Aid Society organised a fund 'to lighten the burden of these broken heroes of our county Regiment'.[134]

For those able to re-join the labour market on demobilisation, future prospects varied. Some employers were generous in re-engaging former employees who had served their country, whilst others were less able or willing to do so. One notable benefactor, a former officer, Captain Rupert Middleton MC, created the Blue Flash Association for demobilised men of the 4th Battalion, whom he employed in his cinemas in Horsham and Shoreham.[135]

Prisoners of War

Compared with the Second World War, few prisoners were taken in the Great War. In the 2nd Battalion, for example, only one officer and thirty-eight other ranks were captured.

Captain Claude Lapworth, 11th Battalion, was taken prisoner on the Somme in March 1918. His diary provides a rare insight into the life of a POW in Germany. His first camp, at Rastatt on the edge of the Black Forest, was a harsh introduction: 700 officers sleeping 50 to a hut, with poor food and sanitary arrangements.

On 4 June he was transferred to Schweidnitz in Silesia, where conditions were better. Several escape attempts were made which, though usually unsuccessful, reflect the imperative to escape, or at least cause problems for their captors. He was freed on 29 November and arrived home on Christmas Day.[136]

One camp with a notorious reputation was Holzminden in Lower Saxony. It held up to 600 British officers. One casualty was Captain Frederick Godman, 9th Battalion, from Wivelsfield. He had been wounded and taken prisoner at Loos and died in October 1917. A report in the *Daily Express* a year later implied he had been deprived of food and attention while sick.[137]

Ex-Sergeant Charles Tulett, 7th Battalion, wearing his campaign and gallantry medals, presented to Queen Mary on her visit to Shippam's factory in Chichester, in July 1924. (WSRO Slides Collection. 'Royal Sussex Regiment in Great War' presentation. Slide No. 95)

Honours and Awards

Official recognition, promotion within the ranks or decoration, was a factor in maintaining morale.

Gallantry medals were appreciated by their recipients. They were proudly worn by Old Comrades on remembrance occasions long after the war, as indeed were the campaign medals, the 1914 or 1914/15 Star, British War Medal and Victory Medal, awarded to all who served in overseas theatres of war.[138]

On 29 July 1924, Queen Mary visited Shippam's factory in Chichester and met the fifty ex-servicemen on the workforce. She congratulated Charles Tulett on his Military Medal, won with the 7th Battalion at Monchy in April 1917. Ninety years after the war, it was still being proudly worn, by his son, at the Cenotaph on Remembrance Day.[139]

Remembrance

The Chapel of St George, the Regimental Association and the Regimental Museum continue to cherish and preserve the memory of the fallen. So, too, do the regimental archives in the

A selection of soldiers' documents of the First World War. From the archives of the Royal Sussex Regiment at West Sussex Record Office. (WSRO RSR Mss. 2/53, 59-60)

County Record Office at Chichester. There will be found that most precious legacy, the thoughts and words of those who answered the call to arms in the War to end Wars. Therein lies the testament of their youth, a tribute to courage and endurance, a memorial to service and self-sacrifice.

Edmund Blunden provides some of our most eloquent and compelling prose of the war. In *Undertones of War*, one can detect, amidst the unspeakable torment of those years, the brotherly fellowship that existed within the county regiment.

He leaves us here with an epitaph to the men of the Royal Sussex Regiment who served their country, and their county, on the battlefields of the First World War and a reminder of our duty to keep their memory alive:

It is time to hint to a new age what your value, what your love was; your Ypres is gone, and you are gone; we were lucky to see you 'in the pink' against white-ribbed and socket-eyed despair.[140]

3

Sussex Goes Khaki: Billeting and Military Installations

By Martin Mace

Billeting

There were so many men in uniform across West Sussex that emergency accommodation had to be found and Chichester became a billeting centre. The Corn Exchange became the temporary home of 140 of the Hampshire Carabineers and a club in South Street was occupied by a unit of the Cyclist Corps from the Isle of Wight.

However, further places were needed, and West Sussex Constabulary's Deputy Chief Constable, Superintendent Horace Ellis, 'with his usual tact and good judgement', invited residents to offer accommodation (rather than using his compulsory powers), sending his officers round to speak to them. As a result, the residents responded 'in the most patriotic manner'. Ellis was awarded the King's Police Medal in the New Year's Honours in 1915. In most houses the residents agreed to accommodate from two to four soldiers and were given an allowance of 2s 3d per soldier per day.

The billeting of troops not only gave an income to those households that took soldiers in, but the local economies received a welcome boost from the influx of so many men. Littlehampton and Arundel promoted themselves as having accommodation available for the troops. In Bognor it was stated that 'if it should be found expedient to billet a thousand or so Troops in that town during the winter [of 1914/15], a good many local householders as well as tradesmen would be very glad'.

Billeted men and housemaids, Wynnestead boarding house, New Steyne Road, Worthing, c. 1914; donated by Stephen Hoad. (Walter Gardiner Photography Collection, WSCCLS, D000101)

There were even complaints that Arundel had missed out on the billeting of troops to other places nearby; one Alderman Whittaker said that representations should be made to the War Office as 'he understood that Horsham only got the troops through the good offices of a well-known military gentleman'. Just 500 soldiers billeted in the town would 'make all the difference to the kind of winter the borough would experience'. Likewise, and eager not to miss out, the town clerk of Bognor wrote to the War Office, stating that the town could provide accommodation for 5,000 troops.

Not everyone welcomed the troops. A Broadwater resident 'ventilated a genuine grievance' to the *Worthing Gazette*:

> … the men took up their billets on Monday afternoon. We were given no orders whatsoever. The poor fellows were wet through and hungry, and the majority of the residents gave them tea and supper, and also breakfast on the Tuesday. On that day we were given to understand that 1s 1d per day for each man would be allowed, for which we were expected to provide bed, vegetables, milk, condiments, and attendance, which I am sure is not overpaying. On the following Sunday, an Officer called and notified us that from and including that day we were to get 2s 6d for each man, to board them; but on the Monday rations were again issued. Greatly to our surprise, on drawing the billeting money we found the payment only started from the Tuesday. We do not want to make anything out of the brave fellows who are going to fight for us, but they on a good many instances felt most uncomfortable at the thought of working people having to provide for them, and not being paid for or any notice taken of it.

The Bishop of Chichester also complained to *The Times* about the practice of billeting the soldiers in public houses:

> It certainly seems most inconsistent to close the public houses earlier at this critical time and yet to select them as desirable homes for our soldiers. I understand that the

payment made in such cases is less than that paid to the owners of private houses; but the saving of threepence a night per head surely does not justify such an arrangement unless it is a matter of necessity.

It was not just soldiers for whom billeting arrangements were made. Home owners in the Littlehampton, Westhampnett and Bognor districts were notified in the autumn of 1917 that, under the Billeting of Civilians Act, room would have to be found for a large number of people working on munitions in the area. This news, it would seem, was not as well received as the billeting of troops was earlier in the war as it was stated that it was hoped that enough accommodation could be found voluntarily – but if not compulsory powers were available to the authorities. There was an appeals procedure against having workers forced upon a household.

Military Camps

Following the outbreak of hostilities in 1914, Lord Kitchener, the Secretary of State for War, sought to raise a volunteer army to reinforce the BEF on the Continent. Young men poured into the recruiting offices and Kitchener was able to form five Army Groups. These men had to be turned into soldiers and large training camps were established around the country. One of those was at **Shoreham-by-Sea**.[141]

With a railhead, seaport and airport in a strategic position on the South Coast, Shoreham-by-Sea was ideally placed. It duly became the location for the formation of much of the 24th Division, part of Kitchener's Third Army Group, or K3 as it was known.

Local Territorial Army soldiers began creating a tented camp on the Oxen Field to the north of Mill Lane but the influx of recruits was so great that churches and even private individuals took in some of the men. As more recruits arrived, the camp was extended into Buckingham Park, where a field kitchen and latrines were dug.

A parade square was laid out on Mill Hill and wooden buildings erected for the headquarters staff, the quartermaster's department and the medical team. So great was the volume of letters handled by the post office at Shoreham that an army post office was established at the camp. One facility that was lacking at Shoreham Camp was a laundry so local people were asked to take in the soldiers' washing.

Evening classes were established in the camp for the troops. These included courses in first aid, cookery (which was compulsory for all soldiers), and a number of foreign languages. There were about 1,350 men taking part in the various classes each evening, including 600 taking French, 80 learning German and 70 taking Flemish.

During the camp's first winter, heavy rain caused mudslides which poured into, through and over the tents. As a result, wooden huts were erected in 1915. These could each accommodate twenty men, in charge of whom was a corporal.

An important part of the recruits' training was, of course, rifle practice. Unfortunately, when the camp opened there were only two rifles for the entire division, these having been borrowed from Lancing College Officer Training Corps. Eventually practice ranges were set up, one of which, complete with painted backgrounds to give the impression of being out in the countryside, was set up on the ground floor of the Marlipins Museum. Others were housed in two greenhouses at East Worthing.

Entrance to the army camp, Slonk Hill, near Shoreham-by-Sea. (WSCCLS; P003437)

Army camp hut interior, Shoreham-by-Sea, c. 1916. (Marlipins Museum, 89.561)

Eventually, outdoor rifles ranges were constructed and, in due course, the area above Buckingham Park and Slonk Hill became a realistic battle zone, complete with trenches and barbed wire.

Gradually the men were turned into soldiers and issued with their weapons. The division, by then some 35,000 strong and arranged into three brigades (the 71st, 72nd and 73rd Brigades) with a Machine Gun Battalion and a Cyclist Company plus supporting artillery and cavalry, moved to Aldershot between 19 and 23 June 1915 for final training.

Shoreham continued to be a training camp, its buildings taking on an ever more permanent nature so that by the end of the war it had all the appearance of a small wooden town. Throughout the course of the conflict, five divisions were trained at Shoreham-by-Sea, the men coming from all across the country to learn the art of war. Often the soldiers could be seen marching down through the High Street and over Norfolk Bridge, singing 'It's a Long Way to Tipperary' or other popular songs as they went for their afternoon dip.

On two occasions the camp was inspected by King George V. The first time was on 3 November 1916. The Royal car took the King and Queen up to the camp through streets lined on either side by Canadian soldiers standing to attention.

A similar camp was established in the grounds of **Roffey Park** in Horsham. The first unit to be based there was the 22nd (Service) Battalion, Royal Fusiliers (the Kensington Battalion). Representing all social classes (bankers and stevedores, writers and labourers) and with a strong colonial influence, the battalion was raised by the Mayor and Borough of Kensington on 11 September 1914 at White City.

The hunt was soon on to find suitable winter quarters for the men. The solution was provided by its first commanding officer, Colonel Archibald Innes. A Boer War veteran, Innes 'owned land in Roffey about 2 miles north of the town of Horsham which he was prepared to hire out'.[142]

The advance elements of the battalion arrived in Roffey the following month, only to be greeted by very sparse, if non-existent, accommodation. Frantic negotiations began to billet the troops in private homes nearby, and 'A', 'B' and 'C' companies were eventually housed in properties in Horsham and the men of 'D' Company in Roffey itself.

The 22nd Royal Fusiliers remained at Roffey until June 1915 when, as part of 99th Brigade, 33rd Division, it moved to Clipstone Camp in Nottinghamshire. As for Roffey Camp, in time it became almost as permanent and extensive as that at Shoreham-by-Sea.

Entrance to Roffey Park Camp near Horsham, one of a postcard series published by the YMCA. (Martin Mace/HMP)

Goodwood Park was also used for training purposes. In September 1914, for example, the 1st Infantry Brigade, accompanied by two batteries of artillery and the 15th Hussars, spent a week under canvas, practising 'tactical exercises' in the Lavant-Singleton area. It was not all serious stuff though, as the camp was visited by citizens from Chichester and a regimental band played each evening for the benefit of the soldiers and Cicestrians alike.[143]

Aerodromes

The civilian airfield at **Shoreham-by-Sea** (which was founded in 1910 and is the oldest airport in the UK) was used for military purposes in the First World War, as a training airfield (see Chapter 4 for further information). It was formally taken over by the RFC in 1915, when No. 3 Reserve Aeroplane Squadron arrived, flying Maurice Farman Longhorns and Shorthorns. Amongst those young pilots who learnt their trade at Shoreham-by-Sea during the First World War was Sholto Douglas who, in the Second World War, became the chief of Fighter Command after Hugh Dowding, and Harold Balfour who became Under Secretary of State for Air in 1938.

In May 1916, 21 Reserve Squadron was resident at Shoreham. After 'working up', the squadron flew its Royal Aircraft Factory RE7s (these were two-seat light bomber and reconnaissance biplanes) to France. This was followed by 53 Squadron, which operated Royal Aircraft Factory BE2cs.

Hangars 3 to 7, Shoreham Aerodrome, with Pashley Bros Farman biplane in the air and an Avro biplane is parked in background left. (Marlipins Museum, 95.2667.7)

It was whilst flying from Shoreham that Lieutenant W.F. Sharpe, a Canadian officer serving with the RFC, crashed near the Sussex Pad public house. Another crash occurred on 21 August 1917, when Lieutenant W.T. Harris' aeroplane suffered engine failure and came down at Ecclesden Farm, Angmering, whilst Lieutenant Aime Leger (a French-Canadian from the Canadian Forestry Corps but attached to 3 Training Squadron RFC) was killed on 4 September that year when he crashed into the sea after his exhaust manifold had fouled his propeller.

There was another fatal air crash, also in 1917 – this time on 22 May. Four aeroplanes were flying in company and an eyewitness noted that one dropped a little behind the others. Then it caught them up, and looked as if it intended to go between them. Suddenly the wings of two of them touched. A woman who saw the crash said that 'the air seemed full of sparks' and then the two aeroplanes fell. Second-Lieutenants William Vince and Cyril Crapp were both killed.

No. 3 Reserve Squadron was re-named No. 3 Training Squadron in early 1917, which more accurately described its function. The following year the South East Area Flying Instructors' School was formed at Shoreham, equipped with nineteen Avro 504 trainers. One of these aeroplanes was involved in a most remarkable incident in early 1918.

It was the practice for mechanics to lie across the tailplane to keep it down while the pilot warmed up the engine. However, it seems that on this occasion the pilot had just landed and so considered a warm-up was therefore unnecessary. He took off again almost straight away – unaware that a mechanic had climbed onto the back of the aircraft and was clinging on to the tailplane. With the machine heavily unbalanced, the pilot somehow managed to circle the aerodrome and, as the tide was out in the River Adur, bring his aircraft down in a flat spin on to the soft mud. The mechanic survived with a broken leg, whilst the pilot broke his nose on the instrument panel.[144]

In November 1916, Lieutenant Geoffrey Dorman of the RFC was flying his Royal Aircraft Factory FE2b biplane when it developed engine trouble on a flight from Shoreham-by-Sea to Gosport. He managed to land the aeroplane in a field without damage and in his report on the incident he suggested that where he landed would be suitable for an airfield. That field, part of a farm on the Goodwood Estate, was compulsory purchased less than a year later to become **Tangmere Station**, RFC.[145]

Altogether, 200 acres of land, including a substantial part of Church Farm, was requisitioned for the aerodrome and a temporary 2 foot-gauge railway was laid from the London, Brighton & South Coast Railway's goods sidings at Drayton, just a mile away. Along this route wagonloads of sand, gravel and other building material were transported.

The first aircraft to operate from Tangmere were those of the RFC's Nos 91, 92 and 93 squadrons, which used the aerodrome for training purposes, flying SE5Aa, Avro 404s and Bristol F2Bs. The RFC, however, was only a temporary resident as, on 1 August 1918, Tangmere became the home of the Air Service of the American Expeditionary Force (ASAEF). It was intended that night-bombing squadrons would be equipped and trained at five airfields in Sussex before being transferred to France. A series of setbacks and delays meant that by the time of the Armistice in November 1918, only Tangmere and Ford Junction were actually operational.

Ford Junction, like Tangmere, was close to completion by the end of the war. It was intended to be a training base for Handley Page O/400 twin-engine bombers. Under the terms of the Handley Page Agreement between the governments of the United States and Britain, it was arranged that the former would fabricate and supply parts for the Handley Page bombers, which would be assembled in factories in Oldham by British workers. The agreement also committed the US to send labourers to construct aerodromes.

Another of the West Sussex airfields was established on 159 acres of land at **Rustington**, an area stretching from Ash Lane to Pigeon House Lane and to the north and south of Station Road. US personnel left in November 1918, as soon as the Armistice was signed, without a single operation having ever been flown.

In a memo signed by the US Air-Service Chief of the Night Bombardment Section, it was noted that on 20 November 1918, the hangars at Rustington were 75 per cent built, the Handley Page building 80 per cent complete, the airstrip 60 per cent, living

Temporary canvas covered hangars, with Farman aircraft in the foreground, at Ford Junction Aerodrome. (Courtesy US Government; Imperial War Museum, Q113464)

quarters 90 per cent, regimental institute 90 per cent, lavatories 90 per cent and the remaining buildings 40 per cent. The hangars were designed for aircraft erection and repair.[146] The main entrance into the airfield was from Station Road, and is now the entrance to Sea Avenue.

The buildings at Rustington had a span of 75 feet and were 408 feet long. The aerodrome was served by a railway branch line so that the bombers could be transported in crated parts to be assembled at Rustington in the sheds at the training depot. A siding off the London, Brighton & South Coast Railway was also constructed, connecting the base to Angmering Station. The aerodrome's official address was: American Construction Detachment, Army Service Component Command, Rustington RAF Training Depot, Rustington, Sussex.[147]

The other proposed ASAEF aerodrome was at Goring-by-Sea, on the then empty fields between Limbrick Lane and Field Place. This, though, was not started before the war drew to a close.[148]

Middleton Aircraft Works

Norman Arthur Thompson, a prosperous layman, became interested in aircraft design before the war. In conjunction with an old school friend, Dr John Douglas Campbell White, he began work on an experimental aeroplane with advice from E.W. Lanchester, a consultant with the Daimler Company. Thompson and Lanchester made a series of trips to the South Coast to find a suitable location for 'a flying ground' and found what seemed to be a perfect location at Middleton-on-Sea. 'Here the foreshore consisted of several miles of good, firm sand about 300 to 400 yards wide at low tide and free of obstruction of any kind.'[149] So was created the White and Thompson Aeronautic Works. Ironically, soon afterwards the ideal landing ground suffered from severe coastal erosion which swept away much of the sand, but the factory remained there.

The Thompson-Lanchester No. 1 biplane, 'The Grey Angel', was their first collaboration and was built as a military reconnaissance aircraft. This did not meet the army's needs but eventually one of their designs was accepted by the Admiralty. This was the NT2B, which became the company's most successful aeroplane. It was the Royal Naval Air Service's main flying-boat trainer. The White and Thompson factory also produced a land-based aircraft, the NT3 Reconnaissance and Coastal Patrol biplane, which was referred to by some as the 'Bognor Bloater'. This nickname came from its unusual monocoque fuselage.

Small America NT4A (plus factory and NT2B behind) at Middleton. (Imperial War Museum, Q63836)

Twelve Bognor Bloaters were ordered, but only ten were delivered to the Admiralty, the other two being kept for spares. The Bloaters entered service with the Royal Naval Air Service in 1915 and had only limited use in communications and training roles but mainly operated on coastal patrols from the air stations including the one at Eastbourne.

It was the flying-boats, however, that provided most of the work for the Middleton works and the Hubert Williams Littlehampton factory. A total of somewhere between 249 and 253 aircraft were built throughout the course of the war and, at the peak of production, between 700 and 900 people were employed across the two sites.

Ports

With the war on the Western Front so close to the English Channel, the Sussex ports were constantly in use by the Royal Navy throughout the conflict.

By 1916 **Littlehampton** had been taken over completely by the military authorities. Enormous quantities of weapons, equipment and assorted supplies passed through the port. Access to Littlehampton port is limited by the bar at the harbour entrance and the fighting on the Continent consumed so much materiel that an attempt was made to improve access by blowing up the bar. Though the high-explosive charge certainly threw sand and shingle off the bar, the tidal flow soon restored the status quo.

Ships were not the only war-related objects to be seen floating at Littlehampton. On Fisherman's Quay, the little workshop of Hubert Williams manufactured the hulls for seaplanes. These were then transported to the White and Thompson works at Middleton-on-Sea (of which the Littlehampton works were a subsidiary) to become part of a NT flying-boat. The completed aircraft could often be spotted on the Arun.

The waters off Littlehampton were also the setting for a review of the Royal Navy's destroyer flotillas. On Monday, 7 September 1914, the flotillas of fifty-seven warships assembled off Beachy Head and then sailed along the coast, anchoring offshore between Littlehampton and Selsey Bill. Large crowds watched as the King then put to sea in the Royal Yacht to inspect the warships before they undertook exercises. It was reported that 'at night their lights could be seen on the horizon like a row of tiny pin-heads'.[150]

Littlehampton was also the scene of much excitement when a seaplane landed just to the south of Beach Hotel. The pilot, Major Gordon of the Royal Marine Light Infantry, explained that he 'required more petrol'.

Possibly one of the most ambitious of all enterprises undertaken in West Sussex during the war was at **Shoreham Harbour**. Germany's declaration of unrestricted submarine warfare on 31 January 1917 meant that ships crossing the Atlantic were the target of German submarines operating out of Bruges. Various schemes were introduced to counter this situation, with varying degrees of success. Finally the Admiralty came up with a plan to prevent the German submarines from gaining access to the Atlantic and the Western Approaches by closing the Dover Strait. This secret project, codenamed 'M-N', was thought up by Royal Navy Captain D. Munro and designed by Admiralty designer G. Menzies.[151] Some sixteen towers were to be sunk across the Strait from the Goodwin Sands (near Dover/Folkestone), via Dungeness and the Varne Shoal, to Cap Gris Nez.[152] Each would have a garrison, be armed with guns and have enormous steel anti-submarine nets suspended between them.

Nissen huts on Southwick Green for workers constructing the 'Mystery Towers', 1918. (Marlipins Museum, Shoreham, 89.558)

Shoreham was chosen as a suitable location to build six of these towers[153] as it was sheltered from the sea and had a shingle beach capable of supplying material for concrete production. A workforce of 3,000 was brought in to construct them,[154] housed in a temporary hutted encampment at Southwick Green.[155]

A railway link was laid from the dock line under the road to the western arm of Shoreham Harbour. This then ran along the bottom of the embankment, across Kingston Lane, crossing the coast road and along the edge of the wharf, traversing what was then a single lock. The structures, known as the 'Mystery Towers' due to the level of security around their purpose, stood 190 feet high, built in three tapering tiers on top of vast hexagonal bases 195 feet wide.[156] The base was to be sunk in thirty fathoms of water. On top of that was a 1,000-ton, 100 feet-high steel cylinder which was where the garrison of ninety or so men and their supplies and submarine-detecting equipment would be housed. The towers would also have their own electricity-generating plant.

When the Armistice was declared, on 11 November 1918, only one tower was complete; a second was almost finished and several bases had been laid. It was decided to complete the construction of the two that were almost finished, but to scrap the others. Each was reported to have cost £1 million (£57 million today). In 1920 the completed tower was transported

Two of the 'Mystery Towers' under construction in Shoreham Harbour, c. 1918. (Martin Mace/HMP)

to the Nab sandbank, off the Isle of Wight, and fitted out as a combined lighthouse. Now known as the Nab Tower,[157] it can still be seen today and did actually serve a military function when, in the Second World War, it formed part of the Solent defences. No civilian use could be found for the second tower and it was demolished. The concrete was broken up and used as hardcore in the foundations of many local buildings, including greenhouses in Worthing.[158]

4

INVASION THREATS AND COUNTERMEASURES

By Martin Dale and Tim Stanton

Introduction

In 1914 the British Government based its home defence plans around countering traditional, small-scale seaborne attacks. If the enemy evaded the Royal Navy and reached West Sussex these attacks were to be repelled by Territorial Army units. Beyond these arrangements, central government initially acted as an enabler rather than an organiser, as local defence was not a high priority. Legislation such as the Defence of the Realm and Special Constables Acts, along with guidance on creating the Volunteer Training Corps (VTCs) and Emergency Committees, was used to harness local desire to help with the war effort.

The Perception and Reality of the Threats

The Royal Navy was the largest navy in the world in 1914 and Britain's first line of defence against invasion. The belief in the War Office and the Admiralty was that the navy could hold off any aggressor, making invasion unlikely. However, Germany's growing military power on land and sea left British military planners concerned that damaging raids might occur on major ports, as could sabotage attacks by small forces on vulnerable points along the coast.[159]

To prepare for this, home defence from 1908 to 1914 centred on the newly formed 'Territorial Force' (fourteen infantry divisions and fourteen cavalry brigades) of part-time soldiers, plus two divisions of the regular army.[160]

At the outbreak of war in August 1914, these territorial forces were mobilised to provide home and coastal defence of commercial ports and naval bases in the South of England. The Territorial battalions of the Royal Sussex Regiment (RSR) duly took up their duties: the 4th went to Newhaven, the 5th assembled at Hastings and the 6th deployed in Brighton, before moving to Norfolk. The Sussex Yeomanry also initially assembled at Brighton before moving to Canterbury.[161]

As the war moved closer to British waters in late 1914, these defence plans looked likely to be tested. In November and December 1914 the German High Seas fleet carried out raids on the East Coast towns of Yarmouth, Scarborough, Hartlepool and Whitby. The Royal Navy proved unable to intercept them. By this time Germany had also captured the Belgian ports of Ostend, Zeebrugge and Bruges, just a few hours' sailing from the South Coast. 1915 saw the Imperial German Navy build up the 'Flanders Flotilla' of ships and submarines in these ports, capable of bringing the war to British waters.[162]

Despite this, by late autumn 1914 the manpower needs of the British Army were so great that Territorial units tasked with home defence were asked to volunteer for service overseas. By 1916 all the RSR Territorial battalions had volunteered to fight or were acting as training units.[163]

To bolster depleted home defences, the War Office created a 'Central Force' held well back from the coast. Formed in late 1914, it consisted of nine Territorial Divisions and two Yeomanry Divisions. From headquarters in Tonbridge, Kent, the Central Force covered the West Sussex coastline as far west as Chichester.[164]

The next four years, however, would see the threat to West Sussex change in ways pre-war planners could never have imagined.

Protecting the Coast: Land, Sea and Air

When war was declared the only place in Sussex with significant defensive armament was Newhaven Fort in East Sussex,[165] which had two 6-inch guns installed to ward off any hostile ships.[166]

Shoreham Redoubt may have been maintained as a military establishment during the war, but with an obsolete gun.[167]

The perceived threat of coastal raids and sabotage led to a popular desire to assist the authorities in a system of early warning and patrol along the coast and inland. Under the direction of the police, special constables, volunteer 'civil guards' and Scouts all assisted in guarding railway junctions, bridges and waterworks from the threat of sabotage in the autumn of 1914.[168]

On the coast the Admiralty put in place a pre-war plan for a 'Coastwatch' in September 1914, to assist coastguard stations manned by the Royal Naval Reserve. Civilian volunteers were to report movements of shipping and aircraft. Under the 1914 Defence of the Realm Act (DORA) they had the power of special constables and could arrest persons thought to be behaving suspiciously around ports.[169]

Across West Sussex much of the manpower for coast and inland watch duties was supplied by the Scouts and Sea Scouts throughout the war. By the end of August 1914 over 1,000 Scouts were engaged in coast watching and inland watch duties. Over 500 were living away from home.[170] The Burgess Hill Troop sent seven Scouts to West Wittering and the Crawley Troop supplied eight Scouts for duty at Normans Bay in East Sussex.[171]

The Scouts' activities continued to be reported with pride in local papers through the war, as this report from Worthing in May 1918 shows:[172]

Many of the boys, straight from School, come to their billet here (an old boathouse in the Coastguard Station), rough it badly without pay, for the good and benefit of King and Country. They take night and day shifts of duties, helping as far as possible the Coastguard in their fine work. One or more of the boys walk over 15 miles each night with Coastguardsmen or coastwatchers in all weathers and are ready at an instant's notice to render first aid, etc, to any needing their assistance. These boys cook, and clean their so-called home entirely for themselves, and by their brightness and eager willingness should be an example to many others!

Scout camp, Crawley Troop, Three Bridges, Crawley, c. 1915. (WSCCLS, P003823)

Royal Navy SSZ airship from Slindon on a patrol flight over Bognor Regis, c. 1918. (WSCCLS, PC001512)

Over the course of the war the threat of attack shifted to the sky as Zeppelin airships began attacking the United Kingdom.

In autumn 1914, No. 3 Reserve Aeroplane Squadron was formed at Shoreham to train pilots; the flying instructors were to have a second role as pilots for home defence duties.[173] From 6 May 1915, Shoreham maintained a single Martinsyde S1 Scout, armed with incendiary bombs for the defence of London.[174]

In 1916 the threat finally appeared over West Sussex when German Zeppelin L31 flew along the coast and attacked Portsmouth naval base on 25 September.[175] L31's return journey took it on a route that passed over Midhurst and Steyning. Although little damage was caused, the event spurred the authorities to further action and further air defences were put in place in West Sussex to protect Portsmouth.

In July 1917 a searchlight post was established in Selsey to detect hostile aircraft en route to Portsmouth and a second one was added by August 1918.[176] A Royal Observer Corps map, dated 24 September 1917, shows an observer cordon in place along the coastlines of East and West Sussex. Set up by No.7 Company of the Royal Observer Corps, the cordon came as far west as Arundel, turning east to Henfield, before continuing on a steep north-westerly arc, leaving the county at Rudgwick.[177]

Another attempted solution to detecting enemy aircraft was the reflection and focusing of the sound of approaching aircraft via concave concrete dishes known as 'Sound Mirrors'. The sound was focused on a collector connected to a stethoscope. The operator would move the stethoscope to find the loudest signal. This allowed a bearing to be given on any aircraft that approached within 25 miles. A 7½ foot Sound Mirror was built at East Beach Road, Selsey, in 1916.[178] Edward Heron-Allen, refers to this 'new' apparatus in August 1918,[179] suggesting that the Sound Mirror was not operational until this time.

On 4 February 1915 Germany declared the waters around Britain to be a war zone, meaning any British or Allied shipping could be sunk without warning by German submarines. In order to prevent German submarines getting into the English Channel, the Royal Navy established the 'Dover Barrage' to protect the vital supply link to France. A network of minefields and indicator nets was laid between Dover and the Belgian coast to destroy ships or submarines entering from the north, or alert patrolling Royal Navy vessels to their presence.[180]

As submarine warfare grew more intense, the barrage defence was assisted by aircraft and airships. The Royal Naval Air Service established an airship base at Polegate in July 1915 and sent out anti-submarine patrols along the Sussex and Kent coast, looking for enemy vessels that had penetrated the Dover Barrage.[181]

Despite these efforts, submarines from the German Navy's Flanders Flotilla were still able to breach the barrage due to gaps in the nets, poor quality mines and a lack of patrol boats. Six ships were sunk by mines or torpedoes off the West Sussex Coast in 1916, rising dramatically to twenty-two in 1917, with many more vessels being sunk off the East Sussex and Kent coasts.[182]

These events resulted in the expansion of the anti-submarine defences based in West Sussex and on the South Coast. A new airship mooring-out post was built as a satellite for the Polegate station in woods near Northwood Cottages at Slindon, opening in April 1918.[183] Slindon station covered 200 acres and had a complement of 14 officers and 200 naval ratings who handled and maintained the airships. The woods of the Slindon Estate screened an area in which to moor three airships in L-shaped bays. Each bay had a maintenance pit and ramp in which to contain the airship car so that the airship envelope was flush with the ground. The nearby 'Folly' housed a wireless post which received signals from airships on patrol.[184] The airships patrolled along the Channel coast of Sussex between Polegate, Slindon, the Isle of Wight and Upton in Dorset.[185]

These and other efforts led to a reduction in attacks, with only eleven sinkings off West Sussex in 1918, most notably the torpedoing of the hospital ship *Warilda* off Selsey Bill on 3 August 1918 with the loss of 123 lives.[186]

Another anti-submarine scheme was the ambitious and top secret Admiralty 'M-N' project, based partly at Shoreham Harbour with the structures involved known locally as the 'Mystery Towers'; a detailed account appears in Chapter 3.

West Sussex Volunteer Civil Guard Duties, 17 August 1914. (WSRO, MP 1235)

CHIEF CONSTABLE'S OFFICE,
HORSHAM,
17th August, 1914.

West Sussex Volunteer Civil Guard.

The West Sussex Civil Guard may be required to perform some of the undermentioned duties :—

1. To undergo elementary drill and musketry so as to become a fit and competent body to assist and support the police and thus to relieve the military. Drill centres will be arranged, and will be localised as far as possible.

2. To guard bridges and other important points, i.e., Water Works, Post Offices, Electric Light Stations, and Gas Works, etc.

3. **BRIDGES.** No persons should be allowed to loiter near a bridge, culvert, or interfere in any way with telegraph poles and wires, etc. Enquire of any person doing the above their business, and if Germans or Austrians their names and addresses. They should be asked for their permit from the police, and if not in possession of one they should be arrested and handed over at once to the nearest Police Constable. The names and addresses of all persons who have been questioned and any information gained should be handed in to the officer commanding their respective districts, who will if necessary report at once to the Police ; or communicate direct t: the police if more convenient.

4. To escort prisoners and to assist the Red Cross detachments.

5. The Civil Guard should report all Germans and Austrians if they know that they have in their possession any of the following articles :—FIREARMS, AMMUNITION, EXPLOSIVES ; or material intended to be used for the manufacture of explosives ; any Inflammable Liquids ; any Signalling Apparatus, any Carrier Pigeons, and Motor Cars, Motor Cycles, Motor Boat, Yacht or Aircraft ; any Cypher Code, any Telephone Installation, any Camera or other photographic apparatus ; any Military or Naval Map, Chart or Hand-book ; they should detain such persons if necessary.

6. Each member of the Civil Guard will be required to sign an agreement form and a nominal roll will be kept at each centre.

7. Members of the Civil Guard are requested to warn all they can to be very careful not to photograph moving troops or to write to people that they have seen troops leaving, or to write anything that may be conveyed to the enemy, and which may prove detrimental to our Army or Navy.

8. Every possible care should be taken to prevent any damage being done which might hinder or delay the action of the War Office and to prevent any assistance being given to the enemy.

A. S. WILLIAMS.
Chief Constable.

The First 'Dad's Army': Civil Guards and Volunteer Training Corps

Once war was declared, a nationwide movement of local defence associations and 'civil guards' who wanted to protect their communities appeared. These groups were formed from men not suited to military service due to age or fitness. The idea rapidly spread across the county in August 1914, with dignitaries such as the Mayor of Chichester, a Sussex barrister and a Worthing lady restauranteur among those organising local units.[187] This enthusiasm was no doubt spurred on by lurid reports of real and imagined German atrocities carried out in Belgium. Many people in Sussex would also have been aware of pre-war fictional accounts of German invasions.[188]

Postcard of inspection of VTC members, Worthing, September 1915. (WSCCLS T000417)

In West Sussex the civil guards placed themselves under the authority of the Chief Constable. They were directed to assist in supporting the 'coastwatch' and guarding vulnerable parts of the transport and civic infrastructure from the threat of sabotage, as well as escorting prisoners and enemy aliens. The *Worthing Gazette* reported that:

The duties of the Civil Guard have chiefly consisted of patrolling the railway and guarding the bridges, etc., the members taking turns in shifts of from twenty-five to thirty on alternate nights; but at the request of the Mayor and Town Clerk the guarding of the Waterworks has now been added to their duties ; and although no question of drill has arisen, it is quite possible that the desirability of turning the new body into an armed and semi-military organisation may have to be considered in the future. ['The Local Civil Guard', *Worthing Gazette*, 19 August 1914, p.4, col.e]

Officially illegal, these groups craved official recognition. In November 1914 the War Office authorised the creation of the Central Association of VTC presided over by Conservative Peer, Lord Desborough and General Sir O'Moore Creagh.[189] Civil guard units were quick to make themselves legitimate. The East Grinstead and Crawley & Ifield Civil Guards all decided to join the Central Association in January 1915[190] although Worthing took slightly longer, only deciding to join in March 1915.[191]

Postcard of VTC motorcycle unit at Littlehampton, April 1915. (WSCCLS, TC001714)

'Notes and Comments.' (Mid-Sussex Times, 26 November 1918, p. 5 col. d.)

Notes and Comments.

It was with a sigh of relief that many business men in the Volunteers opened their papers on Wednesday and saw the announcement of the Secretary of War that it had been decided to relieve all ranks of the Volunteer Force of their drill and training obligations and that, for the present, attendance at drill will be purely voluntary. The sigh of relief was not due to the feeling that the force served no useful purpose, but solely to the fact that the demands of business—often entailing Sunday as well as week-day labour—strained the powers of physical endurance to such an extent that drill and training became a positive hardship. In the early days of the war membership of the Volunteers, to many men, was a real delight, and they confessed themselves greatly benefited by the training and comradeship. The Volunteers have rendered the country great service—greater than many people are aware of. In Mid-Sussex all the officers, we have ascertained, have won the respect and esteem of their men because they treated them as men, and if ties are now severed the associations of the past will ever be a pleasant memory.

* * *

Chichester Emergency Committee poster, instructions in event of invasion, c. 1915. (WSRO, MP 3148)

NOTICE!

CHICHESTER EMERGENCY COMMITTEE.

Regulations to be observed in the event of a Landing by the Enemy on the Coast.

It is thought advisable to issue instructions to the Civil Population as to the course which they ought to follow should any landing of the enemy be made on our shores. That such a landing should take place is MOST IMPROBABLE, but it is well that all necessary steps should be taken to make ready for it should it be seriously threatened.

WHEN a state of emergency is declared by the competent Military Authority:—

1. The Population of outlying and solitary houses are strongly advised to come at once into the Towns or Large Villages, the inhabitants of which are advised to remain where they are. Any persons wishing to leave the district should do so at once, avoiding the main roads. In no case must there be any attempt at resistance by civilians either with firearms or otherwise. Any such attempt could do no good and might bring terrible consequences on the whole district.

2. In the event of any attack by aircraft, bombardment, or otherwise, people are strongly advised to remain in their houses, and where possible to take shelter in cellars or basements. Occupants of houses on the sea front should, in case of bombardment, leave by a back door and take shelter elsewhere.

   Unexploded shells or bombs should not be touched as they burst if moved. The Police or Military Authorities should be informed where they are.

   NO PERSONS EXCEPT THOSE ON DUTY SHOULD REMAIN OUT OF DOORS.

3. All cattle, sheep, horses, carts, carriages, and other means of transport must be driven off in the direction and by the routes already arranged. The drivers will be allowed to take with them in carts their wives and families, and should provide themselves with blankets and three days rations.

4. All motor cars and motor cycles must be loaded up with spare parts, petrol, &c., and be driven away at least ten miles from the coast.

5. All live stock which cannot be moved and all pigs and poultry must be killed. This should be done without using a knife, so that they may soon be unfit for human food.

6. Any motors, carriages or carts which cannot be moved must be rendered unfit for use: motors by removing carburettor, magneto, or induction pipe; other vehicles by removal and destruction of the wheels.

The object of the above regulations is to remove, in the event of a landing being effected, anything which may be of use or assistance to the enemy.

F. B. DU PRE,

Chairman of Chichester Petty Sessional Division
Emergency Committee.

Initially the men wore civilian dress and, other than a badge or armlet, were unequipped. Later a green uniform was authorised.[192] Volunteers often paid subscription fees; for example, East Grinstead VTC charged members a shilling.[193] Public appeals for funds were often made to purchase equipment and uniforms.

Once affiliated to the Central Association, a desire to become more organised often followed. By mid-1915 VTC units around Chichester and Mid-Sussex were holding field training days and regular shooting contests. Several groups had also created motorcycle units.[194]

In the early months of 1917, the requirements of the VTC were changed. Men were asked to agree to serve for the duration of the war, and submit to more definite and strenuous training.[195] For those men who were able to pass a test, the government agreed to provide new uniforms, arms and equipment necessary for an enhanced role, often attached to the RSR.

The military usefulness of the VTC in West Sussex was questionable. In the event of invasion civilians were supposed to hand in weapons and follow the orders of the police and military authorities (to avoid provoking the abuse of civilians by the Germans seen in Belgium).[196]

What the VTC did do was ward against any threat of sabotage and back up a depleted local police force. Although occasionally criticised as a 'funk hole for shirkers'[197] the West Sussex VTC also gave men ineligible for service due to age, fitness or occupation a feeling of usefulness that helped to bolster morale and maintain civic order.[198]

With the signing of the Armistice this extract from the *Mid-Sussex Times* (opposite) probably sums up the feelings of those who served in the VTCs best of all.

Local Authorities and Police

In October 1914, although an invasion was considered a remote prospect, the government gave guidance to local authorities on how to maintain civil order in the event of an attack.[199]

General orders for special constables: air raids. (WSRO, MP 1235)

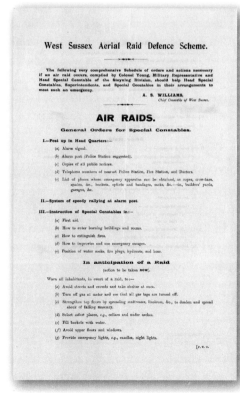
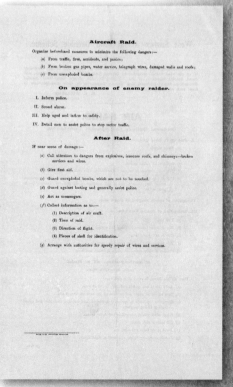

Emergency Committees were set up in every Petty Session District (modern Magistrates Courts) under the auspices of Lords Lieutenants and a Central Organising Committee. If an attack took place the Emergency Committee would work through the police, encouraging people to stay at home and provide manpower for the construction of defensive works. It was their aim to keep the population from fleeing and clogging up the roads as refugees.

In Sussex the Central Organising Committee was chaired by the Duke of Norfolk and the committee were nominees from the mayors of the boroughs of West Sussex, the police chief constables, military representatives and a secretary.[200]

Next in the chain of responsibility were the police constables. The police were tasked with protecting vulnerable points and had access to firearms (even deploying them in Worthing in August 1914).[201] The police were assisted by special constables, the VTC and Scouts. Police stations throughout the county were issued with notices directing what to do if the invasion alarm was raised, including securing civilian firearms and directing civilians to stay put and keep off roads.[202]

West Sussex Police Force was tasked with implementing these emergency duties at a time of falling manpower.[203] During the course of the war, ninety-four regular West Sussex Police officers left to fight in the army.[204] In the Chichester area almost 60 per cent of the police officers volunteered over the course of the war.[205]

This was a nationwide problem and the government passed the Special Constables Act of 1914[206] to allow for the recruitment of part-time officers. Men across the county volunteered in large numbers. Sixty special constables were recruited in Worthing in August 1914. In Chichester 850 had been recruited by January 1915.[207] By February 1918 West Sussex Constabulary had recruited its first women special constables to assist with clerical work. The special constables wore a lapel badge and armlet bearing the words 'West Sussex Constabulary', the crest of the constabulary and the wearer's number.[208]

In the event of attack, the special constables were to pass down the orders given to the civil population and see that they were carried out. They were also to undertake regular patrols of their area, producing lists of items that would be of use to an enemy force. Under the Emergency Scheme individual landowners and householders also had a duty to receive official instructions from the special constables and to obey all orders given to them.[209]

Precautions and Restrictions

Another feature of coastal defence was the implementation of a blackout during night-time hours[210] to avoid giving navigational assistance to enemy ships, submarines, and later, airships and bombers.

The first restrictions were put in place in October 1914, as reported in the *Worthing Gazette*: 'Curtailed Lighting … Yesterday notification was received [from the Admiralty] and the result was seen last night in the darkened streets.'[211]

By early 1916, with a growing threat of air attacks, the regulations became strictly enforced through DORA. Edward Heron-Allen recounted his experience at the hands of the local police in Selsey:

> [31 March 1916] The lighting question has become acute, and Selsey is flooded with comminatory notices on the subject. The local policeman, like an intermittent volcano, has sprung into renewed activity … our 'Sbirro' [Italian slang for Policeman] prowls around levying half crowns upon anyone whose blowing curtains show a streak of light for one moment.[212]

Enforcement was not restricted to coastal regions of the county. It even became an offence, with a penalty of £100 fine or six-month prison sentence, for citizens to have a fire lit after sunset.[213]

By the later stages of the war the restrictions were used not only as a defence against naval and air attack but also as means to conserve stocks of coal and gas. By 1918 the effect of darkened streets in winter was being felt as a serious nuisance rather than a vital act of civil defence. An editorial in the *Worthing Gazette* of

6 November[214] appealed for the end of the total blackout but within days the war was over anyway.

Defence of the Realm Act (DORA) and Enemy Aliens

When war was declared, the government moved rapidly to obtain emergency wartime powers. DORA was passed on 8 August 1914[215] and was amended several times during the war. It authorised trial by court martial and the use of summary justice against anyone communicating with the enemy, sabotaging railways, ports and shipping, or spreading false information. It also gave the government and the armed forces wide-ranging powers to commandeer resources for the war effort and censor the press.

Also in August, the Aliens Registration Act was passed, under which Germans, and anyone who was not a British subject, had to register with the local superintendent of police. Within a fortnight, sixty aliens (fifty Germans) registered in Worthing[216] and well over 100 in Chichester.[217] Enemy aliens were prohibited from living in certain areas in West Sussex, including the rural districts of Steyning East (rural area north of Brighton from Portslade to Patcham, Fulking and Poynings), Westbourne (Bosham, Chidham, West Thorney and the rural parishes to the north) and Westhampnett (largely the area around Chichester Harbour).[218] In late October, however, the whole county was to become a restricted area for alien men of military age and over the following months families and individuals were expelled.[219]

Within days of the outbreak of war came the first arrests across the county. Otto Van der Reche, a German army veteran with twenty-five years of service, was prosecuted in Worthing for failing to register. Despite the suspicious act of dyeing his black hair brown, the court simply ordered him to register and charged him 8*s* 6*d* costs.[220]

Dozens of similar cases can be found in the local press and in virtually every case, ignorance of the law appeared to be the only crime and the miscreants were dealt with sensitively.

More sinister cases followed, however: on 21 August Chichester police, acting on a tip-off from the War Office, arrested Mr Von Grundher of North Pallant House and sent him to the temporary POW camp at Christ's Hospital.[221] This large public school was used to house up to 750 German POWs from 6 August[222] until larger camps were built by the end of the month.[223] Other actions followed, with probable War Office involvement. A group of eight Germans from the Bognor and Chichester areas were marched to the latter's railway station on 12 September, bound for the POW camp at Frimley near Aldershot.[224] From 16 to 18 September Worthing police, 'acting on instructions that had been received', rounded up for transport to Aldershot seventeen alien men between the ages of 19 and 45 'for the most part of the waiter type … [or] … indoor servants'.[225] Arrests were made in other places, such as on 29 October in Littlehampton: 'a couple of waiters … a fairly well-to-do visitor … [and] a doctor of German parentage … conveyed to Newbury, the famous race-course, which is now the scene of an enormous concentration camp.'[226]

In April 1915 the Aliens' Restriction Amendment Order required hotels, lodging houses etc. to keep a register of all aliens staying there. Included in this were those from Allied countries such as Belgium and France, and led to numerous court cases and fines, all reported in the local press week by week.

German and other enemy aliens being marched along Chapel Road to Worthing Railway Station en route to internment, September 1914. (WSCCLS, PC007905)

There was clearly nervousness, even occasional hysteria, among the local population and spy scare stories abound in the local press. Perhaps the most notorious local case was the suing for slander of Lord Leconfield of Petworth Park by Paul Schweder of Courtlands, Goring-by-Sea. Sussex Assizes heard on 5 March 1915 that the former commented in August 1914 that Schweder was 'a dangerous man to this country … when police searched his house … [he] managed to destroy incriminating documents … [and] plaintiff's firm… had a private wire to Germany'. Not only were these sensational claims dismantled one by one but Schweder proved that he had been born in England, his family name was of Swedish, not German, origin and he had had a long British military career. The Chief Constable of Sussex had also pursued a vendetta against Schweder, illegally searching his house the day after war had been declared, and he had previously been fined for supposedly 'emitting mysterious lights from his window out to sea'.[227] The jury took just ten minutes to find for Schweder and awarded damages of £100 to be paid by Lord Leconfield.[228]

The attack on Portsmouth by Zeppelin L31 in September 1916 caused further panic. At a court case in Chichester in October 1916, a London bank manager with a cottage at Sandy Hill, Selsey, was accused by four of his neighbours of using a flashing light to signal to the Zeppelin. Once again the individual's record as an upright citizen was cited and the case was dismissed.[229]

Some incidents were simply amusing. Around the same time, Haywards Heath police rushed to intercept apparent German spies 'who had been seen to be busily employed with a map, apparently engaged in the task of spying out the nakedness of the land'. Members of the Urban District Council and their surveyor were not pleased to be interrupted whilst considering the site of a new cemetery.[230] Edward Heron-Allen of Selsey became obsessed with unmasking a supposed spy, Ford Madox Hueffer (Ford) then living in the village: '… a typical Prussian bully … I firmly believe he is a German spy'.[231] August 1915 saw the name of Worthing's Germanic-sounding Kursaal cinema changed to The Dome, after a contest resulting in 160 different suggestions.[232]

There were no anti-German riots in West Sussex, even after the sinking of the *Lusitania* in May 1915, though those in Winchester were erroneously reported as being in Chichester at one stage.[233]

There were examples though, of low-level unpleasantness, swiftly condemned by local newspaper editors. The *Observer* series editor, defending a Littlehampton resident, condemned '… persons who are taking advantage of the rounding up of aliens to direct their ignorant pettiness by making postcard attacks on certain ladies who, … no matter how British they really are, … happen to bear a German name.'[234] In Worthing a foreign shopkeeper had his blinds daubed with messages 'of a very uncomplimentary character'. He lodged a complaint with police and also put up a recruiting poster.[235]

Conclusion

To protect West Sussex, a vital strategic area, the government developed defence systems that made Selsey, Slindon and Shoreham vital bases for defending the coast against enemy submarines and airships. Local people responded with enthusiasm to the call to protect their localities. The great numbers of men who formed the civil guards, the VTCs, and Special Constabulary across the county were fine examples of the civic pride typical of the period. The changing nature of the German threat saw new military technology deployed in the county. This was to cause inconvenience, interference, loss of liberty and entail personal sacrifice not foreseen in 1914. Despite this, morale seems to have held up in West Sussex and there was widespread support for civil defence.

THE HOME FRONT: CIVILIANS AT WAR

By Martin Hayes

Introduction

This chapter covers the National Relief Fund (NRF), the complex systems of fundraising across our county, national initiatives, local initiatives, goods and services, fundraising events, and how social life was affected through variety shows, cinemas, pubs, social and sports clubs.

Local people understood from the beginning that this was to be a large-scale war which would require a massive and continuous effort by the population on the home front to support it. Activities and events were held every week from 4 August 1914 to 11 November 1918 in towns and villages across the county and browsing the local newspapers brings home their scale and the commitment needed. They involved the whole community, men, women and children, the political and social elite, and those less fortunate. Middle, and some upper, class women came to dominate the planning and delivery of these activities as many could commit the time and had already developed the organisational skills required. Their roles on the home front are further explored in Chapters 7 and 8.

The National Relief Fund and
Fundraising Infrastructure

Responding to a government circular, on 12 August the Duke of Richmond, chairman of West Sussex County Council (WSCC), organised a General Committee for the Relief of Distress to co-ordinate the distribution of war relief funds countywide.[236] All chairmen of WSCC committees were included but not representatives from other local authorities, such as parish councils, small boroughs, Urban and Rural District Councils (UDC and RDC), though they could be co-opted if WSCC felt it necessary. Similarly, despite the need to liaise with Boards of Guardians (administrators of poor relief and workhouses), no representatives were invited to join the committee. The only woman appointed was the Countess of March, chairman of the Soldiers' and Sailors' Families' Association (SSFA) but her organisation was to have a key role in distributing relief. The lack of representation of local bodies undoubtedly irritated some and resulted in, to some extent, less effective fundraising (for more about the SSFA see Chapter 7).

The committee made an appeal to the public for donations to the Prince of Wales' NRF which had been launched on 7 August. From the beginning there was tension between WSCC's policy promoting all fundraising and distribution via the NRF and the desire of many locals to raise money for use within their own area. The Mayor of Chichester's suggestion for a 'local' fund aimed at relieving local people directly did not go down well with the WSCC committee. Both the chairman, and the Lord Lieutenant, the Duke of Norfolk, advised against, saying '… It would be a mistake to have a lot of independent collections started'.[237] The system of centralising the fundraising but delegating distribution to the SSFA West Sussex branch, liaising with the eight Boards of Guardians and parish councils, who knew their villages best, seemed to work well, once in place. There was, however, early confusion – perhaps not surprisingly, given this largely unexpected war. On 28 August the Duke of Norfolk wrote to the press to clarify the fundraising scheme for East and West Sussex.[238]

Many communities collected substantial sums for the NRF and local newspapers reported on these week by week. Chichester had raised an impressive £2,500 (worth £142,500 today) for the fund in eight weeks.[239] In Sullington twenty-two out of the twenty-nine occupied households contributed to the local efforts on behalf of the national fund.[240]

However, many purely local relief funds emerged, reflecting an understandable desire by locals to support people in their own community rather than see money disappear into a national fund, administered countywide, over which they had no control. Horsham UDC's decision not to send money raised to the NRF, but to go it alone was criticised locally.[241] Selsey people had raised nearly £24 (£1,368) by 14 October for their Local Relief Fund and the rector stated, 'We have no wish … to interfere with the work of the NRF, or of the Sailors' and Soldiers' Families Association, but … if the war lasts a long time, there may be cases which neither of these funds may touch, and in which a little help may be very useful.'[242]

Poster advertising Horsham's first fundraising public meeting on 17 August 1914. (Horsham Museum, 1998. 1029)

"GOD SAVE THE KING."

PATRIOTIC FUND.

The Relief of Sufferers through the War.

A PUBLIC

MEETING

Will be held at the

TOWN HALL, HORSHAM,

ON

MONDAY AFTERNOON

AUGUST 17, AT 3.30. 1914.

E. I. BOSTOCK, Esq., J.P., in the chair.

In consequence of the meeting held on Wednesday, the 12th, at Chichester, with the same object, the meeting advertised to take place at Horsham on that date was postponed. To avoid delay in this urgent matter, the **Meeting** will now be held on **Monday Next, the 17th,** at **3.30 p.m.,** at the **Town Hall, Horsham,** when all interested in this Patriotic Movement (Ladies and Gentlemen) are cordially invited to attend.

E. I. BOSTOCK,   E. C. HAWES,
GERALD BLUNT,   A. C. ODDIE.

"WEST SUSSEX COUNTY TIMES," 15, MARKET SQUARE, HORSHAM.

Pulborough showed how many communities balanced the sometimes conflicting concept of raising money for national and local initiatives. Their War Emergency Committee collected £276 (£15,732) by December 1914 and allocated as follows: NRF £109, Belgian Refugees Fund £47, Needlework Fund £45, Christmas Presents Fund £19 and the village General Fund £56.[243]

Haywards Heath UDC acted the most promptly of all, their Relief Committee being formed just three days after war was declared, and £420 (£23,940) was collected at that public meeting.[244] By early September Haywards Heath UDC and Wivelsfield parish had agreed to co-operate to organise a local War Relief Fund.[245] After £849 was collected by summer 1915 they stopped collecting because by July 1916 they had only needed to pay half that sum in relief. Payment examples include rail fares for parents visiting wounded sons in distant hospitals and sums to pregnant women unable to work.

The government circular suggested boroughs over 20,000 in population raise and administer funds independently of county administration and Worthing lost no time in doing this. On the Monday (10th) after war was declared, a packed meeting called by the mayor at the Town Hall in South Street formed a local War Relief Committee and collected an astonishing total of over £410 (£23,370) that evening. Hotelier Walter Howell pledged to donate 100 loaves a week to dependents for the rest of the war. The importance of engaging women in the work of the committee to understand the needs of the families left behind was emphasised.[246] In September, having consulted subscribers after some complaints,[247] the committee decide to split the total, sending a quarter to the NRF and keeping three quarters for local use.[248] By January 1915 nearly £5,000 (£285,000) had been raised, about 200 families relieved and money was also pledged to the Red Cross Society for their hospital (The Cecils) at West Worthing and the Belgian Relief Fund.[249]

East Grinstead residents probably demonstrated the most 'get up and go' in the county. The UDC initially ignored East Sussex County Council's (ESCC) instructions,[250] merged with East Grinstead RDC's villages (Forest Row, Hartfield,

George Hotel, High Street, Crawley, scene of a controversial fundraising meeting, c. 1915. (Frederick Henty Collection, WSCCLS, L000605)

West Hoathly, Withyham and Worth) and suggested to ESCC that they take full responsibility for relieving the social distress in their area. The new Emergency Committee met on 10 August and within ten days had raised £1,374 (£78,318), investigated forty-eight relief applications and made twenty-three payments.[251] By 29 August pressure had been brought to bear and the East Grinstead Emergency Committee came into line and left the relieving of local servicemen's families to the SSFA using money from the NRF operated via the two county councils. This avoided some confusion and duplication of effort though whether it was more efficient than the town's own scheme is debateable.[252] By 17 October they had raised an impressive £2,526 (£143,982).[253]

Not everything went quite as smoothly at Crawley, where class warfare broke out! A newspaper report of the largest meeting ever held in Crawley, at the George Hotel Assembly Hall on 12 August, did not suggest anything amiss. On the platform was the usual mix of civic leaders – JPs, large landowners, businessmen and clergy – 'whilst in the body of the hall all classes of the local community were fully represented'.[254] Letters criticising the meeting appeared in local newspapers: 'unbusinesslike and inconclusive, with a strong suspicion of eliqueism [elitism] …' wrote 'A Well Wisher' and another writer described the meeting as 'a sordid parade of petty local prejudices, rivalries and animosities, which in brighter times would have been treated and appreciated as a comic entertainment …'[255]! This was a rare example of class warfare and factionalism we came across in our research. It set the tone for the war effort and fundraising suffered as a result. By the end of 1914 the town had raised only around £260 (£15,000).[256] As we saw above, East Grinstead, with only double the population of Crawley, had raised nearly ten times that amount by mid-October.

Other National Fundraising Initiatives

Flag and 'Special' Days were occasionally held for a specific cause. The special days involved more than simply selling badges or flags, and could involve concerts, fêtes, sports days and other events. Themes included support for our allies Belgium,

France, Italy, Serbia and Russia, refugees and specialist funds. Refugees are covered later in this chapter. As an insight into the relentless pressure on people to contribute, in just two weeks in July 1916 the Littlehampton area raised over £81 (£4,617) on France's Day (13th),[257] £250 (£14,250) for the Cottage Hospital and over £54 (£3,078) on Russian Flag Day.[258] In June 1918, the sale of roses for Alexandra Day, in aid of local hospitals, made nearly £62 (£3,534) in the Chichester area[259] and £34 (£1,938) in Midhurst, in spite of bad weather, up £25 (£2,425) on the previous year.[260] As late as August 1918, after four long years of war and rationing, Worthing people still supported the Butterfly Day for the RSPCA's Special Fund for Sick and Wounded British Army Horses to the tune of £220 (£12,540).[261]

The **British Red Cross Society** arranged a campaign of 'Our Day' events from summer 1915 with remarkable success. The Burgess Hill event is a good example, held at Oak Hall, attracting 1,800 and making £113 (£6,441). Activities included a baby show, sports, variety entertainments, jigsaw contest, pig and rabbit weight judging, perfume identifying, shop window contest, the playing of a large gramophone and 'an exhibition of the best-looking lady in the district', which comprised a tent with a large mirror inside![262]

Advert for National War Bonds 'Fire Your Money at the Huns'. (Mid-Sussex Times, 9 July 1918, p. 6)

The **War Savings Movement**, namely government-issued War Bonds, War Loans or War Savings Certificates, raised money quickly from people with guaranteed interest, usually around 5 per cent.[263] Many towns and villages formed War Loan Clubs then, from early 1916, War Savings Associations, such as at Findon in July 1915[264] and Littlehampton Elementary schools in August 1916.[265] Promotion following a county conference in June 1917[266] saw the number of associations in Sussex increase from 99 to 404 by September, comprising 112 in West Sussex and 292 in East Sussex.[267] A new scheme for loans from January 1917 were publicised as 'Victory Loans' and promoted across the county.[268] A useful summary for September 1917 of the number of associations, members and purchases appears in the *West Sussex Gazette*.[269] In 1917–18 tanks, based on the 'Bognor Tank', a model designed by Mr O.A. Bridges,[270] were displayed in towns and cities across Britain. These so-called 'tank banks' were to encourage war savings.[271]

Various **War Weapons Weeks** in 1918 saw an increasingly desperate government raising money for a final push to victory. Aeroplane Week in March witnessed Chichester raise over £72,000, apparently enough to manufacture twenty-six aeroplanes, the culmination of which was a big procession light-heartedly 'buzzed' by a brash young pilot as a thank-you.[272] War Weapons Week in June saw fundraising across the county but the outstanding achievement must be East Grinstead's. Having been challenged to raise £35,000, the 7,000 residents (20,000 including the RD)[273] produced an astonishing figure of over £135,000 (worth nearly £7.7 million today). Admittedly £50,000 was given by Sir Thomas Dewar but nevertheless it remains the largest single sum produced by any Great War event in the county and was enough to fund fifty-four aeroplanes![274] This achievement is all the more remarkable due to the challenging conditions in 1918 of shortages of food, fuel and low wages.

Local Fundraising Initiatives

Early in the war several **Tobacco Funds** were started. In September 1914 the *Worthing Gazette* launched an appeal for sixpenny pieces, each of which would buy a pack of ten cigarettes and two cakes of tobacco (dark and light) to send to the front. Backed by relentless weekly campaigning, the fund reached just over £500 (£28,500) and around 20,000 packs had been sent by the time it closed in October 1916.[275] The *Observer* series (Bognor, Littlehampton and Chichester editions) supported national newspaper the *Weekly Dispatch*'s tobacco fund with the added attraction of being able to name the serviceman you wished to receive a pack of thirty-five cigarettes, 2oz tobacco and matches.[276]

Agricultural Gift Sales were highly successful in predominantly rural West Sussex. The Hassocks Branch of the National Farmers' Union gift auction and bazaar in 1915 is well described by an excitable reporter from the *Mid-Sussex Times* and is full of country humour. A mass of detail is provided, over 100 donors named, descriptions of the 500 lots and details of the £251 (£14,307) proceeds.[277] Villages were able to organise such

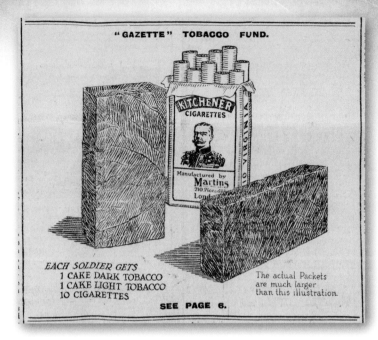

"GAZETTE" TOBACCO FUND.

KITCHENER CIGARETTES

Manufactured by Martins 210 Picca... Lond...

EACH SOLDIER GETS
1 CAKE DARK TOBACCO
1 CAKE LIGHT TOBACCO
10 CIGARETTES

The actual Packets
are much larger
than this illustration.

SEE PAGE 6.

Advert for 'Gazette Tobacco Fund', showing package contents. (Worthing Gazette, 23 September 1914, p. 5)

events too. Cowfold raised about £56 (£3,192) for Netley Hospital (Red Cross facility near Southampton), POWs and Cowfold and District Hospital Supply Depot and nearly £14 (£798) for sailors. Harry Moore, a wounded Cowfold man, came up from Netley as guest of honour. Most villagers attended or organised the day, which included 'buttonholes of choice violets and roses … sold by little girls'.[278] By far the most successful, financially, was the Haywards Heath gift sale in May 1917 which raised over £3,026 equivalent to an astounding £172,482 today.[279]

War Effort: Goods and Services

In addition to fundraising, considerable effort was made to collect and manufacture material and items useful in supporting the war. (Sandbag production, largely by women, is covered in Chapter 7.)

Being a predominantly rural county, West Sussex was able to supply additional **agricultural produce** for the war effort. In 1916 Sussex farmers sent 750 sacks of seed oats and other produce to Verdun to help revive French agricultural production.[280] A gift of sixty Southdown rams, from the annual Southdown sheep show and sale at Chichester, were shipped from Littlehampton to French farmers in August 1915 to replace those destroyed in the fighting.[281] The national Vegetable Products Committee for Naval Supply (VPCNS) appealed for fruit and vegetables to be collected in counties and sent to the North Sea fleet. The local Farmers' Union co-operated with private individuals, usually women, and organisations, to collect and send apples, imported fruit, nuts, artichokes, beet, broccoli, cabbages, carrots, onions, parsnips, sprouts and turnips. Joseph Stratton of East Dean and Miss Long used Barnham Nurseries Packing Shed and Chichester Corn Exchange as assembly points.[282] Haywards Heath had formed a branch of the VPCNS by January 1915 and sent impressive amounts, up to 1.5 tons, of fruit and vegetables fortnightly throughout 1915 and probably beyond. (Egg collecting for the wounded is covered in Chapter 8.)

Reading materials were also required. The Camps' Library movement aimed to supply books to UK training camps, such as at Shoreham and Rusper, and Mrs Caroline Lascelles, of Woolbeding near Midhurst, co-ordinated efforts in West Sussex. Among many men, books, especially light fiction, were more appreciated than tobacco, helping to fill the many tedious hours of inaction. Light fiction was recommended but examples of poor choices included an out-of-date telephone directory and a novel *Killed in Action*![283] Lindfield post office forwarded nearly 3,000 books from August 1917 to July 1918.[284] Used magazines and periodicals were forwarded, from September 1914, by the bookstall owner at Hassocks Station to the Orwellian-sounding Committee of Public Confidence for distribution to servicemen.[285]

Various other initiatives were organised. In 1915 civilians were urged to wear cotton underwear to save wool for military purposes and Hansford of Littlehampton lost no time in recommending their 'Aertex Cellular' cotton briefs.[286] In the same year, the National Council of the YMCA called on amateur photographers to take

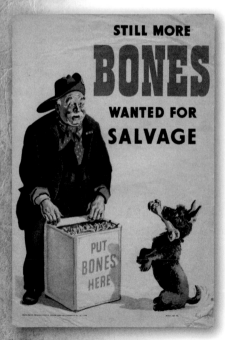

Poster, Still More Bones wanted for Salvage, Horsham Museum, 1998. (1066)

snapshots of servicemen's loved ones and supply the families with prints to put in their next letter to their menfolk. Mr S. Bastow, a chemist and photograph developer of 9 North Street, co-ordinated the scheme in the Chichester area.[287] In 1917 the Horsham UDC donated a steamroller to be used in Macedonia which was later spotted by an officer from the Surrey Yeomanry near Salonika.[288]

During 1918 **recycling** came to the fore. With efforts to win the war becoming desperate, local people were urged to save rags, metal and waste paper,[289] sheep's wool left on fences, hedges etc. for making blankets,[290] food bones to make glycerine for shells[291] and even date stones and hard nut shells for use in gas masks.[292] Boy Scouts ran the Crawley waste paper collection service from April 1916.[293] The Bognor Waste Paper Depot, started by the Hothampton Court War Workrooms Committee, had recycled £407 (£23,199) worth in 1917–18 and distributed various sums to local and national charities.[294]

Fundraising Social Events

Social life became almost indivisible from the war effort in general. Most social events held had some element of fundraising or collecting for the war effort. There were many types, such as concerts, dances, garden fêtes, jumble and white elephant sales, and whist drives. Many clubs and societies suspended their usual peacetime activities or re-structured them so that they contributed to the war effort. Local newspapers cover all of these, often in great detail, and we have space for a selection only.

Concerts, or variety evenings, were not just a means of fundraising but also important social events at which to be seen. They were more frequent in the early stages of the war, before financial hardship and rationing took their toll.

At Horsted Keynes a packed Parish Room witnessed, on 26 August 1914, a successful evening of variety.[295] It was the usual mixture of patriotic, popular and classical songs, plus violin solos. Tableaux were put on, that is 'living' pictures, with people dressed as historical or representative figures, such as Britannia. Mrs Leonard Boyne played two piano solos, and must have found the evening hard to bear, for her only son, Lytton Leonard Boyne, was already at the front with the RSR. Thankfully he was to survive the war, serving with the 2nd and 3rd Battalions, and rising to the rank of captain.[296] The proceeds were £18 (£1,026), an impressive sum for a village of around 931 people.[297]

On 14 October 1914, a concert at Chichester Corn Exchange included classical, popular, patriotic and humorous songs, a comedy act, and literary recitals including one by a 15-year-old French refugee boy. The audience included the Duke of Richmond, the Duchess of Norfolk, the bishop, mayor, RSR officers and many others from the social elite, indeed over forty people were named in the article.[298] It was noted, rather patronisingly, that 'not only was the audience composed of … the better class of residents; the rear of the hall included many not over blessed with this world's goods …' Over £49 (£2,793) was realised but rigid class distinctions were apparent.[299]

Garden fêtes were held, such as that at Winterton Lodge, Littlehampton, on 16 August 1916 for the local War Supply Sub-Depot which made medical supplies. Recovering wounded

Chichester Corn Exchange advert for a patriotic concert. (Chichester Observer, 7 October 1914, p. 4)

CORN EXCHANGE, CHICHESTER

(By kind permission of Messrs. Mayer and Somers).

THE MAYOR OF CHICHESTER HAS PLEASURE IN ANNOUNCING A GRAND

Patriotic Concert

(Arranged by Messrs. Pillow, Son and Lewis), on

WEDNESDAY, OCTOBER 14th, 1914, at 8 p.m.

THE WHOLE PROCEEDS will be devoted to the

British and Belgian Relief Funds.

Artistes—

THE ARGYLE QUARTETTE.	MR. HARRY SIMPSON (Chichester Cathedral)
MADAM EDITH WELLING (Soprano).	(Bass). (First appearance in the City).
MADAM ETHEL HARMAN (Contralto).	MR. WASHINGTON ALLEN (Reciter).
MR. HERBERT ORBELL (Tenor).	MR. ARTHUR MANT (The Yokel Comedian).
MR. ARGYLE GALLOWAY (Baritone).	MR. NAT ABATT (Humourist).

At the Piano—Mr. F. J. W. CROWE and Mrs. PERCY LEWIS.

Doors open at 7.30.   To commence at 8 p.m.

Prices—Stalls, 3s. ; Reserved Seats, 2s. ; Admission, 1s.

Plan of the Hall now ready, and Tickets obtainable of PILLOW, SON & LEWIS, 31, East Street, Chichester.   Telephone No. 126.

soldiers attended and the attractions included a fortune-teller, fishing pond, butterfly painting, clock golf, 'mouse town', an auction, frog races, Aunt Sally (throwing game), candle lighting and cake weight guessing.[300] Most **flower shows** were cancelled, but some were revived as fundraising opportunities and to encourage more vegetable growing for the war effort. The Poynings Flower Show of 16 August 1916 was supported by Albourne, Edburton, Fulking, Newtimber, Poynings and Woodmancote and raised over £15 (£855) for the British Prisoners of War Fund. As well as the usual flower, fruit and vegetable competitions, there were contests for the twelve heaviest hens' eggs, best cottage industry products like hand-knitted socks, duchess set (decorative needlework) and raffia baskets, plus pig weight guessing. The Southdown Brass Band provided music and there were traditional attractions such as hoop-la stalls and coconut shies.[301]

Many **dances, jumble sales and whist drives** (a social version of the card game) took place. Whist drives at Shipley raised over £5 (£285) for St Dunstan Home for Blind Soldiers and Sailors between October 1916 and February 1917.[302]

White elephant sales, that is the donation of unwanted items which are then sold to raise money for various causes, were also commonplace. Perhaps the most prestigious was that at Arundel on 3 May 1916 which was opened by the Duchess of Norfolk and raised £142 (£8,094).[303]

Many **children and schools** were involved in the war effort. (The role of Scouts and Guides are covered respectively in Chapters 4 and 7.) Many concerts, sports days and other events were dedicated to fundraising. Eastergate schoolchildren gave half the proceeds of their Christmas concert to the Belgian Relief Fund.[304] In 1915–16 Burgess Hill Council School gave money to the French Relief Fund, sent fruit and vegetables to the Fleet and comforts worth £1 12s (£91) to servicemen at Christmas by collecting pennies.[305] Children at Copthorne and Crawley collected 20cwt or 2,240lbs of blackberries, worth over £27 (£1,539), in September 1918 which were sent to the jam factory in Newick.[306] Children at Goring School 'knitted socks, scarves and balaclavas for the soldiers. Older children were taken out to gather rosehips, elderberries and blackberries and to collect acorns for the pigs. They were paid a penny a pound for them. The fruits were used for jams and jellies and some were canned and sold at a shop in Montague Street, Worthing ...'[307] Public schools, notably Ardingly, Christ's Hospital, Hurstpierpoint College and Lancing College, cannot be covered in the space available in this limited book but most are well served by published histories. They contributed greatly, both in terms of men who served, particularly officers, and by raising funds, comforts and goods for the war effort.

Refugees

There was great public support locally for Belgian refugees in particular, given the suffering experienced during the German invasion. The local *Observer* newspaper[308] started a Shilling Fund in November 1914 to support the *Daily Telegraph*'s Belgian Refugees Fund national appeal and by the time it was closed at Christmas, 1,128 shillings (£3,215) had been donated.[309]

Boy collecting for Belgian Relief Fund, Worthing, c. 1915. (WSCCLS, PC008750)

Many towns in the county received Belgian, and the occasional French, refugees. Larger towns such as Chichester, Horsham and Worthing set up special relief funds to help house, feed and clothe the former group.

Worthing received fifty (later fifty-two) Belgians on 16 October and Saltley Lodge, a large house in Broadwater, was lent to accommodate some, with the rest being dispersed to boarding houses and residents' homes. The *West Sussex Gazette* reported 'Gifts of furniture to make Saltley Lodge habitable – it has been empty and unoccupied for some time – were sent by many householders the instant they knew of the need'.[310] Many had trades and some were able to be employed, for example, in market gardening. By the end of 1914 the town had raised £4,250 (£242,250) for the national Belgian Relief Fund and also £700 (£39,900) to aid the local refugees.[311] An account of the Worthing War Relief Committee meeting in March 1915 has more detail of the refugees who'd arrived.[312] Fundraising events and appeals for clothes continued throughout 1915 to 1917. As the refugees returned home, the number in the town reduced and the only sour note came with criticism of the remainder being moved from Saltley Lodge to Canterbury House, part of a butcher's shop, in Montague Street by March 1918.[313] The work of Miss Napper, of Oxford Lodge, Farncombe Road, on behalf of the refugees was recognised by the award of the Medaille de la Reine Elisabeth to her by the Belgian King.[314]

Horsham received the first Belgian refugees on 17 September at Albert Lodge, a large detached house in King's Road, supplied and fitted out by Sendall Bros.[315] Some fifteen had arrived by the end of September and families are described in detail in a *West Sussex County Times* article.[316] The same newspaper reported the overwhelming public support: '… there has been no abatement in the … kindness and generosity shewn day by day to the poor refugees.'[317] On 30 December, at the Albion Hall, a Christmas high tea, concert, a present for every refugee and a magic lantern show was provided for the very grateful group.[318] Later Mr King lent a house at 22 Carfax where ten of them went to live, leaving two families at Albert Lodge. A series of interesting documents in the *County Times* details their living expenses and the list of donors during 1915,[319] 1916[320] and 1917.[321] A statement in the last report reveals how positive the experience had been: 'The Masson family left Horsham for Calais some months ago. They wished to express their great gratitude for all the kindness shown to them by their friends in Horsham during their stay.'

Half a dozen Belgian and French refugees had arrived at Chichester by mid-September 1914 and were accommodated in private houses.[322] Another eighteen arrived in early October and Farm Cottage, Summersdale, was converted to be a hostel for them and was furnished with items supplied by local shops and private donors.[323] Within a week another house in the same area, 'The Poplars', had also been converted[324] and a week later Dr Buckell's ex-surgery in North Pallant[325]. The last article also mentioned that three of the Belgian boys attended Prebendal School and were very popular with the local boys.

At East Grinstead three large houses were offered for refugees[326] and the Belgians began arriving on 5 October 1914, the first being a family of ten.[327] Within a week another two families had been brought from Portslade and settled into the house lent by Mr Dixon (12 Railway Approach). This prompted the only sign of discontent towards refugees this research project found in the local newspapers. A War Relief Fund collector wrote to the *Sussex & Surrey Courier*:

> They [working class people] consider the sum to be allowed the Belgian refugees is most extravagant and out of all proportion to that allowed the families of our own men serving at the Front. To allow a family of six people £1 16s a week, exclusive of rent, when under the relief scheme a British family of the same size would get only 17s has, I am afraid, had the effect of greatly reducing my collection and has also stopped many of us contributing to Mrs Russell Reid's [Belgian] fund.[328]

It was a fair point because in Littlehampton a refugee family of seven was receiving 9s 6d a week.[329]

Other towns and villages took Belgian refugees too. Bognor had several families and one of them, Paul Leyder, expressed his gratitude in a letter: 'Never shall we forget the many kindnesses shewn to us, and we shall take care that our children also remember the hospitality we have found here, while all Europe is in flames. Again thanking you a thousand times for all these benefits, which will always be remembered gratefully.'[330]

Littlehampton received twelve wounded Belgian soldiers in October 1914, large crowds welcomed them and they were treated at the temporary hospital at the Sailors' Institute.[331] By April 1915 the town was looking after three Belgian refugee families.[332] Burgess Hill's dozen refugees settled into a large house (Lea Copse) in Birchwood Road, and they included a peasant farmer, a penniless diamond cutter, a caretaker, plus their respective families, an orphan girl and two nuns. An appeal for money had raised £135 (£7,695) within a month, enough subscribers signed up to insure a weekly income of 22s and three local doctors offered their services free of charge.[333] There are references to individuals and families being given refuge at Arundel,[334] Bosham,[335] Haywards Heath,[336] Pulborough[337] and Three Bridges.[338] A comprehensive search of local newspapers would probably find other examples.

Occasional events were held to support the Continental War Victims Relief Fund, French Red Cross, Russian POWs Help Committee, Serbian Relief Fund, and other charities.

Social Life

Servicemen contributed significantly to **concerts and variety shows**, both at military camps and in town and village venues. At Roffey Camp the newly formed 27th Battalion of the Royal Fusiliers entertained locals from the Horsham area with popular songs and comedy acts.[339] In February 1917 Lieutenant Gurteen organised a concert for children and old people at Steyning Union Workhouse in Shoreham. The packed programme featured bayonet juggling, clog dancing, comic acts, escapology, military band, ventriloquism and songs, including ones by 'Private Wilson (22nd Royal Fusiliers), the possessor of a very high, sweet tenor, which seems to have been in no way impaired by a lung wound received at Vimy Ridge …'[340]

At Balcombe in February 1916 local people were entertained by 'The Camp Followers', a dramatic and concert party, influenced by French 'pierrots' with pointed hats and clown-like costumes who danced, juggled, told jokes and sang. Their leader, Alderson Burrell Horne, lived at Ditton Place in the village, and they had just returned from eighteen months of touring convalescent hospitals, munitions factories and military camps at home and abroad.[341]

Silent film **cinemas** were on the rise; 4,000 were opened in Britain between 1907 and 1912[342] and every town, and even large villages, in West Sussex had one or more purpose-built building or adapted village hall.[343] Bognor and Worthing were particularly well served: the week before war was declared the brand new 860-seat Picturedrome was opened[344] at Worthing, joining the Winter Hall, St James's Hall, Cinema Elite and the Electric Theatre at the Kursaal (re-named The Dome in 1915).[345] In 1914 Bognor boasted the Pier Pavilion, Pier Theatre and Kursaal Theatre as film venues.[346]

Miss Kate Carney's entertainment show for wounded soldiers, Bungalow Town, Shoreham Beach, August 1915. (Marlipins Museum, 96.2843.10a)

Mobilised Territorials march past Whitehall Picture House (Theatre) on the left, London Road, East Grinstead, 5 August 1914. (East Grinstead Museum, 2340.80)

As well as being a profitable business and providing employment for locals, many cinemas organised occasional fundraising evenings for the war effort. Typical was the programme at the Haywards Heath Picture House on 16 September 1914 in aid of the Local War and Belgian Relief Funds. This featured 'Britain's Bid For Supremacy, a Gaumont topical, showing actual scenes from the Front … The Baby Spy, a cleverly acted drama … and The Misadventures of a Mighty Monarch', a US comedy short starring John Bunny.[347] Charlie Chaplin had begun his illustrious career in films the year before and *His Musical Career* was a guaranteed crowd puller at Bognor's Pier Theatre in summer 1915.[348]

Attendances were very good early in the war and seem to have held up later thanks to the presence of the military. All four of Worthing's cinemas reported good audiences, with standing room only in some in mid-August 1914, despite the competition from the new Picturedrome.[349] In 1915 the diary of Frederick C. Maplesden, manager of the Whitehall Picture House (Theatre) at East Grinstead, indicated that billeted soldiers helped keep numbers up.[350] From 1916 the War Tax put a penny on tickets, an increase of up to 25 per cent, putting, for example, Horsham's Central Picture Hall prices up to 4*d*, 5*d*, 7*d* and 11*d*.[351] These increases may have reduced numbers somewhat but we found no examples of cinemas closing on economic grounds in 1914–18.

In the absence of radio and television broadcasts, cinema played a crucial part in influencing the public and maintaining morale. Realising this, the government set up the War Propaganda Bureau in September 1914 to control information received by the public and to generate its own publications, including films.[352] As early as September 1914 a series released by the War Office depicted the life of 'Tommy Atkins', a new recruit being equipped, trained and fed and the *Warwick Chronicles* showed London scenes, including mass recruitment rallies.[353] The execution of British nurse Edith Cavell shocked the nation and the film *Nurse and Martyr* released in 1916 told the British side of the story.[354] The best known example is *The Battle of the Somme*, possibly the longest film local audiences had ever sat through, such that, at over seventy minutes, it was shown in five parts. It provoked controversy nationally, given some of the graphic images of the fighting, but seems to have passed off without widespread criticism locally, possibly due to censorship. Some cinemas chose a somewhat insensitive programme. The Worthing Picturedrome, for example, added: 'A Nestor Studios comedy, a two part drama "Paid With Interest", an interesting educational film illustrating the life and habits of the cormorant, and the customary instalment of the Gaumont Graphic [newsreel].'[355] Whether relatives of servicemen on the Somme stayed on to see the second half of the programme is unrecorded. Some excitement was caused in March 1917 by the follow-up film which featured a new weapon, tanks, in action at the Battle of the Ancre, the final large-scale attack of the Somme offensive.[356]

Sunday closure controversies best illustrate what a mainstay of social life the cinema was. Two examples took place in 1914 at Littlehampton and from March to September 1917 in Worthing. A 'Daughter of the Empire' wrote 'The Church opposition to … cinema displays … on Sunday evenings, after Church hours, is another of the … examples in which Clergy

Picturedrome advert for The Battle of the Somme film. (Worthing Gazette, 13 September 1916, p. 4)

WORTHING GAZETTE.

GO TO

THE PICTUREDROME

AND SEE THE

Official War Film of

THE BATTLE OF THE SOMME

(PERFECTLY SCREENED)

As exhibited before Their Majesties the King and Queen at Windsor Castle.

SHOWING

September 18th, 19th, and 20th, at approximately 3.20, 5.50, and 8.20 pm.

THREE DAYS commencing September 21st,

The Celebrated London Comedy,

OFFICER 666. Featuring DAN MOYLES.

Grand New Pathé Serial,

THE PERILS OF PAULINE. Episode No. 1. Twixt Earth and Sky

Featuring PEARL WHITE, the Heroine of "The Exploits of Elaine."

Also SPECIAL FILM OF

THE BURNT ZEPPELIN

"The Strafer Strafed" (the Fate of L21).

IMPORTANT ANNOUNCEMENT.

MR. ARTHUR MALDEN,

THE WELL-KNOWN LECTURER,

Will give a series of Lectures on

"*RUSSIA, our Eastern Ally,*" and "*ITALY, our Gallant Ally,*"

On September 26th and 27th.

SEE SPECIAL ANNOUNCEMENTS.

and Ministers exhibit intolerance, jealousy and ignorance of the needs and conditions of the ordinary people …'[357] The latter ban provoked widespread criticism, particularly from the Provost Marshal, in charge of discipline at Shoreham Camp. Letters to the local press pointed out '… it is not fair to our fighting men that, on wet and windy days, the street and the public houses are the only places for them to go to. They deserve more consideration and the best we can give them'.[358] Finally the magistrates relented and revoked their order.[359]

Public houses remained an important element of social life for many, particularly working-class people.[360] Drunkenness was a major political issue before the Great War and fear of servicemen and workers corrupted and made inefficient by alcohol prompted government action. DORA, passed on 8 August 1914 and amended six times,[361] enforced the watering down of alcoholic drinks and restricted pub opening times to six hours a day, normally noon to 3 p.m. and 6.30 p.m. to 9.30 p.m. Local magistrates could specify the opening times in particular areas. Beer production in England and Wales fell from nearly 30 million barrels in 1914 to 11.3 million in 1918[362] as there were fewer young men to drink it and agricultural production was re-focussed on to food production. The duty on alcohol was also increased several times to restrict consumption and raise more money to fund the war.[363]

The beer drinking versus temperance issue was debated occasionally in the local press. Jerome Deigman, from North Bersted, wrote: '… public houses … afford a vent for the exuberance of those patriots' whose deeds of daring do 'begin and end at the front – of the bar'!'[364] Whereas Edward J. Huntley of the Locomotive Inn at Littlehampton retorted: 'The wealthy man has his Club. To the working man, the Public House serves as a club, a place to frequent in the evening after a day's work, to meet a friend or two, and perhaps to have a pint of beer, in which action he can feel he is helping to bear a portion of our great financial burden'.[365]

The restrictions seem to have had an effect. In March 1915 Albert Thomas wrote: 'In the Steyning Division, which includes Shoreham Camp, drunkenness charges fell from 53 the previous year to 32; in some districts of Sussex the proportion was still better.'[366] Worthing's mayor reported in June 1916 that 'in Worthing there had been a wonderful diminution in the prosecutions for drunkenness so far this year, and last year had shown a great decrease'.[367] The Licencing Sessions for Midhurst area reported only one case of drunkenness in the year from February 1917.[368] Adverse effects were reported in some areas. Some pubs probably closed due to a combination of staff shortages and increased duty, such as the King's Head at Cuckfield in August 1916.[369]

Social and sports clubs were substantially affected by the war. Some carried on, with depleted membership, as men joined up and women became involved in war work, paid or voluntary. Many switched their focus so that their activities and events became geared towards the war effort, either in terms of fundraising or voluntary tasks. The Men of Sussex, a socially prestigious society, used social events to raise money for their RSR Comforts Fund[370] and by 1918 had visited 686 wounded Sussex men in hospital.[371] Rifle clubs flourished as obvious breeding grounds for military recruits. Ashling Miniature Rifle Club enjoyed a successful year 1915–16 with thirty boys enjoying free use of the range.[372] Prompted by the Board of Agriculture's financial rewards, Rat and Sparrow clubs, such as at Bolney, were formed to destroy these animals in the campaign to safeguard crops.[373] The Worthing Sailing Club sent off a weekly parcel containing tobacco, pipes, chocolate, handkerchiefs, newspapers, peppermint, knives, pencils, postcards and boracic ointment.[374]

Sports clubs lost most of their players, being of the right age to volunteer, and abandoned competitive fixtures from 1915. Friendly matches between the military and established or ladies' teams took their place. The mood of the nation and county was summed up by a Turners Hill article in the *Sussex and Surrey Courier*: 'Football: there will be no matches in this village during the current season, owing to just over 50 young fellows having gone to do their country's work against the Scarborough baby-killers.'[375] Some forty Haywards Heath Rangers FC players joined up and by 1917 nine were dead; the *Mid-Sussex Times* gives details of most.[376] Cricket followed the same pattern. Horsham Cricket Club abandoned fixtures in June 1915, instead arranging friendlies against locally billeted Fusiliers.[377] Horse racing finished at Goodwood in July 1915, when the Duke of Richmond called off the (Glorious) Goodwood meeting, run since 1812.[378] Priory Park Bowling Club hosted regular afternoons of bowls, tennis, cricket and croquet for the wounded from Graylingwell War Hospital and elsewhere.[379] Boxing took place across the county, to keep servicemen fit. Typical were bouts at Selsey's Cinema Hall between servicemen from a Cyclists' battalion (probably 1/9th Hampshire Regiment) and one involving local lad Ray Harmsworth.[380]

Perhaps most unusual were the first ever games of baseball, prompted by the arrival of Americans based at the Rustington aerodrome. Games were played frequently on Littlehampton Common, and occasionally in Worthing, in the summer of 1918, 'although it is an open question whether the game itself, or the excited and outspoken comments of the soldier spectators, prove most interesting to the civilian onlookers'.[381]

6

THE LOCAL ECONOMY AND CIVILIAN MORALE

By Martin Hayes

Economic Background

Economic changes during the Great War were staggering, both on a national and local level. The standard rate of income tax rose from 6 per cent in 1914 to 30 per cent by 1918, which, together with a higher rate for the rich, increased governmental income from £47 million (£2.679 billion) to £293 million (£16.701 billion). Most of this burden fell on the middle classes as personal allowances for taxpayers increased to £160 per year.[382] Most agricultural workers and manual labourers in West Sussex earned much less than 30s a week or £78 p.a. and some less than 20s or £52 (see below). An Excess Profits Duty clawed back excessive profits that some firms had made from the war effort. With this and other tax increases, the government's income rose to over £580 million (£33.06 billion) by 1918, that is seventeen times the 1905 figure of around £34 million (£1.938 billion).[383]

Many businesses struggled to survive the war as men volunteered and later were conscripted into the services. To some extent women stood in but many companies existed on fewer staff and lower turnover. The latter was largely caused by people generally not spending as much on themselves either through necessity or choice. The middle classes, in particular, expended a great deal of effort, money and time on fundraising, goods production and voluntary work rather than on consumer goods for themselves, such that the civilian economy shrank. Prices rose by almost 100 per cent between 1914 and 1918, meaning that the average price of products costing 1*s* before the outbreak of war would cost nearly 2*s* by the end.[384] The price of raw materials in particular increased substantially.

On a more positive note, these enforced conditions led to increased wages in some sectors, at least outside agriculture, though probably not sufficient to offset the effects of inflation. Also, almost universally, men's jobs were kept open for them, awaiting their return, though of course around 15 per cent to 20 per cent never came back.

Tough Times

Family incomes were down and prices were up, therefore times were tough. The *Worthing Gazette* reported in 1914 '… the number of little ones who cluster round the bakers' shops in the early morning, to buy the remnants of the previous day's baking at a cheap rate, is now greater than it was a few weeks ago'.[385] Following rationing from 1917, people became increasingly desperate. The Maypole Dairy Company in Worthing was mobbed by impatient customers and had to be closed, while a public kitchen in Chapel Road served about 500 meals a day by March 1918.[386] A letter from a Bognor housewife in 1918 mentions 'wives at home have to stand for hours in a queue fighting for food for their children'.[387]

Some jobs were lost. By September 1915 the Mayoress of Chichester's Relief Fund had 'proved such a great success last winter in preventing distress and providing employment for a large number of women and girls who were thrown out of work on account of the war'.[388] People were urged to keep spending in the local area to prevent unemployment. For example, W.B. Knight appealed to Worthing ladies to use local laundries instead of sending their washing to the cheaper London steam laundries.[389] Despite this, some businesses failed and people lost their jobs, for example the bankruptcy of Miss Lilian Onion's Norfolk Sanitary Steam Laundry in Littlehampton by June 1915.[390] (Chapter 7 has more examples of women's unemployment.)

There were appeals from tradesmen for prompt payment and for people to keep spending to support the local economy.[391] There were some early reports of profiteering and bad service. Those who believe that bad service is a purely modern phenomenon may wish to ponder the following quote from a Littlehampton shop worker: '… an assistant, who is known for his ordinary and extraordinary want of civility, told a poor old lady threateningly: "If you don't pay this price you'll have to pay more on Tuesday – that is, if we like to serve you at all!"'[392]

Wages, Labour Shortages and Strikes

Labourers building St Symphorian church, Durrington, Worthing, 1915. By kind permission of the New Life Church. (WSCCLS, L000100)

There are many examples of wage rises in West Sussex not keeping pace with inflation, despite the labour shortage as men joined up. In March 1915 Littlehampton Urban District Council (UDC) turned down a request by carters and other workmen for an increase on their wages of 22s a week, saying they did not wish to put a penny on the rates and there were some people living on less.[393] In October 1916, twenty-two workmen from

the Surveyor's Department petitioned in Horsham UDC for an increase in pay due to the increased cost of living and received an increase of 4s per week. The Finance Committee commented that 'a man earning 22s or 23s a week, with his family to keep, could not find it sufficient. The food bill had now increased by about 65 per cent [since 1914]'.[394]

Some local factors did push up wages in some areas. Bognor UDC were forced to offer their workmen a wage increase of 4s a week in 1918 because 'the men can get more elsewhere, so there is no alternative'.[395] The alternatives were probably aerial construction at Yapton (see below) and the aircraft factories at Middleton and Littlehampton employing up to 900.

Despite the growing labour shortage, agricultural labourers' wages were generally lower than for other male jobs. Evidence of this is provided by the meeting of the Cuckfield Guardians in April 1916:

> … a woman requiring relief … said her husband was only earning 16s a week, and had to provide a house. The House Committee thought that such a man was not getting as much as a farmer ought to pay … William Wood of Hurstpierpoint … said … others [cases] had come before them lately. He knew what he had to pay his own men … 22s and 23s a week and a house.[396]

A minimum wage of 25s a week was not guaranteed until 1917.[397] WSCC's Education Committee amended an emergency resolution in February 1916 enabling boys over 12 to finish school early to work in agriculture, market gardening and fisheries[398] and this may have undercut agricultural labourers' wages too. By August 1918 some 1,511 boys and 128 girls were so employed.[399]

Some businesses began to use volunteers. The *West Sussex Gazette* revealed in 1916 that out of their fifty-six staff, twenty-nine were of military age of which twenty were serving, three had been rejected on medical grounds and six were attested and expected to be called up shortly. So, with the loss of nearly half of their total staff, the editor appealed for volunteers in communities across the county to submit reports.[400]

Unlike in large cities late in the war, and despite the relatively low wages for labourers in the county, strikes seemed to have been rare in West Sussex. Those which took place were small-scale affairs over quickly. In March 1915, some sixteen labourers, working on the Littlehampton railway wharf development, asked for a wage increase from 5d to 6d an hour. Employers J. Linfield refused, most of the men found work elsewhere within a day or two and several returned for the same wage.[401] Later in the year the National Union of Railwaymen secured bonus payments for their workers.[402] In August 1916 the Haywards Heath branch voted to support any (strike) action deemed necessary by the NUR National Executive Committee to obtain a wage rise of 10s a week.[403]

Local Industries

Postcard of Worthing beach sent on 17 July 1918. (WSCCLS, TC002303)

The tourist industry, on which the coastal towns in particular depended, seemed to hold up, though statistics are hard to come by. The London, Brighton & South Coast Railway Company shareholders' annual meeting in 1915 mentioned 'during the Christmas holidays … the first-class traffic showed considerable increase over last year at such places as … Worthing …

presumably [because] travellers who migrate to France and Switzerland for the winter months have this year taken their holidays on our South Coast'.[404]

In 1915 Littlehampton experienced 'a large number of visitors'[405] and Bognor 'has been fuller of visitors than it has ever been before ... with many visitors having been booked for furnished houses and apartments [to] the end of September and October'.[406] The following year, destinations not normally regarded as tourist places reported good trade. In August Cuckfield was 'Full of visitors: persons who let apartments are full up and some of them say that if their houses were four times the size they could have filled them'.[407] An editorial in the *Mid-Sussex Times* commented: 'Haywards Heath, Balcombe and Horsted Keynes are among places in Mid-Sussex which have benefitted by the presence of a large number of visitors.'[408]

The market gardening industry in West Sussex, and particularly Worthing, was hit hard by the war, because demand for its luxury products, flowers and grapes, fell away badly. Cucumbers and tomatoes made little profit too as their retail price fell as people concentrated on buying the food essentials.[409] Maintaining the workforce was also a problem throughout the war as men joined up. Military tribunal records have many interesting cases.

William Frederick ('Fred') Young at his nursery in Goring near Worthing, taking on his children to help during the labour shortage, 1917. (Copy supplied by Malcolm Linfield; WSCCLS, P003380)

For example, a 31-year-old fruit grower in 1916 had 'lost all my men and have only two women and some boys left to work two acres of ground with 1,100 feet of glass'.[410] Later in the war even more were attracted to munitions production and other war-related construction. For example, several market gardeners earning up to 8*d* an hour left to take jobs on 'aerial construction at Yapton'.[411]

Builders found business hard to come by as local authorities postponed or down-sized building projects. Frank Sandell & Sons of Worthing, building extensions to Midhurst Grammar School, asked WSCC to pay an extra £35 (£1,995) 'owing to the rise in the prices of materials and labour difficulties'.[412] WSCC refused as they had funding problems of their own.

Some established industries increased their production and changed some products to support the war effort. Workers at The Tannery in Chichester were thanked by the Minister of Munitions for their efforts in making boots and other leather equipment for the military. Singled out for praise were Tom Egerton, a 77-year-old who'd come back after retirement, and West Sussex agricultural labourers who'd been drafted into coalmines.[413] Rice Brothers of East Grinstead were originally saddlers, expanded to manufacture carriage and motor car bodies and switched production to shells for the war effort.

Rice Brothers' workers making shell cases at their London Road premises, c. 1915. (Joseph Rice Collection, East Grinstead Museum, 2100.4)

Some new businesses were set up, associated partly with the war effort, such as toy making companies at Bognor, Chichester and Worthing (see Chapter 7 for more details of these new businesses). The Littlehampton economy was boosted a little by the London, Brighton & South Coast Railway Company's cross-Channel ferry service for freight during 1915–16.[414] The three boats a week had limited impact and the service ended when the harbour was commandeered in 1916.[415]

Local Authorities and Postal Services

The general effects of the war on public services are well expressed by the annual meeting of the Sussex Public Officials' Association in 1916:

> ... public work had been reduced to the lowest possible minimum ... constructional work ... drainage and water supply schemes had been suspended, road-making had been delayed and there had been a cessation of building operations in most districts. In ... public health ... there had been a similar state of affairs.[416]

Local authorities not only released men to fight but often paid them an allowance of part of their wages. West Sussex County Council kept all employees' posts open and made up the pay of married men and single men with dependants.[417] East Sussex County Council agreed to keep all posts open, married men received full pay, less allowances, and single men half pay.[418] These patriotic actions had consequences for both county councils as, to maintain these payments and other services when prices for most goods doubled, they felt obliged to put up local rate charges. On 20 November 1914, WSCC increased rates from 5½d to 7½d in the pound, which prompted angry protest letters from Boards of Guardians at Chichester, East Preston, Midhurst, Petworth, Steyning and Thakeham.[419] In April 1915 L.P. Johnston, Overseer for Warningcamp, resigned rather than sign off the new rates of 3s 6d imposed on people who were suffering: '... heavy income tax, heavy food and living expenses, and ... generous contributions ... to War Funds'.[420] Six weeks later, Horsham Board of Guardians passed a resolution 'to call the attention of the West Sussex County Council to the very serious and continuous increase in the rates in recent years, and especially ... of the Education Committee'.[421] The war caused major, if temporary, changes in education services: many male teachers joined up, causing such a shortage that married female teachers were employed for the first time, whilst new school buildings and evening classes were cancelled.[422]

Other local authorities were under pressure too, as we saw in the 'Wages, Labour Shortages and Strikes' section above. Despite this, both Westhampnett Rural District Council (RDC) in 1916[423] and Bognor UDC in 1917[424] were able to send workmen to reconstruct French roads damaged in the fighting.

Postal services were depleted by a loss of staff, for example Bognor's daily deliveries were cut from four to three.[425] Littlehampton's postmaster explained why the town's second delivery was so late in the afternoon: '... his staff was limited for delivery, and more so indoors, and they were now working very long hours indeed ... The second delivery was very heavy ... For fourteen months he himself had not had a day off except one Sunday, ordered by the doctor ...'[426]

Prisoners of War at Work

Late in the war, a more pragmatic policy was introduced of putting to work the large number of resident German POWs to support the local economy. By July 1917, POWs from the Naval Prison in East Sussex were reported to 'work well and willingly and seem to be perfectly contented'.[427] Perhaps they were pleased to be out of the prison! By 1918 several hundred were employed in a variety of tasks. At East Grinstead a large, empty shop was used to house some.[428] Some 100 to 150 were engaged in tree-felling in the Findon or Washington area,[429] agricultural work especially ploughing near Horsham[430] and near Lindfield,[431] unloading coal at Midhurst Station[432] and at Chichester,[433] repairing roads at Littlehampton[434] and East Lancing sea defence work.[435] In the

German prisoners of war felling trees at Longbury Hill Estate, Washington, 1918. (By kind permission of Geoff Goatcher; WSCCLS, L001064)

summer more were deployed in agricultural work: seventy-five at Angmering, fifty at Henfield, thirty at Wisborough Green and fifty at Hove.[436]

Although generally working well, there were some problems. A general report on POW workers, pay, conditions and problems, particularly strikes, appears in the *West Sussex County Times* in July 1918.[437] In early November some 150 POWs working on the land near Worthing went on strike, objecting to sleeping in tents. They were disciplined by having their food cut and were moved to another camp.[438]

Shops

Traditionally shops had long opening hours, usually from 8 a.m. to 9 p.m. and even later on Fridays and Saturdays. Some local shopkeepers, struggling with fewer staff, reduced profits and higher energy bills, began to cut their hours, although the trend was patchy across the county. Some Worthing shops began closing at lunchtimes as early as September 1914.[439] Chichester shopkeepers began closing at 7 p.m. (Monday to Wednesday) in winter 1914–15 and continued this into the summer, apparently without much public complaint.[440] A detailed review in the *Chichester Observer* supported the move, pointing out the energy savings and better working conditions for employees.[441] Burgess Hill's Chamber of Commerce was praised for deciding shops would close at 6 p.m. weekdays from October 1916 and continue the hour lunch closing, whilst Haywards Heath traders were criticised for not following suit.[442]

Also of note is the Summer Time Act of 1916 which established British Summer Time, with clocks going forward one hour then and back in autumn, and local newspapers reported no particular problems for shopkeepers on 21 May.[443]

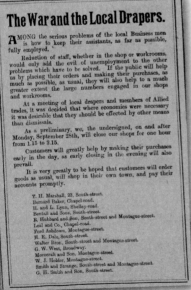

The War and the Local Drapers.

AMONG the serious problems of the local Business men is how to keep their assistants, as far as possible, fully employed.

Reduction of staff, whether in the shop or workrooms, would only add the evil of unemployment to the other problems which have to be solved. If the public will help us by placing their orders and making their purchases, as much as possible, as usual, they will also help to a much greater extent the large numbers engaged in our shops and workrooms.

At a meeting of local drapers and members of Allied trades, it was decided that where economies were necessary it was desirable that they should be effected by other means than dismissals.

As a preliminary, we, the undersigned, on and after Monday, September 25th, will close our shops for one hour from 1.15 to 2.15.

Customers will greatly help by making their purchases early in the day, as early closing in the evening will also prevail.

It is very greatly to be hoped that customers will order goods as usual, will shop in their own town, and pay their accounts promptly.

T. H. Marshall, 23, South-street.
Bernard Baker, Chapel-road.
H. and L. Lynn, Shelley-road.
Bentall and Sons, South-street.
R. Hubbard and Son, South-street and Montague-street.
Leal and Co., Chapel-road.
Ford Ashdown, Montague-street.
H. E. Dale, South-street.
Walter Bros., South-street and Montague-street.
G. W. West, Broadway.
Morecraft and Son, Montague-street.
W. J. Holder, Montague-street.
Smith and Strange, South-street and Montague-street.
G. H. Smith and Son, South-street.

'The War and Local Drapers' an appeal in Worthing Gazette. *(*Worthing Gazette, *23 September 1914, p. 4 cols d–e)*

The 'co-op' movement was an important feature of the local economy, in which members shared any profits made in their shops selling groceries, bread, coal, clothing, draper, boots and shoes. The Haywards Heath and District Industrial Co-operative Society half-yearly meeting in July 1916 reported '… trading conditions being trying and difficult … enhanced prices of goods', yet sales of nearly £11,729 (£668,553) were up over £500 on the previous half-year and membership up to 1,199.[444]

Food shops came under particular pressure in 1917–18 (see 'Morale' later in this chapter).

Coal, Gas and Electricity

Local coal, electricity and gas supplies were affected by the war and shortages increased as the war went on. The Haywards Heath Gas Company supported the war effort by releasing ten of their employees to fight and giving large gas stoves to the new Red Cross hospitals at the town's Public Hall and Lindfield's King Edward Hall.[445] As early as March 1915 Littlehampton Gas Company reported its profits were down due to a big increase in coal prices and difficulties obtaining supplies.[446] Later the same year, the Ministry of Munitions required companies to extract benzol (benzene) and toluol (toluene) from coal gas for use in explosives –[447] which local people would have noticed in dimmer lights – and urged people not to use coal for this reason.[448]

Haywards Heath Gas Company's price increases in March 1915 and in September 1916 provoked strong criticism from consumers and the UDC and an equally robust reply justifying the increase from the company.[449] In March 1918 East Grinstead Gas and Water Company's annual report mentioned a probable price increase due to these factors: 'Coal has cost more … considerable increase in wages and the greatly increased cost of materials.'[450] The same report compared price increases of the neighbouring companies and them-selves: Haywards Heath pre-war 3s 6d now [1918] 5s; Horley [serving Crawley area] 4s now 5s; Horsham 3s 11d now 4s 7d; East Grinstead 3s 6d now 3s 10d.

In April 1918, a new order by the Board of Trade under DORA meant users of gas and electricity had to reduce their consumption by one-sixth.[451] The government also took out a series of adverts 'Notes on Saving'[452] in local newspapers. Right up to the end of the war people were being urged, via these adverts, to save coal by having fewer hot meals and baths, smaller fires, going to bed earlier etc.[453] Electricity prices also went up. Worthing was lit by electricity via a Corporation-owned works but a £1,925 deficit by June 1918 forced a price rise of about 10 per cent.[454]

Morale

The morale of the civilian population is difficult to measure, but it is largely based on economic and family issues or concern for loved ones. Local newspaper articles give only a partial, sanitised, relentlessly upbeat account of the war effort which does not allow us to come to firm conclusions on morale generally. Newspapers do cover all local court cases, however, and we found no serious offences in West Sussex under the DORA, unlike that of the Seaford man jailed for 'making certain statements likely to prejudice the recruiting, training, and discipline or administration of His Majesty's Forces'.[455] A more thorough examination of surviving court records is necessary.

There are, however, hints that all was not well with all of the people all of the time. We have already seen open class warfare at Crawley during the attempts to set up the fundraising body there[456] and in the same area apparent profiteering was also a source of discontent. 'Frisco Jake' (possibly not his real name!) wrote:

At the end of the war Crawley will be a mass of millionaires and the roads will have to be widened to accommodate their cars ... the war has caused an advance in prices but when you come to 100 per cent ... it is time to bestir in this matter ... a man that will use the war as an excuse to bleed his less fortunate neighbours is a traitor to his country.[457]

At Littlehampton[458] and Worthing[459] there was widespread discontent at the Sunday closing of cinemas which suggested a serious breakdown of communication and lack of sensitivity and misunderstanding of popular culture by some in authority.

White feather and verbal attacks were also an insidious problem. Veteran E. Hopkins of Chichester wrote, 'What unkind, thoughtless person is it who is wasting time and money ... sending to discharged soldiers and also rejected men, a white feather? I myself enlisted in the 7th Battalion, RSR on the outbreak of war, but was invalided out ...'[460] Another soldier returned from the front in 1915, writes: '... it is only at home that some people prefer to get, and to spread, the doleful dumps'.[461] L. Skinner from Lingfield wrote:

> I was walking into East Grinstead with a young friend, only 18 years of age ... and was ... disgusted at the way in which people ... sneered at him ... my friend ... had been on active service both in France and at the Dardanelles, where he was wounded, and is ... recovering from ... dysentry.[462]

The incessant demand for donations for the war effort took their toll. The *Worthing Gazette* commented in 1915 that 'Certain people who have promised to subscribe to the Local War Relief Fund ... have failed when the time of performance arrived'.[463] In 1917 Mr Lane of Horsham UDC remarked '... there was no question that flag days were getting very slow ...'[464] Edward Heron-Allen of Selsey wrote in his diary: 'Sometimes now there are four of five Flag Days in a single week. It has become an intolerable nuisance' and the 'lambs with minx sauce ... have largely given place to elderly and ugly persons of a kittenish exterior, who unblushingly attempt to imitate the wiles of their predecessors.'[465] This last jibe by the waspish writer was a claim that some flag-sellers were prostitutes![466] By 1918 Haywards Heath UDC members felt an understandable weariness with the war, particularly the financial burden and, unlike other towns, did not organise a War Weapons Week.[467]

Certainly the scarcity of foodstuffs after the German submarine campaign of 1917[468] caused some panic which is only partially reported in local newspapers. We get a hint of how many people felt in a letter from a soldier's wife, in the *Observer* series, criticising workers at Middleton aircraft factory, who had complained about their accommodation:

> These men do not know what hardships are. When their work is finished they can go to their comfortable lodgings and a good bed to sleep on, whereas our dear brave soldiers have to give up every home comfort for the battlefield. What would some of them give to have their families with them? They have to fight on one shilling a day (with a contented mind at that) while their wives at home have to stand for hours in a queue fighting for food for their children. Many of these men have gone to work at Middleton for the simple reason of dodging the khaki.[469]

A Women's Institute (WI) member remembered, 'Mother took up work at Goring-by-Sea … Food was very short … and there was no rationing as such, so we were lucky if we got something to eat. Fuel was very short too, which meant we were often very cold'.[470] A letter from 'A Soldier Home from the Front' complained about the lack of a cottage hospital in Bognor '… a thing which is badly needed for all. But, there, I suppose Tommy's wife must put up with all illness etc in her own house'.[471] (Further evidence of the struggles of maintaining family life is covered in Chapter 7.)

A study of suicide statistics and cases would throw more light on the issue of morale. Certainly there are cases brought on by the pressure of the war. For example, Thomas Dare, a Poling farmer, who shot himself, was apparently '… greatly perturbed by the war. He has a son in the Army, which apparently occasioned him some anxiety …'[472]

Much more research remains to be done, particularly on archival material such as court records and any surviving diaries and letters, before we'll be able draw firm conclusions about the morale of West Sussex people during the conflict.

7

WOMEN AT WAR

By Justin Burns

Themes explored in this chapter include changes in family life influenced by the war, voluntary work, unemployment, employment opportunities, the new WIs and the Women's Land Army.

Family Life

When war broke out, a key role for women was to encourage their menfolk to join up and fight for King and Country.[473]

This recruitment appeal was made directly to women: 'When the War is over, and your husband or son is asked, "What did you do in the great War?" is he to hang his head because you would not let him go?'[474] At a patriotic meeting in Durrington, women were urged to co-operate together 'to fight the enemies we have at home, while the men are doing their part for us in the field.'[475] Women were seen as the moral backbone of the country, looking after the family and the nation. The girls of Chichester High School were urged to uphold their strength of character with bravery and courage.[476] Patriotic fervour led some women to issue white feathers to the men not fighting as a symbol of cowardice. Discharged veteran E. Hopkins wrote to the *Chichester Observer* criticising the white feather campaign. He argued that women would be better spending their money making badges for discharged men to wear, allowing the army to know who to canvass.[477]

TO ENGLISH WOMEN.

Mother, give up your brave young son,
  Your pride and joy though he may be;
Think of the glory to be won,
  Pray for him now on bended knee.
Young girls, be great and true of heart,
  Be first to let your lover go;
Help him, for his country's sake, depart,
  Cheer him, whate'er may be your woe
Sisters, use your best persuasion,
  Speed your brother for England's sake;
This is now your great occasion,
  Do not miss it, all's at stake.
Wives, help your men great men to be,
  Trust God when danger overtakes;
Spare them to serve on land or sea,
  Be hopeful, strong, for their dear sakes.
                                F.C.

Recruitment poem appealing directly to women. (Mid-Sussex Times, 8 September 1914, p. 1)

Many women were now bringing up a family and running a household alone. Food prices rose throughout the war, sugar, potatoes and bread became scarce and rationing was introduced in 1918. At a meeting in Horsham, Mrs Peel from the Ministry of Food advised that mothers 'should give no bread to any child who did not want it'.[478] As one child remembers, 'food was hard to come by. I remember my Aunt and a friend being gone all day to Bognor trying to get some kind of food. ... and come back tired and sometimes disappointed.'[479] National kitchens, such as at East Grinstead, were set up to serve healthy and nourishing food to the poorest families.[480] Schoolchildren in Haywards Heath were able to enjoy a half pint of nourishing lentil soup and tasty suet roll with jam sauce for three pence.[481] Women and girls were urged to 'practise economy and go without things that were not absolutely necessary',[482] including being economic with their consumption of food and fuel, and having to make do and mend with household items and clothes.

Money was usually tight and separation allowances and pensions often did not cover family needs.[483] Within a week of war starting, the Soldiers' and Sailors' Families' Association (SSFA) West Sussex branch opened an office in South Street, Chichester. Between 4 and 12 August 1914 the SSFA gave financial help to at least seventy local families of servicemen and a further twenty families a day were coming forward for assistance. The SSFA's aim was to make up income to 12s 6d a week.[484] The SSFA was divided into divisions, Arundel, Bognor, Chichester, Horsham, Midhurst, Petworth, Steyning and Worthing, each with a formidable lady in charge.[485] In Chichester, the Mayoress' Relief Fund was set up in the winter of 1914 to prevent distress and provide employment for local women. All applications for relief had to go to the Local Distress Committee whose money came from the NRF. Only people specifically referred by that committee would be helped. By September 1915, the Mayoress' Relief Fund income was nearly £621 (£35,397 today).[486] When employment opportunities improved in 1915, many women had to go out to work for the first time. (More information on fundraising is in Chapter 5.)

There were concerns about young women liaising with soldiers and drinking in public houses. Police Superintendent Avis from Shoreham commented, 'we are infested with these young girls since the Troops have been here.'[487] By 1915, the Chichester Diocesan Purity Association reported the need to increase its preventative work among girls in areas where there were military camps.[488] Residents of Chichester were so concerned about the welfare of the girls that patrols of women were set up to help maintain order.[489] For a small minority, the excitement and emotional intensity of war did result in a change of behaviour. Other groups offered a different approach for women. The League of Honour, holding its first meeting in East Grinstead, asked women and girls to join in 'prayer, purity and temperance'.[490] Most local women focussed on keeping the family unit safe and supporting their men and country.

Voluntary Work

Many voluntary groups emerged to aid the war effort. Some of these were existing organisations, such as the National Union of Women's Suffrage Societies which suspended its political work during the war to help 'the sufferers from the economic and industrial dislocation caused by the war'.[491] New organisations emerged, while others were driven locally by determined individuals or groups.

On the outbreak of war women began making and supplying comforts for the troops. Comforts were small gifts parcelled out to the men at the front to make life more bearable. This included foodstuffs like chocolate, cocoa, tins of confectionery and tobacco, as well as soap, books and stationery. Clothes were an important part of the comforts, including shirts, vests, underwear and knitted gloves, scarves and socks.[492] The Manhood Aid Society (Selsey) was formed on 17 August 1914 to help with the crisis. By 14 October articles such as pyjamas, nightshirts, towels, bandages and pillowcases had been supplied to the

British Red Cross, to hospitals in Southsea and Chichester and to the Belgian Refugee Committee. Members were also knitting scarves, hats and gloves for troops overseas.[493]

The Royal Sussex Regiment (RSR) made direct appeals via local newspapers, stating confidently that they knew the 'ladies of Sussex will do their best'.[494] Items required by the 3rd Battalion included cigarettes, pipes, tobacco in small pouches, socks, soap, handkerchiefs, plain chocolate, woollen gloves and woollen belts.[495] These gifts were greatly appreciated by the men at the front. The commanding officer of B Company of the 2nd Battalion wrote, 'it is quite impossible to describe how valuable such things are to us all … in view of the cold weather ahead nothing can be more appropriate than gloves and scarves.'[496]

Special collections were made for Christmas. From Lavington Park near Petworth, Miss Catherine Buchanan's efforts saw the delivery of 1,000 boxes, one for every member of the 2nd Battalion, RSR. Each contained plum cake, sardines, coffee, butterscotch, soap, towel, handkerchief, pencil, writing pad and envelopes.[497] Over two years, from November 1914, Mrs Slavin sent 21,000 cigarettes to the fifteen sailors and fifty-five soldiers on active service from Fernhurst and began a Christmas parcel service for them from 1916.[498]

As the war continued, Voluntary Work Organisations (VWO) were formed in regions to help co-ordinate and prevent waste in comforts being sent to the troops.[499] At a branch meeting of the VWO at Hurstpierpoint, Miss Parez, honorary secretary of the Mid-Sussex Organisation, explained, 'although local efforts were well managed and sent in many excellent articles, some were found useless, and thus time, material and transport were wasted … showing that an organization was needed to put the supplies to their best use …'[500] During 1917, the War Work Association of East Grinstead made 32,390 articles in its work-rooms for the soldiers and sailors, an increase of 4,475 items on the previous year.[501]

Women voluntary workers played an important role in providing medical supplies. The Chichester Aid Society was set up to supply bandages and splints for the Red Cross.[502] As organisation improved, many areas set up war supply depots and fulfilled orders from the War Office. Chichester's depot banded together 'every class of woman, to work for one common cause, which should appeal to all, and that is to make comforts for the wounded.'[503] Women paid one penny to 'alleviate some of the terrible sufferings our soldiers and sailors are called upon to bear'.[504] Women responded promptly to appeals. In one day, nine Chichester women made 235 respirators urgently needed by the RSR.[505] Volunteers were also required in military hospitals; attached to a VAD, they provided field nursing duties including elementary nursing, cooking, cleaning and driving ambulances.[506]

From early May 1915, Miss J. Anna Keatinge of Horsham began a campaign to produce sandbags. She was initially deterred by a War Office circular that decried private efforts, citing transportation and quality control issues.[507] Letters in the *West Sussex County Times* from the front, however, suggested that the men fighting desperately needed them.[508] In July 1915, hearing of a specific need in the Dardanelles and the inability of the War Office to supply, she arranged transport via a container ship of 1,580 sandbags, produced locally by Rusper war workers, Denne Road School and Chichester girls schools.[509] Through the second half of 1915, and beyond, the local sandbag campaign continued apace; Miss Tyler's campaign in Crawley was able to produce around 500 a month[510] and totalled nearly 5,000 for 1915.[511]

Miss Jessy Annette Peake from Horsham exemplified someone who contributed greatly to the war effort. Firstly she set up a Parcel Fund for Horsham's Soldiers and Sailors. 'No one could carry out the work, more efficiently, more thoroughly or more energetically' was how she was described at a fundraising whist drive.[512] Letters of gratitude from soldiers were printed in the *West Sussex County Times*. Private H. George said, 'I have just received your very nice parcel I want to thank you, the whist drive and the Horsham people for being so good and kind.'[513] Miss Peake was also active in the *Daily Express* 'Cheery Fund', sending gifts to soldiers including footballs, musical instruments and sweets.[514, 515] Through her organisation and determination, Horsham led the country in collecting silver foil, the tin from which was used in munitions and other products. Her final total was over 29cwt.[516]

CARFAX THEATRE

Parcels for Soldiers.

A Grand . Musical **Matinee**

With Attractive Films,

Will be given in the above Theatre (kindly lent by the Proprietors, Messrs. H. F. & P. C. Bingham) on

THURSDAY, JAN. 10TH, 1918,

Doors open at 2.30, commencing at 2.45.

The whole of the proceeds for

MISS J. H. PEAKE'S SOLDIERS' PARCELS FUND

MUSICAL PROGRAMME ARRANGED BY

MISS ANNIE TATE

BOMBARDIER F. S. ROBERTS

GUNNER GARRETT

&c., &c., have consented to assist.

MR. HERBERT RUTLAND will accompany the films on the Pianoforte.

Tickets - 2/6, 2/-, 1/- & 6d.

Plan of the Room can be seen, and Tickets obtained, at Messrs. PRICE & Co.'s, West Street.

Plants kindly lent by Messrs. Jupp & Sons, West Street.

Fundraising poster, Horsham, 10 January 1918. Note mistake in Miss Peake's name (see page 149). (Horsham Museum; 1999. 689)

Fundraising was a key part of activities, with women and girls organising concerts, fêtes and jumble sales. In June 1915, wild roses were sold on the streets of Chichester, Midhurst, Selsey and Bosham in conjunction with a gigantic jumble sale at Priory Park. Over £408 (£23,256 today) was raised for the Royal West Sussex Hospital.[517] In April 1916, the local Girls' Friendly Society provided entertainment for the RSR POW Comforts Fund at the Iron Room congregational chapel, Petworth, making over £13 (£741). The programme included popular and costume songs, piano duet, comedy sketches, a *Sleeping Beauty* pantomime sketch, patriotic tableaux and the National Anthem.[518] The Girl Guides were expected to spend 100 hours voluntary service to achieve their war service badge. Activities undertaken included entertaining soldiers in Chichester[519] and collecting waste paper to sell in Worthing.[520]

Some women organised themselves into **civil defence** groups. The Women's Corps at Rustington were the first female volunteer reserve in the country and undertook physical exercise and marching in readiness for attacks.[521] The Horsham Women's Emergency Corps was established as 'a trained body of women to carry out the instructions of the local Emergency Committee in case of a raid'.[522] Classes were run on a range of subjects, including camping, cookery, sanitation, first aid and signalling.[523]

Employment

In 1914, female workers were traditionally employed in domestic service, including in boarding houses and hotels, and trades such as millinery and laundry work. At the outbreak of war, as people concentrated on the war effort, the need for domestic help was reduced and unemployment grew. In September 1914, a letter to the *Worthing Gazette* appealed to customers to continue using laundry services to help prevent unemployment and poverty: 'it is far better to provide for these women and their dependents by means of wages than by the distribution of charity.'[524] Similarly, the Women's Social and Literary Club in Horsham noted that many seamstresses were out of work because people were volunteering to do needlework. Readers were urged to continue using the seamstresses, again, to help prevent unemployment.[525]

Toy making as part of the Work for Women Fund in Chichester. (Chichester Observer, 21 April 1915, p. 5)

The emerging voluntary organisations were able to offer some help. In Worthing, a Women's Work Bureau was set up to organise paid work for those who had lost it owing to the war.[526] Toy making was introduced to keep women employed and fill the gap created by the banning of German imports. In Chichester, local women raised funds to set up workrooms to employ women and girls to make toys via their Work for Women Fund.[527] The enterprise was a success, with Chichester Toys Limited being formed on a commercial basis.[528]

By mid-1915, with increasing need for men at the front, women were needed to fill their jobs. There was resistance from many men for two reasons. Firstly, women would take home less money, bringing down general levels of pay which would

WORK FOR WOMEN FUND.

TWO CHICHESTER PHOTOGRAPHS.

THE MAYORESS'S SPLENDID SUCCESS.

TOYMAKING AT CHICHESTER. A WORKROOM AT DR. PAXTON'S SCHOOL.

We have pleasure in reproducing here two photographs of the Workrooms at Chichester, where, for several months past women and girls have been employed in the art of toymaking in connexion with the Work for Women Fund, which achieved such a splendid success through the efforts of the Mayoress, Mrs. Garland, and those who have been associated with her.

The first photograph shews a workroom at Dr. Paxton's School (very kindly lent for the purpose), with the Mayoress and Mrs. Close in the back of the picture, and the second depicts a workroom at "Ivy Bank," the resi-

dence of the Mayor and Mayoress, where the scheme made its practical start.

As already announced, the house to house collections for the Work for Women Fund have now ceased, and the balance is being placed on deposit in the names of trustees for future needs.

Preparations are being made to place the toymaking industry on a business footing, and for this purpose a local Company is shortly being formed which will take over suitable premises in Little London for the work.

TOYMAKING AT CHICHESTER. A WORKROOM AT "IVY BANK."

WORTHING GAZETTE

AT THE TICKET BARRIER

THE NEW LADY COLLECTORS

NOW ON DUTY AT THE RAILWAY STATION.

[From a "Gazette" photo]

REFERENCE was made in our last issue to the fact that the lady Ticket Collector had made her appearance at Worthing, and we are this week enabled to reproduce a snapshot of the two new female officials of this grade of the service on duty at the Railway Station.

In their neat blue serge uniforms and peaked caps they present a very smart appearance, and considering the comparatively short training they have had, they are proving themselves admirably adapted for the work that is being entrusted to them.

First female ticket inspectors at Worthing Station. (Worthing Gazette, 21 July 1915, p. 3)

also threaten male employment. Secondly, able-bodied men feared being dismissed and coerced in to joining the army.[529] Trade unions ensured that men's jobs were safe when they returned from the war.

Some women entered the workplace as a replacement for their absent husband. In Haywards Heath, a wife learnt how to cut hair and became the barber at her husband's shop.[530] New trades opened to women. The *Worthing Gazette* reported that two lady ticket inspectors at Worthing Railway Station were 'proving themselves admirably adapted for the work that is being entrusted to them.'[531]

Five women were taken on at Haywards Heath postal service; 'so far they have given satisfaction' was the underwhelming endorsement reported in the *Mid-Sussex Times*.[532] Commercial and clerical work expanded, with West Sussex Education Committee establishing training classes across the county in 'book-keeping, arithmetic, shorthand, commercial correspondence and typewriting.'[533]

International Stores, grocers with branches across West Sussex, advertised the fact they had released 2,000 men to the army and were employing lady grocers.[534] The *Mid-Sussex Times* commented, 'it really is remarkable that the lady grocers should step in and fill the position vacated by the hero at the front in such a capable manner'.[535]

The munitions industry particularly welcomed female workers. Light munitions work was being offered via Worthing's Labour Exchange in June 1916.[536] Opportunities were available outside West Sussex, particularly for female engineers in the Ministry of Munitions. Training would be undertaken at Tunbridge Wells and women could be sent to any factory in Britain.[537] Jobs in wartime industries were often better paid. Miss Rattey resigned her Assistant Mistress post at Ferring village school to become a clerk at an aeroplane factory in Farnborough for double the money.[538] The Middleton-on-Sea aircraft factory provided a local opportunity for employment (see Chapter 3).

As the war continued, so more female workers were needed. The Women's Army Auxiliary Corps (WAAC) was formed in December 1916 to allow women to take the place of soldiers in non-combatant roles. A recruitment drive in Bognor was advertised:[539]

Shoreham-by-Sea postwomen, with Mrs C.D. Page, centre at back, 1917. (Marlipins Museum, 89.1317)

If you are able to drive a motor car, then you will be a useful unit in the corps either at home or overseas. Perhaps you are a good clerk or typist, there are plenty of openings for you. If you are not suited for this, then your domestic training can be utilised as waitress, cook, storewoman …

Adverts in local newspapers encouraged women to enlist.[540]

For some West Sussex women, employment meant working overseas, close to the front, often in difficult and dangerous conditions. In a letter sent home to Arundel, one WAAC worker in France complained about the dangers of drowning in the mud and described her office job as 'useful work, that is indisputably going to help on the ending of the war'.[541] Nurses worked close to the battlefields and received awards for bravery and courage.

Advert showing lady grocers working in International Stores. (Mid-Sussex Times, 18 July 1916, p.2)

Recruitment advert for joining the WAAC. (West Sussex County Times, 13 October 1917, p. 3)

Nurse Constance Colt-Williams from Ifield was awarded the Croix de Guerre for refusing to leave wounded soldiers when Germans attacked her hospital and she was taken prisoner.[542] Some women ultimately lost their lives. Very few women are listed on war memorials and Worthing has such a rare entry: 'nursing sister Nellie Foyster, drowned when the hospital ship *Salta* sunk.'[543]

Women's Institutes

The first English branch of the Women's Institute (WI) was formed at Singleton, West Sussex, when a meeting was held at the Fox Inn on 9 November 1915.[544] The organisation embodied women's voluntary role, and placed strong emphasis on the land and home: 'without good homes the nation could not do its very best …'[545] It was founded as a 'group of women banded together to help their country and themselves'.[546] Their main aims were to 'release men from the land, increase the food supply, prevent waste, start a War Savings Association, consider the question of rural education, encourage village industries and make the Institute the centre of village life'.[547]

For a small fee, women from all classes and all backgrounds met together to help the war effort and be part of an organised group. In Bognor, the WI was started 'with good promise of support … many ladies are taking strong interest in the project'.[548] Activities included embroidery, knitting, shoe-repairing, toy-making, upholstery, cookery demonstrations, growing herbs, preserving fruit, jam-making, rabbit clubs, poultry-keeping and bee-keeping. Some went in for co-operative marketing of food, with Danehill WI having a stall at East Grinstead market.[549]

As the war progressed, so the movement grew in West Sussex. The WI did have its detractors, including existing women's organisations and some men. Strong organisation, by women, for women, was crucial to its growth with neighbouring Institutes working together to form co-operative programmes. In September 1917, Institutes from Mid-Sussex[550] met to encourage others to increase interest in 'the War Loan, waste paper, horse chestnuts, wool and blackberries, and the conservation of food …'[551] From this meeting, the Federation of Sussex WIs was born, organising and advising local Institutes, and was the first Federation in England.[552] The women of Handcross commented at the end of its first year in 1918, '… there was no end to the good the Institute had done for them'.[553] The *Mid-Sussex Times* was a strong supporter, 'things are going to be different after the war, we are told. Women's Institutes are going to make them different'.[554] Emerging from the war, the WI movement had a strong identity and defined role which has continued to this day.

The Women's Land Army

As the war progressed, with food shortages growing there was an increasing need for female agricultural labourers. Farmers' attitudes were not always favourable towards women working on the land. One Haywards Heath farmer told the *Mid-Sussex Times* that women 'would bring plague more than profit'.[555] Another farmer felt that women 'could not do hedging, ditching, stacking, ploughing, manure carting and handling machinery – all necessary work'.[556] Mr J.T. Strong, a local farmer and chairman of the East Preston RDC, argued that 'he could not help feeling that work on a farm was not a woman's place'.[557] He believed it would be better to allow boys to be released from their education earlier than aged 14 to be able to learn farming.[558] Indeed that happened – see Chapters 6 and 10. Mr J.H. Uridge, chairman of The East Grinstead Farmers Union, believed using women would reduce productivity.[559] In July 1915 the *Worthing Gazette* reported that a shortage of workers was impacting on the production of milk in West Sussex.[560]

To help overcome the prejudice of farmers and to encourage women to work on the land, different local organisations worked together to increase participation. Following a meeting at Worthing in July 1915, called by the National Union of Women Workers, a local committee was set up to organise

Agricultural workers at Town House Farm, Thakeham, near Storrington, 1 July 1917. (WSCCLS, P003378)

agricultural work for women.[561] In East Grinstead, a register was compiled of all the local women willing to be trained in farm work with farmers agreeing to take them on if they had been suitably trained.[562] During a recruitment meeting at Ashurst Wood fifty women registered to go wherever they were needed.[563] In Bognor and South Bersted women were asked to offer their services through the Women's Farm and Garden Union. They needed to 'produce and harvest as much food as possible during the war, by being trained in farm work, and in this way doing their "little bit" in assisting their country'.[564] Under the chair of the Countess of March, the Women's Agricultural Committee for West Sussex was formed to help organise and promote the employment of women. The committee began work at the beginning of 1916 and by July they were reporting that 2,000 women had registered with over 1,000 actively involved in farm work.[565] Typically women undertook milking and dairy work, ploughing, working in the field and market gardening.

By 1917, as demand increased, the State began a national campaign to employ women on the land. 'An appeal is now being made for women, their service on the land being most urgently needed … It is the women who are healthy and fit and who have their heads screwed on the right way who will find agricultural work congenial.'[566] The terms of service included board and lodging, one free outfit (high boots, breeches, two overalls and a hat) and a wage of 18*s* per week. They were called War Land Workers or Land Lasses, and formed part of the Women's Land Army.[567]

There were, however, local shortages of labour. 'West Sussex is the worst county in England as regards its contribution to women's work on the land'[568] claimed the *West Sussex Gazette*. Miss Leys of the Women's War Agricultural Committee explained, 'Land Lasses are doing extremely well. But there are not nearly enough of them, and lately the farms in West Sussex have had to be recruited by girls and young women from London, Bucks and Norfolk.'[569] One of the difficulties for recruiting women in West Sussex was the need for accommodation close to the farm, often in short supply.[570] There is little written evidence of women's experience of working on the land, but for many being away from home, working long hours and doing physically hard work would not have appealed. 'Town Girl' writes of her experiences working on a farm on the Sussex/Surrey border. After a day driving horses in the field, she goes to bed very tired Saturday night and then needs to be up at 5 a.m. Sunday morning to milk the cows. Her writing emphasises the demands of the role, but also illustrates her determination to make the most of the opportunity by understanding the animals and cultivating her own plot of land.[571]

However, in October 1918, an examiner commented that 'the West Sussex Land Girls have come out of the ordeal with flying colours … One of the most pleasing observations … was the fact that the unwarranted prejudice of the average farmer with regard to woman labour is rapidly disappearing'.[572] The following year, the Women's Land Army was disbanded as men returned home to their old jobs. (Further information on agricultural change is covered in Chapter 10.)

Legacy

The First World War was a watershed period for women. The national need for vastly more money, munitions and food to support the war effort saw them emerge from traditional roles of wife and mother with official encouragement. This chapter has described the wide range of roles undertaken, and economic, organisational and social demands placed on West Sussex women during wartime. 1918 saw their political aspirations rise as the vote was granted to propertied women over 30. Although it was to be post-1945 before the female social revolution happened, it has its roots firmly on the home front in the Great War.

TREATMENT OF THE SICK AND WOUNDED

By Katherine Slay

By the end of the war more than thirty locations across West Sussex had been used as hospitals, treating sick and wounded soldiers, sailors and airmen. These hospitals were located in a variety of buildings, some of which already had a nursing role:

Hospitals: Royal West Sussex, Chichester; Littlehampton; Worthing.
Cottage hospitals: Crawley and Ifield; Haywards Heath; Horsham. (Both hospitals and cottage hospitals continued to receive civilian patients.)
County asylum: Graylingwell Hospital, Chichester.
Convalescent homes: Sunshine Home, Hurstpierpoint; St Mary's, Westbrooke, Worthing; The Grange, Heene Parade, Worthing.
Workhouse infirmaries: Steyning Union Workhouse, Shoreham; East Preston (also including a nurses' home).

Other hospitals were in public or private buildings:

Public halls: Queen's Hall, Cuckfield; Public Hall, Haywards Heath; King Edward Hall, Lindfield.
Private houses: The Knowle (later Tower House), Balcombe; Bignor Park near Pulborough; East Lodge (later White House), Crawley Down; Brewery House, Felbridge Place and Stildon House, East Grinstead; Goring Hall; Broadhill, Hassocks; Beechhurst, Haywards Heath; Oldland, Keymer; Belgrave House, Littlehampton; Slindon House in Slindon; The Cecils

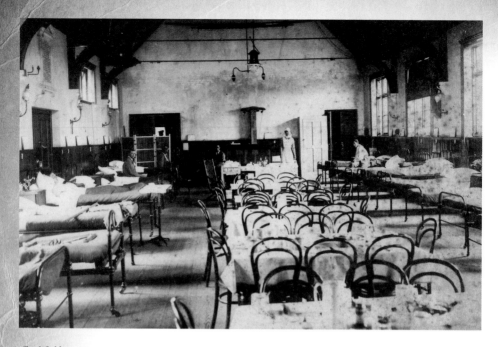

Cuckfield VAD Hospital, Queen's Hall; note chairs and tables for mealtimes, along with beds. (Cuckfield Museum)

(which had three locations in Worthing, in Manor Road, Mill Road, and Clifton Road), and 8-9 Heene Terrace, Worthing. *Girls' club room in a convent*: Arundel.
Sailors' Institute: Littlehampton.

Some hospitals were in military surroundings:

Camp: Roffey (Horsham).
Barracks: Chichester.

Finally, there were some private houses that were converted to become temporary convalescent homes, such as those at Sennicotts House near Funtington, and Cawley Priory in Chichester.

Background

The Boer War had made the War Office realise the need to plan ahead for treatment of the sick and wounded in the event of another war. In 1909 it issued a 'Scheme for the Organisation of Voluntary Aid in England and Wales'. The Red Cross and

the St John Ambulance each began setting up separate male and female Voluntary Aid Detachments (VADs). Each female detachment generally consisted of a commandant, a quartermaster, a lady superintendent (a trained nurse) and twenty women, including four qualified cooks. They were to staff auxiliary hospitals in Great Britain, and were unpaid. The women had to gain certificates in home nursing and in first aid. Male detachments had fifty-six members, some of whom might be ambulance drivers or orderlies in hospitals.

VAD, Auxiliary and Red Cross Hospitals

Once war was declared in 1914, houses and public buildings were offered as hospitals. Not all offers were taken up by the authorities. Location was a major consideration, with a nearby railway station being particularly useful. Storrington had expected to have an auxiliary hospital, but did not, for this reason.

With private houses, the owner and/or his wife was often the commandant. There were different coloured uniforms: scarlet (commandant), grey (quartermaster), pale brown (cook),

The Knowle VAD Hospital, Balcombe, June 1918. From left to right, back row: Nurse Duff, Nurse Adamson, Nurse Booth, Nurse Meredith, George Muddle. Middle row: Nurse McCall, Nurse Reid, Minnie Terry, Nurse Davis, Nurse Cobban, Nurse Orange, Nurse Oxley. Front row: Mrs Messel (commandant), Sister Bartlett, Mrs Oxley (quartermaster). (WSRO, PH 28161-28162)

and pale blue or grey (VAD nurses, attached to Red Cross or St John Ambulance respectively). Nurses had white headgear and starched detachable collar and cuffs. They made and sewed the red cross onto their aprons.

Once approved and furnished, hospitals (referred to variously as Red Cross, auxiliary, or VAD hospitals) were opened and dealt with up to 100 patients at any one time. The Knowle in Balcombe was 'entirely equipped by the kindness of friends who lent, or gave, most of the beds etc necessary to start a hospital of this description'.[573] Donations for the split-site Hassocks Hospital at Broadhill and at Oldland (in Keymer) were listed in detail down to matches, hot water bottles and toilet paper. Bignor Park, and The Cecils and St Mary's in Worthing had operating rooms, and The Cecils also had an X-ray machine. A certified masseuse (physiotherapist) visited regularly at The Cecils and at Belgrave House.

The VAD nurses did whatever work was necessary, including dressing, undressing and washing the patients. In an age when an unmarried girl could not be alone with a young man (other than her brother), this was initially embarrassing for both.

Bignor Park VAD Hospital. Patients in the drawing room enjoyed a variety of art on the walls. (WSRO, Add Mss 45230)

Unlike the tarmac surrounds of many hospitals in big cities, West Sussex hospitals were fortunate in being able to offer parkland and gardens or a small town location. Meals at The Knowle, and maybe at other hospitals, were taken outside in fine weather. After the horrors they had experienced overseas, the open space surroundings must have contributed to the men's recovery.

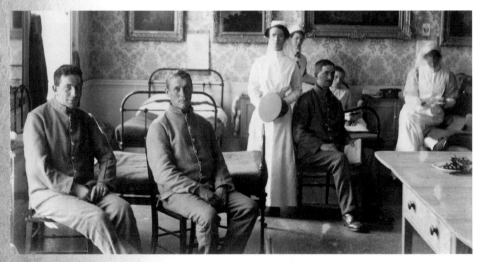

Graylingwell War Hospital, Chichester

West Sussex had only one war hospital, which took men direct from the front line. This was in the county asylum, whose existing patients had previously been transferred to other asylums in the south-east. It opened in May 1915, when the War Office had realised that there were insufficient war hospitals and more were needed. There were over 1,000 beds, and the first 490 patients arrived in three batches within the space of thirty hours. Qualified nurses were supplemented by VAD nurses from Chichester, Bognor and Lavant. During the four years that it was open, Graylingwell dealt with 29,412 patients, fairly evenly divided between medical and surgical cases. Over 6,000 operations were performed in the three operating theatres, and only 142 men died.[574] Donations to the Gift Fund and Gift Room were listed weekly in the *Chichester Observer*, as were 'items needed', outings and entertainments.

Auxiliary Hospitals

Affiliated to Graylingwell War Hospital were six auxiliary hospitals. These were the Royal West Sussex in Chichester, Arundel, Bignor Park, Littlehampton, Slindon House, and (briefly) The Grange in Worthing. The remaining auxiliary hospitals in West Sussex received patients from war hospitals in Brighton. Patients were generally transferred by car, but ambulances were used when the men were on stretchers.

Officers were housed separately from the 'other ranks'. There were two hospitals for officers: Slindon House (opened October 1917) and Heene Terrace in Worthing (open by 1917). There was also a convalescent home for officers at Goring Hall (opened mid-1918).

The first soldier patients in West Sussex arrived at Worthing Hospital in early September 1914. The last patients to leave travelled in April 1919 from Graylingwell War Hospital to a convalescent hospital in Eastbourne.

The smallest number of hospital beds in any one building was at Oldland (part of the split-site Hassocks Hospital), which opened with four beds, later increasing to six. The shortest-lived was the Sailors' Institute in Littlehampton (twelve beds), which closed after six weeks because it was deemed too small.

The most dramatic end to a hospital was at Stildon House in East Grinstead, which was destroyed by fire in March 1918,

Red Cross ambulance, in a yard off Victoria Road, Worthing, c. 1917. (WSCCLS, TC0336)

Dorothy Hewer's (Graylingwell nurse 1915–17) autograph book; Private W.H. Williams, no.2813, was in the 1/6th Battalion, Royal Welsh Fusiliers and occupied bed 17 in Queen's A1 Ward. (WSRO, HCGR/3a/1/5)

fortunately with no loss of life. The patients were rehoused locally in Brewery House Hospital, in nearby houses, and in the commandant's own home. The hospital subsequently re-opened in Felbridge Place.

The youngest patient was probably a 14-year-old drummer, the son of a soldier on active service in France. Falling sick (in England) he was sent first to hospital in Brighton, and then transferred for convalescence to St Mary's Hospital in Worthing. No 'hospital blues' could be found that were small enough to fit him, so he was allowed to wear khaki trousers.[575]

The King and Queen visited the hospital in Shoreham in November 1916, prior to inspecting the nearby camp. 'Many men in the hospital were engaged in remedial exercises at the time, and the fun which the soldier introduces into everything caused the King to laugh heartily.'[576]

Building Alterations

Additions were made to buildings: a recreation room was added to the Haywards Heath Cottage Hospital so the convalescent patients would not disturb those confined to bed, and it proved a useful location for concerts. Once the room at Beechhurst was no longer available as an annexe to the hospital, the recreation room was requisitioned as a ward in October 1916. The Conservative Club's billiard room was purchased, and relocated as a replacement recreation room. By February 1917 the War Office required more beds, and the whole of Beechhurst was offered and accepted, providing space for forty more patients. The sum of £1,000 in donations was requested to furnish the hospital and pay salaries.

In 1915 both The Grange and Belgrave House increased their capacity by expanding into the house next door. The hospitals in Hurstpierpoint, Crawley and Crawley Down all had recreation rooms added.

The King Edward Hall in Lindfield had a tiny kitchen which was much too small for all the cooking and washing up required for patients. An extension was built with a scullery, cloakroom, two more baths and a small extra room for patients.

Patients

Sick and wounded soldiers travelled on hospital ships back to England, not just from the Western Front in France and Flanders, but from places much further afield, such as Greece, Mesopotamia (Iraq), Gallipoli (Turkey) and Palestine. They then travelled by ambulance train across Britain, going to whichever war hospital had space for them. There was no attempt to send a man to a hospital that was near his family home.

Some came straight from the battlefield, presenting 'a rather sorry spectacle, with several weeks' growth of beard and their uniforms dirty and torn, but their transformation was complete after the first day in hospital. How they enjoyed their first night in comfortable beds after weeks of hard work and exposure on the battlefield can well be imagined.'[577]

Wounds were to all parts of the body, from bullets and shrapnel and burns from flame-throwers. Treatment included skin grafting and amputation of badly damaged arms and legs. Illnesses included dysentery and malaria, with some men dying from cancer. Shell shock affected a number. Comparatively few patients died in hospitals in West Sussex: the most severely

Wounded Indian soldiers, Worthing, 1915. (WSCCLS, P003438)

affected had already died in foreign hospitals, on the sea crossing, or in hospitals at British ports.

Patients came from all three services and also from the Labour Corps. They originated from the British Isles, Belgium, France, Australia, New Zealand, Canada and the United States. The Belgians, who arrived mostly in 1914, were nursed at a number of hospitals, particularly at Cuckfield, Lindfield and Littlehampton.

Six German prisoners of war died of pneumonia and influenza in hospitals in Chichester in November 1918. Indian soldiers were patients in Brighton, and much interest was caused by their appearance in West Sussex, whether on a train passing slowly through Chichester Station in 1914 (their khaki turbans were noted) or when taking a stroll along the promenade in Worthing in 1915 (their autographs were much in demand).

Violet, Lady Beaumont of Slindon House, was the Official Searcher for missing and wounded soldiers for the Chichester division of the Red Cross. She visited hospitals, armed with a list of 'missing' men and their units, and interviewed other men

Graylingwell War Hospital, Chichester; patients in fancy dress with three nurses and an orderly, Christmas 1915. (WSRO, HCGR/3a/4/19)

167

from these units to try to establish whether the missing men were in fact dead. By April 1916 she had spoken to 4,000 men.[578]

After treatment in a war hospital, a man would be sent either to an auxiliary hospital for further treatment or on leave, before returning to his depot and being sent back overseas. Some, however, were too badly injured physically or mentally to be able to continue fighting.

Hospital Life

Hospital life was much the same for patients whether they were in a war hospital or an auxiliary hospital, but in the former they were under military discipline. All patients wore 'hospital blues', a uniform of blue suit, white shirt and red tie. When they were out of the hospital grounds, this showed that they were service personnel.

The West Sussex hospitals were favourably reported on in the local papers by their occupants. One patient in Lindfield said it was 'top-hole' and the first hospital (of the five he had been in) where 'you could send your plate up for a second helping of vegetables and meat'.[579]

The annual report of the Haywards Heath Cottage Hospital noted that the average length of stay of soldier patients during 1915 was 29.63 days, and 39.65 days in 1916. In Lindfield it was 27.27 days in 1917.[580]

Fancy Dress

Fancy dress was popular in all the hospitals, and there are photographs showing a wide range of attire including dresses, hats and parasols. The Pram Parade in 1917, part of Arundel's 'Baby Week', included a nurse pushing a large baby – this was in reality two wounded soldiers appropriately dressed, and with a bath chair serving as the pram. At the Petworth Baby Show in 1917, soldier patients from Bignor Park presented one of their number as a baby in a carriage, 'a very fine specimen of a child, just under twenty years'.[581]

Gifts

Crawley and Ifield Cottage Hospital, Robinson Road, Crawley, c. 1910. (WSCCLS, L000591)

Hospitals were given a sum of money to cover each patient's costs, but this was never enough, so there were regular appeals in the local newspapers for items, and acknowledgements of what had been given. Cuckfield patients benefited on one occasion from an Ansty WI competition 'war cake' where the ingredients had to cost under one shilling. Among the items thanked for by the quartermaster at The Knowle were rabbits, butter, onions and jam. Fruit, vegetables and flowers were donated following Harvest Festival services in parish churches.

Eggs, an important supplement to the hospital diet, were collected and distributed through depots. Occasionally eggs were collected at local events; each person attending a 1918 whist drive in Haywards Heath was asked to bring an egg, and the contributions were passed to the cottage and VAD hospitals. Parish rivalry was encouraged in the Chichester area by reporting totals in the local paper and the Chichester Egg Depot collected an astonishing 407,149 in the three years up to January 1918.[582]

The Crawley and Ifield Cottage Hospital acknowledged repairs to linen, the sweeping of its chimneys, and car rides for the patients. In Hurstpierpoint, local schoolgirls darned the socks of patients at the Sunshine Home VAD Hospital there. Deck chairs and an awning were requested for patients at the Public Hall in Haywards Heath so that they could enjoy fresh air on the green at the rear of the hall. As many soldiers arrived in hospital with no money, donations of items such as writing paper and stamps were requested.

By mid-1917 Haywards Heath Cottage Hospital and Beechhurst Annexe had opened a Gift Room, having found that inflation in food prices had rendered the daily per capita government grant totally inadequate. Graylingwell, on the other hand, had opened its Gift Room and Gift Fund before its first patients arrived. War Hospital Supply Depots also donated items: in the year to March 1918, the Littlehampton Branch made 25,600 swabs for the hospital at Belgrave House.

Concerts

Concerts were held both to entertain the wounded and to raise funds for the hospitals. In March 1917 a large audience in Petworth was entertained by Scottish songs and a farce, the proceeds going towards providing easy chairs for the wounded soldiers at Bignor Park. The *Mid-Sussex Times* in particular lists every item performed at concerts, showing what was popular at the time. One-act plays, tableaux, recitations, instrumental pieces and songs all featured, with the patients joining in the choruses. Among the more unusual acts in hospital concerts were a young woman performing whistling solos (Arundel), a soldier playing the spoons (Balcombe), and an Irish hornpipe dance (Cuckfield). Occasionally the concerts were organised by the soldiers, showing a wide range of talents. Each concert ended with everyone singing 'God Save the King'.

The entertainers were usually local, but patients at East Preston were entertained in 1918 by a party of American soldiers 'engaged on construction work in the neighbourhood'.[583] (See Chapter 3 for information on the US aerodrome at Rustington.)

Fundraising

In addition to concerts, money was raised in a variety of ways. These included carol singing by the Balcombe Church Sunday School boys, whist drives (some with more than 300 players), flag days, house-to-house monthly collections, football matches (East Grinstead), Pound Day (donations of either money, £1, or weight, 1lb), and pay a penny to guess the number of seeds in an 88lb pumpkin (Lindfield). Donors' names and their gifts were listed in the local papers, presumably both to encourage some and to shame others.

Games were popular at local and hospital fêtes, including hat trimming (some soldiers proved unexpectedly competent with a needle and thread), eating a suspended bun covered with golden syrup while their hands were tied behind their back, and faces getting blackened while trying to remove a five shilling piece from the centre of a frying pan (both Haywards Heath).

Outings

Outings were arranged to a wide range of locations. These included a group from Slindon House attending a 'juvenile dance' at the High School in Chichester; patients from Hurstpierpoint visiting the Camp at Hassocks; river trips (Littlehampton); visits to the seaside (Graylingwell) and to local large houses (150 patients from the three Chichester hospitals were entertained to tea and games at Cawley Priory, where music was played by Chichester City Band).

People in Worthing could even see films of patients from The Grange on outings to Arundel, as well as footage showing the outside of the hospital and some of the patients.[584] What the 'several hundred' Graylingwell patients made of the Somme films they were taken to see at a special matinee in Chichester in October 1916 is not recorded, but it was stated that the films 'have not fulfilled expectations'.[585]

Occupational Therapy

Patients were encouraged to make items for sale. These included needlework (cushions, table covers, mats, bags) at Balcombe; fretwork, black and white drawings and pen painting at Worthing; and tray and basket making at Haywards Heath.

The superintendent of The Grange rented a quarter of an acre of land from the Corporation at West Worthing for the purpose of cultivation, where about a dozen patients worked for two hours a day.

Weddings and Funerals

Soldier patients attended weddings and funerals. A former patient from the Crawley Down Hospital was married in Copthorne, and he and his bride left the church under an archway of walking sticks held aloft by patients. When a soldier died elsewhere and was brought home to be buried, soldiers from the local hospital attended the funeral as a mark of respect. In June 1917 six patients from the Sunshine Home VAD Hospital carried the coffin out of the church, and others walked on either side of the carriages taking the mourners to the burial ground.

Sports

Matches were played against other hospitals, locally-based soldiers or local people. Cricket was the most popular: batting was not a problem, but several patients had to have others to run for them. In a match at Haywards Heath against young ladies, the men batted with broomsticks and used only one hand. There was shooting at Arundel Rifle Club, bowling at Lindfield, football, and games against teams of women for hockey at Haywards Heath and for stoolball at Littlehampton, where 'despite their handicap, [the men] readily adapted themselves to the game and won easily'.[586]

Smoking

Smoking was very much part of everyday life at this time, and it was expected that soldier patients would smoke in hospital. Announcing a collection of cigarettes for the soldiers in Graylingwell Hospital, Mary Maxse wrote, 'smoking, as we all know, is an immense consolation to [wounded soldiers] in their pain'.[587] In the absence of pain-relieving drugs (aspirin and morphine were the only options), tobacco had a vital role to play. Vast quantities of tobacco and cigarettes were distributed to patients: an order for 20,000 cigarettes went in from Graylingwell for Christmas 1917. A collecting box was placed at the Royal West Sussex Hospital (also in Chichester) labelled 'Smokes, Soldiers, Sailors' for money to provide its patients with cigarettes.

Christmas

A special effort was made by the hospitals at Christmas to give their patients a good time. The wards were decorated, turkey and plum pudding were eaten, and presents were distributed. Stildon House was decorated in 1917 with paper chains, bunting, holly and evergreens by the patients. In 1917 at the Barracks Hospital in Chichester, the main meal was high tea, with crackers. In 1916, a telephone message from the King was received during dinner on Christmas Day at Belgrave House, and the men stood at attention while it was read to them by the commandant. At Graylingwell War Hospital each patient received a stocking containing about ten small presents such as oranges, writing paper and leather purses. At Haywards Heath Cottage Hospital in 1915, soldiers were allowed to choose a present. One soldier did not receive what he had asked for, but since it was 'a wife' this was not really surprising!

Patients from the Sunshine Home VAD Hospital in Hurstpierpoint attended a Boxing Day party, where the tea tables had small Christmas trees decorated with coloured bells and lighted candles. Father Christmas paid a visit, bringing musical instruments including drums, bagpipes, fifes, bugles and Jews' harps. The men returned to the hospital along the 'usually quiet street' playing their instruments, 'which lent a festive air to an otherwise quiet Christmastide'.[588]

Armistice

On 11 November 1918, the town of East Grinstead saw particularly lively celebrations of the Armistice:

> The wounded soldiers from the VAD Hospitals decorated their wheeled chairs with bunting and flowers, and, ringing bells and singing popular choruses, they were drawn up and down the streets for hours by a cheering crowd of youngsters, who had been given a holiday in honour of the occasion.[589]

Graylingwell War Hospital, Chichester; Queen's E2 Ward was an exclusively surgical ward. (WSRO, HCGR/3a/4/60)

Patients from hospitals across West Sussex attended services of thanksgiving in the open air, at local churches and at Chichester Cathedral. The Duchess of Norfolk held a dance at Arundel Castle for patients, nurses and helpers, with everyone given champagne with which to drink the health of the King.

Closure

Although peace had been declared, there were still sick and wounded patients in hospitals across West Sussex. Convoys were being taken to Graylingwell War Hospital as late as March 1919. However, hospitals were gradually emptied of military patients from late 1918. Commandants then had to arrange for the return of loaned furniture and items, and hand private houses and halls back to their owners.

9

THE ROLE OF THE CHURCHES

By Dr Caroline Adams

There is an apocryphal story of a man who, on being asked to give directions to a place, said 'I wouldn't start from here'. This chapter, perhaps more than any other in this book, emphasises the gulf between the culture of today and that of the Great War period. Two different times only 100 years apart have been so removed in outlook from each other that it is essential to appreciate the wholesale change in culture in order to understand how the churches reacted to the events of the war in 1914–18.

In the January 2014 issue of the *BBC History Magazine*, Jeremy Paxman headed his article 'The war finished Britain off in many respects'.[590] His title emphasised a lost community. That the war has passed from memory to history is obvious to those working in local history, but Paxman also emphasises that it is:

> ... seen through a particular coloured prism of the 1960s social revolution, with the satirical musical *Oh, What a Lovely War!* and *Blackadder* in the 1980s and irreverence generally – a belief in individualism, general truculence with governments, distrust of authority, and the rest of it ...

Deference to authority, reverence of tradition, the establishment of one's place in the community, an awareness of class – all these factors contributed to attitudes of both society and its church, and the questioning and breaking up of these as the war progressed led to the phrase 'a war of ideas'. It was a world where sermons were reported in full in local papers, and the wellbeing of the nation came before the needs of the individual. Alan Wilkinson points out that the average secular historian forgets that for more than a millennium, thousands of priests in thousands of parishes preached the gospel, reminding ordinary people of the bigger issues of life. This regular assimilation of religious belief as part of everyday life affected people in the way they thought and ran their lives.[591] There are two parts to this chapter: we explore the lead given by the Church of England and the Free Churches in the moral questions of war – and then the role of the parish churches in encouraging their flocks through this distressing period.

In 1914, British society was insular and ignorant of the outside world. In many ways it was an innocent society: conditions at the front line as related in letters home and in parish magazines upset people and needed explaining. Nobody in 1914 doubted that Britain would win, however long it took, and so the carnage that took place in 1915 and 1916 was viewed as regrettable but necessary. Both the established Church of England and the Free Churches colluded with this standpoint to a point which seems shocking to us today. Religious and secular authorities were allied with each other, particularly in Sussex where the rural community was dependent for its livelihood on the estate owner, and it was usually the latter who held the patronage of the parish incumbent. The nation was considered more important than the individual, and to show signs of being unpatriotic was to go against nature and the state that God had ordained.

In 1914 therefore, the churches preached a just war – it was a solemn duty laid upon the nation by God.[592] The *Chichester Observer* reported a service at St Paul's Cathedral, when Canon Alexander had prayed for victory over their enemies: 'If England is defending an unrighteous cause, then God break the sword in her hand.'[593] The *West Sussex County Times* quoted the Archbishop of Canterbury saying that the nation had a clear conscience.[594] This brought out the best and the worst in some of the clergy. A lecture, 'Why we are at War', given in Burpham by the Revd Prof. Tyrrell Green spoke of a war of ideas, of high spiritual ideas against the baser, material conception of international politics. Consequently, he said, it was not right to just blame the authorities in Germany, whose profession was war, but 'all the blame for the present gargantuan struggle, and all the horror and misery it involved, must be equally laid to the door of the German people themselves'.[595] At the same time, the Revd C.H. Gough, speaking in Littlehampton, spoke on the 'typical German':

Kaiserism stood for the ruin of everything an Englishman held dear, the end of his freedom, the death of his liberty, and whilst the men of Germany upheld the aggressive policy that had caused so much misery and made so many widows and orphans, whilst they connived at the crushing of weaker nations, it was impossible for them to talk of extending the hand of brotherliness to them and not right that they should love them ... they should have a holy hatred ... Could they be certain that they were not the instruments in God's hands to punish the German nation?[596]

Patriotism turned into bad nationalism cannot have been popular amongst a rural community who had lived and worked with many Germans as agricultural labourers. It was evident that this was happening at national as well as local level, as Diarmaid MacCulloch comments:

Some Anglican bishops could be heard making equally remarkable statements. The Bishop of London, Arthur Winnington-Ingram, in one sermon in Advent 1915 called on the British Army 'to kill the good as well as the bad, to kill the young men as well as the old'. At least Herbert Asquith, British Prime Minister, did not share the Kaiser's enthusiasm for bellicose sentiments from scholars and clerics, and styled Winnington-Ingram with elegant distaste 'an intensely silly bishop'. But the killing on all sides was as thorough as the Bishop of London had prescribed.[597]

Not all clergy were quite so superficial. The vicar of Horsham, the Revd John Bond concluded a sermon in the autumn of 1914 by saying:

> It is our duty to pray to God that even yet the cloud may be dispersed, and to pray also, publicly and in secret, for those many homes which will be overshadowed by grief and anguish in the near future. None of us who have not been there can realise the horrors of war. There is a discreet conspiracy of silence among those who have been in the fighting line, and we can feel for others, we can realise the horror that overspread Egypt in the old days, when there was not a house where there was not one dead.[598]

The Free Churches were equally troubled by the dichotomy of Christ the Peacemaker being on the British side of the war. A more grounded view of the war from the home front was given by the Revd E.W. Howes, the minister of the congregational church in Littlehampton:

> We were passing through a time of great difficulty, of great storm and stress, which had lasted during the past few weeks. He thought it had taken a good many of them some time to adapt themselves to the new condition of things. Certainly it had taken him a good time, and he was not quite sure that he had yet found his bearings … They had thought that, as far as civilised, let alone Christian, nations were concerned, war was a thing of the past, and that they had arrived at a stage where it was no longer possible. He believed that God was testing them and refining them as by fire, and so what they needed was a more real and stronger faith in the living God … the self-sacrifice now being exhibited was one of the most hopeful signs of the present time.[599]

Other signs of hope that the churches found were a new patriotism in the nation, and a new morality. In 1915, the Dean of Chichester, J.J. Hannah, perceived a new upright spirit:

There [used to be] numbers of young men who apparently had nothing better to do than loaf about the Cross or skulk behind hedges playing cards and betting for small coins. That had been stopped now. There were no loafers now … whenever they saw those young fellows, how happy they looked … They were better dressed too, for they were wearing the King's uniform … The crisis had made men of them … It was the same with the women … whom they had looked upon as the most frivolous creatures in the world had ceased to worry about their pleasures. England was a better country than a year ago …[600]

Enlistment was voluntary until 1916, but the churches saw it as a patriotic duty and the responsibility of a Christian. The vicar of Bosham made an impassioned plea for new recruits from the village, dishonour being worse than death.[601] In Chichester, the Free Churches provided entertainment for soldiers billeted in Chichester: games, writing materials, light refreshment and musical evenings were offered.[602]

On Friday, 21 August 1914, when the war was only a fortnight old, a special national day of intercession was held, and kept by both the Church of England and the Free Churches. Several of

'Numbers of young men who apparently had nothing better to do than loaf about the Cross', Market Cross, Chichester, c. 1910. (WSRO, PH 1054)

the local papers reported that there was a 'noble response': 'The nation in arms was the nation on her knees'.[603]

Rousing hymns were chosen, and the congregations were larger than usual (some 200 in Cuckfield), and the sermons were reported in depth.

The churches also preached firmly that the war was a divine punishment for national sins. 'Days of humiliation' were introduced from the beginning of 1916 to induce the nation to come to special prayers. In his pastoral letter to the diocese, the Bishop of Chichester, C.J. Ridgeway, asked people to examine their conscience. The war had brought forth 'healthy and happy ways' to do their duty for King and Country, but in contrast people should examine the amount of room

The Bishop of Chichester, from The Chichester Kalendar, *1912. (WSRO, Lib 317)*

they were giving God in their lives. This was a grave responsibility laid on each and every one, for just as a river was clear or muddy according to each drop that made it up, 'each and all of us make the nation' – what our character is will the nation be, and such will the national character be. The war could therefore be blamed on any individual's lack of godliness.

The theme of chastisement seems extreme to us; and one can imagine how a bereaved family felt on being told they were at fault. It was preached at both national and local levels: the Dean of Chichester summed up the war after a year as a:

> Fearful struggle … we have lost our dearest and best – the greatest of the worst of our losses. We have lost our easy and luxurious lives … We needed that chastisement. We were too happy, we were too prosperous, we were too comfortable, we thought the good Lord would continue all those things throughout our lives.[604]

As the war developed, showing no signs of ending, the simplicity of this doctrine began to be questioned. Because the Church of England was a national authority, it was criticised as casualties grew and the stalemate deepened. It was natural that people, shocked by the scale of bereavement, should need a scapegoat for their anger, and the Church failed to give an adequate explanation for the absence of victory. The *Worthing Gazette*, reporting on the discussions over closing cinemas on a Sunday, printed a letter which ran thus:

> … another of the sadly too frequent examples in which Clergy and Ministers exhibit intolerance, jealousy, and ignorance of the needs and conditions of ordinary people, while assuming the right, which they do not possess, of representing an entire town and population … In Littlehampton there were hundreds of young people away from home looking for entertainment … ministers were not taking into account the people who have to work on a Sunday to provide them with milk, hospitality etc. Signed by 'A daughter of the British Empire'.[605]

People were finding the Church's official stance unsatisfactory and out of touch.

In fact, national prayers did change over time, and became less condescending and nationalistic. An interesting exchange of letters between two former vicars of Arundel showed two opposing views within the Church: one disapproved of a form of prayer which attempted to bend God to our will; the other vilified him for suggesting the war was not just.[606] The lack of a single view by the churches is something which the Church of England recognises today. Now, we prefer to think that the Church of England can accommodate all-comers; then, the churches were saddened by their failure to make their traditional views seem relevant to post-war society. In Worthing at the end of the war, Church leaders commented on the state of the Church: there had been a 'great searching of spirit in the army, and new accessibility to religion', but this did not add up to a great revival. What was obvious was the problem of appealing to returning soldiers; 'we have tried to bind our young people to the churches with cups of tea and Bath buns; and there is not a man here who can say it has been effective.'[607]

Other moral questions, such as those of reprisals against German non-combatants, were handled by the churches along the traditional limits of a just war, and they did not always support the government. From 1914 to 1924, George Bell was chaplain to Archbishop Randall Davidson, and was strongly influenced by the archbishop's stand against reprisals, and this influenced his thinking as Bishop of Chichester in the Second World War.[608]

Similarly, the churches did not take a strong line against pacifists and conscientious objectors. Although they officially exhorted its congregations to enlist, they did not condemn those who did not, and at parish level, there were instances of the clergy being much more tolerant than their parishioners.

While the churches had things to say to the nation, they also had a more private responsibility towards the individual in the parish communities across the county. The early twentieth century was still a time when life revolved around the parish church and the rhythm of the seasons: Advent, Christmas, Lent, Easter, Harvest, Michaelmas. Whether people internalised Christian belief or not, the custom was to go to church on Sundays and holy days, to engage with parish community life and to mark the rituals of life – baptism, marriage and burial – within its doors. Consequently, the parish church had a unique role within the framework of the war, as comforter, encourager and sympathiser. The priest could encourage the community to consider its morale responsibilities in the war, and exhort families to part with their sons. Conversely, he could do what others could not – enter the home of a family, whether he hardly knew them or they were almost family, and administer comfort in bereavement. He could reassure about the meaning of life and death and the next life, and he could offer a tangible recognition of their suffering through burials, war memorials and remembrance services. His was the voice who gathered the community together as a pseudo-family in times of distress, and interpreted national Church doctrine for use in common practice.

As Keith Grieves has shown,[609] the parish magazine played a special part in this story, and a century later it is these documents which give us the quality of village church life during the period, and its optimism and despair. This chapter will use the Fernhurst parish magazines[610] of the time, to show a Sussex parish's role in the war.

Fernhurst is probably typical of many of the rural parishes in the county at the time, and its parish magazines provide wonderful examples of local clergy keeping daily life going, raising morale and encouraging optimism. For example, in the magazine for January 1917,[611] the churchwarden wrote that the Social Gathering on 12 January had been a success and that:

> We feel that Social Gatherings such as this help to promote that good feeling amongst Church people which is so much to be desired, but which is often conspicuous by its absence … When Q.M.-Seargt. Holmes was at home the other day he said the boys at the Front are in much better spirits than we at home, and he thought we ought to be a bit livelier. But there's all the difference between living the 'simple life' of a sailor or soldier on Active Service in a great war and living in security at home knowing that your dearest relations are in danger while you are safe … We have a feeling that we are onlookers in the greatest game that was ever played.

Fernhurst church, c. 1912. (WSCCLS, P009798)

Parish churches tried to foster community spirit. The same author pointed out that, whilst comradeship happened naturally at the front because of the war conditions, here in the parish the only united activity was meeting together in prayer. The church community included the whole village.

The family feeling was fostered by publishing letters and news from the front, so that a son of any family belonged to them all: 'it is with deep regret we record the death of this young soldier who was very popular and respected in the parish. He was a member of our C.E.M.S. and a real good fellow.'[612]

By the autumn of 1917 the Roll of Honour had grown ominously long.[613] The fallen were listed first, through the viewpoint of the bereaved widow:

> It is with deep regret we learn that Mrs Nobbs, of Hogshill, Fernhurst has received notification that her husband, Rifleman S.H. Nobbs, Rifle Brigade, previously reported missing, is reported killed. It is a particularly sad bereavement as Mrs Nobbs has only just lost her two brothers, killed in action.

Then 'The Wounded' were reported, with their whereabouts, followed by 'The Missing'. 'Additions to the Roll of Honour' listed, with pride, the latest to enlist: 'Mr and Mrs Talbot now have four sons serving with the forces.' Finally those 'Home on Leave' were welcomed, with information on prisoners of war. These monthly lists served to bind the community together, however distressing the news.[614]

Parish priests had to apply national messages to the local view. The vicar wrote:

> The Government have made a three fold appeal to us. (1) For more men. (2) For more money. (3) For greater economy, not only in food, but in everything. Are there any men left in Fernhurst who are not doing work of national importance, or who could do work of greater importance, and either leave their present work undone or let it be done by a woman or older man? As to money, it is rumoured that

> Fernhurst people have brought their savings and lent them to the country at this hour of need.... As to economy... During the Season of Lent there is always the call of the Church to self-denial: and men can cut off or reduce their beer and their tobacco, and women can perhaps deny themselves in some other ways. It is a shame to go to any unnecessary expense in dress.[615]

Practical advice for Lent followed this appeal, and the admonition that Good Friday was not a holiday but a Holy Day – 'do try to keep holy week, try to attend some of the daily services'. Fernhurst seems to have had good attendances, but the Lynchmere and Camelsdale magazines were full of appeals:

> I could wish to see our Sunday Morning Services better attended ... We seem to have grown tired of our Wednesday evening Service of Intercession. I am afraid the thought of an empty Church at the time of Intercessions would not be a very helpful one to those soldiers who have gone from this District ...

George Ranking, vicar at Fernhurst parish church. (WSRO, Par 82/7/10)

Fernhurst possessed a remarkable vicar, George Ranking, whose letters and advice played a similar role for those at home as Woodbine Willie did for individual serving soldiers.

During the course of 1917, he first told his parishioners that he felt it was his duty to join up, and then he wrote from the front in familiar letters, as one might address one's own family, about his life in France, the conditions and the course of the war. He ruminated on a shell killing one soldier while the man next to him was unharmed, and on how war made men open to religious influence, even if they were not overtly devout. He used his experiences to draw spiritual lessons for those at home, and he was typical of the general feeling that to understand the war properly, serving clergy needed to be with the soldiers.

His letters to the parish magazine ceased in the November, when his death was reported. He had been out at the front for six months.

The effect of the war on the churches was far-reaching: it showed clearly that they no longer had the hold upon the nation that was supposed in 1914. Both the Free Church Council and the Church of England brought in reforms in the 1920s, but the trend continued. This brief overview shows that the churches' role as spiritual leader in West Sussex was similar to other parts of the country, and that the harder and more trenchant aspect of faith portrayed in official teaching did not necessarily correspond with the care given by the parish church. Newspapers and parish magazines show that the parish church still had its place in the village community, that it could offer succour to bereaved families in the parish, and that the ministration it offered continued to be appreciated.

10

Agriculture and Food

By Professor Brian Short

'This is no ordinary war. It is a death grapple of nations rather than of armies ... I believe that this issue will really be determined in the more prosaic region of the human belly.'[616]

On 4 August 1914 war was declared as the harvest season was upon West Sussex. Lord Lucas, president of the Board of Agriculture, declared that there was 'no occasion whatever for public alarm over food supplies' and the *Farmer and Stockbreeder* commented that 'Agriculture of all industries is the least likely to be affected by the war'.[617] Britain was the world's greatest importer of food but faith in the Royal Navy's ability to protect British shipping was unwavering. This chapter investigates the war's impact on West Sussex farming and food supply.

Laissez-faire Years

Arable farming had been on the decline in Sussex since 1875 and by 1914 a generation of farmers had grown up with dairying and livestock on grassland farms. After the outbreak of war there were, in fact, soon worries about the reliance on imports of food, fertilisers and feedstuffs. By September Lord Milner was urging that more wheat be grown, more fertiliser applied, rotations modified, and that farmers rise to the emergency, bene-fitting themselves from higher market prices.[618] The same points were made by William Lawson, County Agricultural Organiser, at a meeting of West Sussex farmers at the Chichester Corn Exchange.[619] But there were also precautions to be taken against the threat of invasion in this front-line county. Arrangements were made for the despatch of livestock, motors, cycles, forage and provisions towards Buckinghamshire and Berkshire.[620]

Meanwhile, farmworkers rushed to enlist, leaving farms precariously short of labour, with many from the Goodwood Estate attending the Chichester recruiting office. By August 1915 it was clear that 'the best of our farmers' sons and the best of our young agricultural labourers are already at the front or training to be there'.[621] And now the army moved swiftly to requisition horses in unexpectedly large numbers, together with fodder. There were also concerns about military training affecting farming operations: one Shoreham farmer had lost land to the military camp, and now reported troops damaging crops, 'sham fighting' in his lambing yard and among in-calf cows.[622]

Nevertheless, no government action came; only calls for voluntary ploughing and for assistance to offset the loss of farmworkers. But during 1915 German submarines threatened imports, prompting the establishment of the Milner Committee to consider food supplies, assuming now that the war might last beyond the 1916 harvest. Milner's interim report in July 1915 recommended guaranteeing wheat prices to stimulate production, and establishing War Agricultural Committees (WACs) by county councils, with district committees to report on farm capacity and farmers' willingness to produce additional food. The WAC would then have to consider whether compulsion was needed.

Such State intervention would be on a scale never before attempted and the government baulked at the idea, only sanctioning WACs and district committees. In West Sussex by November 1915 these new committees quickly expressed concerns about shortages of fertilisers, prohibitive covenants against ploughing, and the need for women and children to help with milking and light work.[623]

Labour problems multiplied as conscription began in March 1916 for single men aged 18–41, and although farmworkers were supposedly in 'starred' or 'certified occupations',

Women help with hay-making at Redgate Farm, Sidlesham, in 1916. (WSCCLS, P001645)

there were further losses, amounting nationally to about 10 per cent, although rather lower than the more conventional figure of over 30 per cent.[624]

Exemptions were sought at tribunals: in July 1916 a Birdham farmer with only his wife to help, was given twelve months' exemption from military service, to which he replied, 'Thank you sir, and I hope the war will be over by that time'.[625] The tribunals frequently faced difficult decisions: the Worthing glasshouse workers, after some deliberation, were deemed eligible for exemption, although the military authorities subsequently won appeals against some of the men concerned.[626]

William Jutsum Passmore at Applesham Farm, Coombes, a member of the WAC, lost eleven men to enlistment, about one-third of his labour force, entailing harder work for him personally: 'Last spring [1915] I had to lamb 500 ewes myself during the night. For 6 weeks I was up every night with the exception of 4. That rather prevents you going to listen to your neighbour's little stories.'[627]

Dairy workers at Wyckham Farm, Steyning, c. 1917. (Courtesy of Steyning Museum, 1992.122)

From February 1916 Women's War Agricultural Committees were formed, led in Sussex by Lady Cowdray and the Countess of Chichester, urging farmers to provide free training for milking, hop picking and fruit growing. Lady Frances Wolseley worked from her women's agricultural training college at Glynde to stimulate women's contributions. But farmers' prejudices were often very real: one 'experienced farmer' wrote, 'The talkative women imagine there are only light duties to be done on a farm. I fear they have no modesty left or they would not interfere with this work'.[628]

A Women's Land Army was not to begin until March 1917 and only reached about 16,000 nationally by September 1918, despite the condescending inducement offered of 'a beautiful complexion and splendid rosy cheeks'.[629] (The Women's Land Army is covered in more detail in Chapter 7.)

Other labour came from boys released from school before the official leaving age of 14 years, although provoking suspicions of exploitation. By October 1915, 528 local boys had left school on this scheme.[630] There were also a few interned aliens, conscientious objectors, 'War Agricultural Volunteers', schoolteachers, Portsmouth residents, policemen and older or less able men. By June 1916 there were also 6,000 convalescent soldiers in the county, many fit enough for some work.[631] At Steyning, farmers were keen to obtain German prisoners of war: as one newspaper inelegantly commented, there was a 'scramble for Hun prisoners', this in Sussex, a supposedly coastal 'prohibited area'. They were also sent to work in the nurseries at East Preston.[632]

Intervention at Last

On 7 December 1916 Asquith's government was superseded by Lloyd George's new coalition, with R.E. Prothero as president of the Board of Agriculture. Both men favoured intervention. It was noted that increasing tillage in 1915 had left behind weeds and abandoned rotations, with many therefore resting their land in 1916. This was also a poor harvest, ever more shipping was being diverted for military uses, and the winter threatened to be severe and prolonged.

And so State control began. A new Ministry of Food was followed by a Food Controller and Food Production Department (FPD) in January 1917. The FPD became the pivot of the campaign, coordinating and enforcing cultivation.[633] The 'plough policy' aimed to extend arable through compulsory inspections, enforcing cultivation, and requisitioning property in cases of non-compliance. Under DORA, these new powers were drastic. WACs could require specific fields to be ploughed, or plough them themselves, and failure to comply could lead to fines, even imprisonment. No appeal was allowed.

In February 1917 a minimum agricultural wage of 25s per week was announced, and rents were not to be raised during the period of guaranteed prices. All was incorporated in the Corn Production Act of August 1917, also guaranteeing prices for wheat and oats.[634]

The WACs proved unwieldy for executive action, so not more than seven members now formed County Agricultural Executive Committees (CAECs). The West Sussex chairman was Francis Herbert Padwick from West Thorney, barrister, county councillor, advisor to Prothero, and president of the National Farmers' Union 1919–20.[635] Other members were farmers, land-owners and agents and included the Countess of March as chair of the Ladies' Committee, until her resignation in August 1918. Support came from William Lawson, executive officer, and his staff. The committee first met on 22 January 1917, and considered survey forms enquiring what ploughing and sowing could be undertaken in spring 1917. Prothero later said that 'their diffi-cult and invidious duty was performed with a discretion which reduced friction to a minimum'.[636] Sub-committees oversaw surveys, cultivation, supplies, labour, machinery, horticulture, finance, and by 1918 even army recruitment.[637]

Westbourne District Committee actually pre-empted the CAEC and on 21 December 1916, sent three prominent farmers to report on land not being properly cultivated. Well-known local farmers helped deliver the survey forms. The three then categorised farms as 'satisfactory', 'unsatisfactory' or 'derelict', and reported back to their district committee on 17 January 1917.

West Sussex was the first county to complete the survey.[638] From over 2,000 farms, few were considered derelict but about 25 per cent of farmland was 'unsatisfactory' (Table 1). Lawson estimated that 3,573 acres of grassland could be ploughed for

First meeting of the West Sussex War Agricultural Executive Committee. (WSRO, WOC/ CM82/1/1)

oats and another 347 acres for potatoes. There were just twenty-seven tractors in the six districts returning figures at that time.[639]

Table 1. West Sussex Land Survey 1917

Condition	No. of Farms	Arable	Market Garden	Orchard	Pastur
Satisfactory	2,171	95,165	3,732	247	97,00
Unsatisfactory	698	27,911	71	72	34,70
Derelict	27	34	0	0	154
Total	2,896	123,111	3,803	391	131,8

Land use figures are in acres. Pasture excludes open downland.
Source: WSRO WOC/CM82/1/1.

The plough campaign did not always run smoothly. Some land-owners and their agents refused to comply. Frank Aman, agent to Viscount Cowdray, refused permission for Selham Manor Farm, Midhurst, to be ploughed for oats, precipitating an order in February 1917. Wilfrid Scawen Blunt had little regard for the CAEC, being more concerned for his Crabbet horse-breeding programme, but finally conceded 20 acres for ploughing 'by way of giving a good example'.[640] Much work in 1917 was devoted to areas classified as unsatisfactory or derelict and farmers from Rudgwick, Partridge Green and Pulborough thus came to the committee's attention.[641] One case in particular stood out. The Coolhurst Estate of C.R. Scrace-Dickins near Horsham, covering 573 acres, was reportedly 'in a deplorable condition':

> The mansion house is in need of repair, and is apparently quite useless to the owner... the Park is neglected ... the hay stacks are not thatched and are partly rotten. In some of the fields the hay has not even been carried in and tons of good hay, which could have been used for the army or cattle, have been absolutely wasted.

On the estate's farms cattle were 'the only sign of habitation' and roofs were damaged. Goldings Farm was derelict and over-run with game. Scrace-Dickins apparently promised much but did little, and the CAEC took over from the end of 1917 until January 1921.[642]

Changes in West Sussex Farming after 1916

To combat manpower losses, some Sussex farmers looked to machinery. On the heavy Wealden clays ploughing was something of a lost art. The 50-year-old double-engine steam ploughs, worked by cable across the field, proved best for breaking up old grass and drawing mole ploughs through heavy soil. Contractors also supplied steam engines for threshing, although in West Sussex some refused to accept contracts for ploughing exceptionally heavy land or small fields.

The tractor was in its infancy. At an arranged exhibition at Barnham in August 1916, only one tractor, a 'Mogul', appeared.[643] Many farmers remained scornful, and anyway lacked drivers, mechanics and spares. But Mr Corp of Broomlands Farm, Horsham, employed a 'Moline Universal Tractor' by February 1918, requiring just one man, resulting in a considerable saving for which he was publicly praised by Professor Dunstan, principal of Wye College.[644] The Chichester area had more tractors by early 1918, but they were referred to even by the FPD as 'the least reliable of all ploughing instruments'. There were also, confusingly, more than thirty different models supplied by the FPD to CAECs nationally, although Fordsons came to be favoured following advice from the well-known S.F. Edge, the pioneering pre-war motorist from Ditchling.[645]

Threshing machine gang and farm workers at Steyning, April 1916. (Steyning Museum, 1992.8.5)

In 1917 the Board of Agriculture was able to promise more help, and asked CAECs for estimates about resources needed for an anticipated record harvest that year. The West Sussex demand, even without allowing for the expected increased output, was for 1,417 men (carters, ploughmen, machine operators, stockmen, labourers and thatchers) and 240 women. A further request was then submitted for 1,600 additional horses and 800 carters to deal with any further increased output in 1918. Now 16hp 'Mogul' tractors were distributed to Pulborough, Horsham, Steyning, Petworth and Angmering, although more powerful machines were requested in future.

But the machines still needed men to work them. In West Sussex by early 1917 it was reported that 'there is tackle lying idle close to 100 acres of land in a fit state to plough, but it is impossible to get men for the work'.[646] Steyning District Committee organised six sets of motor ploughs with two men each, appealed to the Mayor of Hove for car drivers, and to the Shoreham army camp for ploughmen. Ploughs were soon working dawn until dusk.[647]

Although the requested extra men and machines didn't actually materialise, the mood was (temporarily) changing: a Billingshurst stockman was exempted for six months because ploughing was imminent and 'the production of food was now of more importance than sending men into the army'.[648] There were many claims for exemptions: at a CAEC meeting in October 1917 no fewer than 900 cases were considered.

The 1917 harvest added a million new acres of arable nationally. But by November 1917 only half the promised men had been released from military duties; the War Office now removed 18 year olds; and more men were threatened with conscription as the German offensive on the Somme was countered. Furthermore, the tractors were delayed. All was met with bewilderment and anger from the CAECs, and rendered quotas for 1918 practically unobtainable. Instead, those having the resources were asked to plough even more, making the CAECs very unpopular.

However, there was good weather in spring 1918, allowing sowing of the largest grain area in living memory.[649] But yields on newly ploughed land were below those on older arable land, especially in South East England, with Sussex having the lowest wheat yields on new tillage of any English county (18.3 bushels).[650] Undoubtedly mistakes were made: it was the least fertile land that was ploughed; inexperienced persons were sent to plough unsuitable fields; local knowledge was ignored and operations delayed.

The overall farming changes in Sussex wrought by the war included the expansion of wheat, oats and dairy cattle, accompanied by corresponding declines in numbers of sheep, as grazing was lost, and pigs (Table 2, overleaf).[651]

Table 2. Farming Changes in Sussex 1914–1919

	1914	1919
East Sussex		
Wheat	17,868	28,067
Barley	2,245	2,940
Oats	23,398	31,525
Cattle	79,430	87,283
Sheep	234,399	189,999
Pigs	21,845	17,407
Horses	14,427	13,566
West Sussex		
Wheat	26,333	36,756
Barley	6,161	6,505
Oats	29,061	31,200
Cattle	47,897	51,991
Sheep	134,280	101,781
Pigs	19,534	13,271
Horses	11,505	10,728

Crops in acres, livestock in numbers. Source: R.H.B. Jesse, *A Survey of the Agriculture of Sussex* (Royal Agricultural Society of England, 1960), pp.100–104.

There was also a considerable expansion of allotments. In December 1916, the government authorised local authorities to requisition unoccupied land for allotments, irrespective of owners' wishes. By mid-January 1917, Chichester, Littlehampton and Horsham councils were seeking extra plots and urging men (and sometimes wives of serving soldiers) to take on allotments for potatoes or other food crops.[652] Lord Leconfield made land on the edge of Petworth available for allotments, which were taken up enthusiastically.[653] Bognor Council advised on seed potatoes, on ridging land, and on legal requirements.[654] CAECs formed horticultural subcommittees promoting the keeping of rabbits, bees and poultry, and distributing seed potatoes, and preserving sugar and bottles for fruit bottling.[655] Nationally, such efforts possibly produced a million tons of food as allotments increased from 530,000 in 1914 to 1,350,000 in 1917–18.[656]

Food Control

However, stimulating production alone would not suffice without a parallel policy of food control. Hoarding by 'food hogs' was reported as early as 6 August 1914 and in West Sussex wealthier residents, such as Edward Heron-Allen at Selsey, were suspected of panic buying.[657] Consumer unrest gradually mounted. Shortages of fresh meat were felt: at Worthing Workhouse the residents refused to eat the substitute tinned meat, causing one of the Board of Guardians to suggest that they should therefore go without, since tinned meat was deemed good enough for troops at the front.[658]

From April to June 1917, over 2 million tons of Allied shipping was lost, causing lengthening queues for bread, potatoes, and butter, and shops being emptied. High prices and accusations of profiteering provoked protests, and it was estimated that the average cost of food had more than doubled. At a meeting of Horsham UDC, one councillor stated that:

> Although there was a necessity for rationing he thought the best way would be by voluntary rather than compulsory steps. Many families among the working classes were going short of food and he did not think there was need for anything to be done in that direction. If anything was done with the better class of people they could choose whatever way they liked best.[659]

Mercifully this class-ridden view was not officially replicated. Lord Rhondda became Food Controller in July 1917, with the aim of fixing prices of most essential foods – not entirely to farmers' liking. Indeed, a farmers' meeting in Chichester in 1918 was addressed by Prothero, following which Lord Leconfield stated that 'they required a great deal more of Mr Prothero and a great deal less of Lord Rhondda (applause)'.[660]

Price control was decentralised to local food control committees to register retailers, recommend local price variations, develop economy campaigns and administer sugar distribution. National and communal kitchens were established, and Sussex children set to work gathering fruit and horse chestnuts as replacements for grain.[661] The milling extraction rate was raised from its peacetime level of 70 per cent to 91.9 per cent by April 1918. Wheat flour was also diluted with barley, maize, beans or potatoes, to give the unloved 'government bread', but at least it remained unrationed. But in December Lord Rhondda introduced sugar rationing, then meat and fats by April 1918.[662] Wednesdays were to be meatless. Ration books were introduced for sugar, butter, margarine, lard and meat, and weekly rations fixed: 15oz beef, mutton or lamb; 5oz bacon; 4oz fats; 8oz sugar. Despite complaints about unfairness, and Chichester shops having to be guarded against 'the attitude of the populace', this achieved something of a levelling of consumption, rather than a general reduction, but adequate food energy supplies were maintained.[663]

Conclusion

Despite official pronouncements in 1914, it actually soon became clear that the war would impact on farming. William Wood, farming on the heavy clay at Twineham, certainly saw things differently: 'then came the convulsion that shattered all that went before, and at one stroke severed completely the life we lived from the life that lay in front of us … the war robbed us of a generation'.[664] He lost his own son in Mesopotamia in 1916.

Overall Sussex farming was little changed until 1917, when the FPD began its work. Then harvests in 1917 and 1918 were full although the campaign was not completely successful: national targets were set at 31 per cent above the 1916 level but by 1918 only reached 22 per cent. Nevertheless, 1.4 million acres nationally were ploughed up, and, given the depressed state of farming in 1914, the losses of manpower, feedstuffs and fertilisers, this remains a considerable achievement.[665] But the South East increased its tillage by only 17 per cent, since there was generally less grassland here to be broken up, and only East Sussex exceeded 30 per cent. Furthermore, by 1918 much of the Weald was in foul condition through lack of labour and depleted fertility, although the cornlands of the Coastal Plain had profited.[666]

Fear of famine was never far from the minds of those who controlled British war plans.[667] Nevertheless, the belated introduction of the plough policy, the actions of thousands of allotment holders and the government's food economy campaign ensured that there would be sufficient food in West Sussex and elsewhere to last out the war.

11

Peace Celebrations and War Memorials

By Professor Keith Grieves

In their imagination, men and women on active service from West Sussex were never very far from home. In precisely known localities of everyday scenes and familiar sights pre-war lives had been ordered, routinised and safe. Recollections of home, often defined as parishes, provided soldiers with antidotal memories to the strange, nightmarish topographies of modern battlefields.[668] It might be enough to return home and secure some slight social betterment in towns and villages, which were defended in the 'immortal salient' and elsewhere. Reciprocally, civilians at home also knew 'King and Country' to have a very local meaning. After 1918 they strained to celebrate peace and commemorate the fallen through acts of public remembrance which might be meaningful to relatives of the fallen, returning ex-servicemen, religious institutions and local associations in the context of existing and changing social structures. The decisions to construct war memorials connected the localities for which the war was fought, such as Sussex-by-the-Sea, to the abstractions of King and Empire. The war memorial landscape in West Sussex is diverse but its meaning is always local. War memorial committees sought to bring the 'Absent Dead' home amid paradoxical and conflicted views on what might be a 'fitting' tribute. By the 1930s it was impossible to motor or ramble through Wealden, Downland and coastal communities in West Sussex without encountering new sites of memory and mourning, which invited the passer-by to give thanks for victory and be sorrowful for sacrifice. Importantly, these sites cast the Great War's long shadow across much-loved corners in villages and towns which were known to departing soldiers. This chapter will focus on the years for which Armistice Day had first meaning, until another world war required the adoption of Remembrance Day and the addition of further names on panels to existing stone monuments and wall tablets.

During the Great War rolls of honour were prominently displayed in church porches and at **temporary wooden shrines**. In the churchyard at Holy Trinity church, Lower Beeding, the late-Victorian memorial cross to Jane Clifford Hubbard became the parochial war shrine and twenty-seven names were listed on three sides of the shaft.[669] The Roll of Honour at St Peter's church, Slinfold, still survives in situ. It has 213 names, including three nurses, of whom twenty-six were killed in action and seventeen were wounded.[670] Formulaic underlinings, in black and red, denoted men and women who would not return to the parish and men who were wounded or missing, according to the latest news available to the rector.

There are many carefully folded rolls of honour in parochial records for the Diocese of Chichester, such as the incumbent's list for Broadwater, with amendments which reflect a 'living document' under weekly and monthly review.[671] These rolls of honour and their location were known to men on active service. Major Christopher Stone served in the 22nd Battalion, Royal Fusiliers, which, although recruited in Kensington, trained at Roffey Park and was known locally as the 'Horsham Fusiliers'. On 26 July 1916 he wrote with grim humour to his wife, 'I'm sorry to say that poor [Capt.] Grant was killed yesterday, whose mother is at Warnham you know. I was talking to him about the Roll of Honour in the Church there & whether Warnham would be satisfied if only one of us were killed'.[672]

Vestry minutes sometimes recorded that general memorial decisions would be left until the end of the war, as at Boxgrove Priory on 13 April 1915.[673] Nonetheless, the commemorative impulse to use traditional ecclesiastical memorial designs early in the war was evident in numerous requests by influential parishioners to approve memorial designs for fallen relatives. In October 1915 a Special Vestry Meeting at Boxgrove approved

Peace celebrations, High Street, Crawley, 19 July 1919. (Frederick Henty Collection, WSCCLS, L000512)

a new stained-glass window of a chivalric knight in a Gothicised frame in memory of Lord Bernard Gordon Lennox, which was funded by his widow.[674] More generally in West Sussex, the fourth anniversary of the declaration of war was a day of remembrance. On Walberton Green a combined service of 'Church people and Nonconformists' took place in the open air.[675]

In Selsey, Edward Heron-Allen had long planned his own peace bonfire to mark the **Armistice**. 'The autumn prunings of five years' made a fine blaze on 16 November 1918, assisted by two cans of 'hoarded' petrol.[676] A Service of Thanksgiving for safe return and Memorial of the Dead was held at St Paul's church, Worthing, on 11 May 1919, which reflected local variations in the timing of Welcome Home events.[677] Peace Day was on 19 July 1919 and at Southwick sports were held in Croft Meadow and dinner took place in the Green School playground.[678]

The peace celebrations at Warnham on 19 July 1919 included the pealing of church bells, a twenty-one-gun salute at the manor house, an open-air church service, sports for the children on the cricket pitch with returning officers co-opted as judges, tea for all, music and dancing for adults and flares at 10 p.m., which were dampened by a deluge of rain in the late evening.[679] The dinner for returned soldiers, comprising 'feasting, song and speech' was delayed until 22 November 1919, when it was held at the Village Hall. In the name of the parish, 134 men were welcomed home by the principal landowner and his two sons at the head of the table, supported by local clergymen and a general officer newly resident in the parish. After dinner, tobacco and cigarettes were circulated, toasts were made to the Royal Family and the armed services, a tribute in silence to 'The Glorious Dead' ensued, followed by an entertainment of comic songs and sketches, which included 'Sussex by the Sea' with topical verses.[680]

In Horsham a thanksgiving and welcome home event took place on 3 March 1919, when the vicar noted that the 200 invitations had been difficult to organise. It was the first public thank you to returned soldiers and each guest was presented with a souvenir picture of the parish church.[681]

The strands of thanksgiving and sorrow, victory and remembrance, were often interwoven in **dual-purpose committee structures**, which raised funds to erect memorials and celebrate peace. The subscription fund at Steyning met the cost of peace festivities of £80 and the wall tablet of £114, which was designed by the churchwarden. Without controversy, the work of the War Memorial Committee was completed by October 1919.[682] At West Lavington the balance from the peace celebrations of £6 was transferred to the war memorial fund.[683]

Invitation to Welcome Home Dinner at Horsham. (WSRO, Mitford MSS MPD 455, 1919)

At Tillington the vestry meeting decided, on 14 May 1920, that a brass tablet near the chancel arch would commemorate 'men of the Parish who died for England'.[684] The residue of the Welcome Home Fund was complemented by seven further subscriptions and a donation from the WI.[685]

In these instances **'indoor' war memorials** embellished the ancient parish church. Primarily, the names of the fallen were inscribed on stone or wood to place, in perpetuity, the National Deliverance and Great Sacrifice of the war alongside the local records of noble deeds in past centuries. Nowhere was this more apparent than at the St George's Day service at Chichester Cathedral on 23 April 1919. The Order of Service emphasised that at the altar, 'The Lists containing Names of all the Men in Sussex who have laid down their lives during the Great War will then be presented to the bishop'.[686] The names were placed in hallowed custody in the cathedral. Regimental flags which connected great wars were presented to the cathedral for safe-keeping in well-established commemorative rituals, amid the sublime play of light on ancient stones and the muffled toll of bells. They included the colours of the West Sussex Local Militia, raised for home defence in the Napoleonic War, which the late Duke of Norfolk had deposited shortly before his death in 1917, and the Mons Banner, presented to the 2nd Battalion, RSR, as part of the original BEF, at the choral commemoration at the Royal Albert Hall on 15 December 1917.[687] Throughout the 'funeral' service the warrior St George was evoked to exemplify justice, righteousness, freedom and honour, which was enshrined in the selfless deeds and loyal service of the generation of 1914.

Shortly after the St George's Day service in 1919, a fund was initiated by the RSR to refurbish the Chapel of St George at Chichester Cathedral as a thank-offering to all ranks who fell in the war. It was rededicated by the bishop and unveiled by the Lord Lieutenant on Armistice Day 1921.[688] The alphabetical lists of names of 'Our Glorious Dead' are recorded by battalion in oak panels on cases which line the chapel walls. The names of 6,800 (later increased to 7,302) fallen comrades in twenty battalions were located near the regimental colours, which were re-hung horizontally, high in the roof space, in 1963. The magnitude of loss is simply and starkly conveyed, using Sussex timber from Colonel Courthope's Whiligh Estate at Wadhurst. In the 1920s there were complaints that the chapel's sepulchral space was so dark that pilgrims could not read the names on the panels in winter. In 1934 the St George's Chapel Fund replaced the candles with electric light as a concession to modernity.[689]

Naming the fallen alphabetically, and often regardless of rank, was of the greatest importance in localities known to the Absent Dead. This requirement had a significant influence on the siting, design, materials and cost of war memorials. At the west end of Boxgrove Priory the stone tablet is inscribed with nineteen names, 'To the glory of God + in proud memory of the Boxgrove men who died in the Great War 1914–1919, their neighbours + friends have placed this stone'.[690] At West Lavington an invoice for seventy sepia prints in September 1922, totalling £3 10s, demonstrated the intention to ensure that all subscribers and relatives of the fallen would have an image of the memorial tablet for their mantelpiece.[691] For the parish war memorial at St Paul's church, Worthing, the space beneath the portico was described by the vicar as a 'site second to none'.[692] The names of eighty parishioners were collected. However, unspecified design issues occurred and the 'War Shrine' was eventually erected in the garden on the north side on the advice of the diocesan architect. The Slinfold War Memorial Committee encountered considerable difficulties in funding an indoor church memorial which cost £247, namely, a traceried oak tower screen with carved names. However, the rector was determined to secure a permanent list of the fallen in St Peter's church. In its parallel utilitarian scheme to contribute to the Horsham Cottage Hospital Building Fund, sufficient to endow a bed for 'poorer brethren', the committee sought reassurance that a plate would be fixed which stated 'War Memorial from Slinfold'.[693] The protracted and contentious debate at Horsham, where a figurative sculpture was proposed, caused deep concern among the bereaved. They feared that there would be insufficient space for the names of the fallen on the plinth and that the panels of names might be placed at the Town Hall. A referendum on the issue ensured that homage to the war dead prevailed over a prestigious design commended by local arbiters of taste.[694]

War memorial debates sometimes intensified in larger villages and small towns, where there was sufficient political and social leverage for concern regarding the health and happiness of returning ex-servicemen and women to be voiced. Where traditional social leaders were willing to contribute to high-cost schemes, aspirations for social improvement were embraced. William Sellens undertook a photographic survey of war memorials in Sussex and imagined 'the heated arguments that must often have taken place'.[695] In an unusual intervention, the *Sussex Daily News* appealed for mutual respect on 10 July 1919: 'Meetings on the question of war memorials shew a very definite cleavage between two schools of thought, those who believe in something beautiful and uplifting in memory of the fallen, and those who want to see something helpful and useful for the living.'[696]

Remarkably, some local debates added a **war memorial hall** to the village landscape of well, pound, church, rectory, school, post office and meadow. The auction sale at Shoreham Camp in 1919 provided some districts with the opportunity to purchase, transport, reassemble and beautify army huts as recreation halls and clubrooms to memorialise the fallen and provide social facilities for returning ex-servicemen and women.[697] These utilitarian war memorials acknowledged the importance of recreational soldiers' huts behind the front lines in France and Flanders and were direct expressions of the need to 'brighten' village life in the aftermath of war. Unlike school and parish rooms, they were designed to provide evening amenities for all inhabitants and were to be managed by elected committees who might be free from territorial patronage.

The public meeting at Balcombe Working Men's Institute on 17 January 1919, chaired by Lord Denman, decided to construct a Victory Hall, to be managed by a committee representative of village associations as a non-denominational recreational space. The rector indicated his intention to place a war memorial tablet in the parish church, but the meeting was dominated by the prospect of a memorial hall, at a cost of £1,200, which the Denman family largely funded.[698] This locally designed and managed scheme of rural social improvement was adorned by frescoes of War and Peace by Major Neville Lytton of Crabbet Park, who recruited men for the Southdown battalions in 1914–15 in Crawley and served with them in France. The peace fresco depicts the hall's construction by estate workers, the view to Chanctonbury Ring and scenes of music-making and dancing, including the artist's self-portrait as a flutist of classical airs. He wrote to his brother, 'You see it is as it were my Sistine chapel. These frescoes are a sort of war Canterbury tales'.[699] The names of all men who served, including those who returned, are on two wooden panels in the foyer of the Victory Hall, whereas the names of the living were not generally commemorated in parish churches.

In January 1919 the Duke of Richmond was contacted because 'Lavant people' wanted an accessible 'bit of ground' on which a room could be built. He was unceremoniously informed, 'I don't think the people will be contented now-a-days without a room where they can meet, and one is badly wanted for entertainments and meetings, especially as the women have so many meetings now, and the Public house is not desirable'.[700] Land near the cricket ground was conveyed to Lavant Parish Council on 12 December 1921. The hall was valued at £1,300 and included sanitary conveniences.[701] This useful memorial reflected the 'fitting' application of the wartime hut habit to rural communities, which so desperately lacked social spaces for leisure and adult education.

Peace and War frescoes, detail, by Neville Lytton, Balcombe Victory Hall. (Keith Grieves' private collection)

In Felpham the public meeting wanted a parish hall but had insufficient funds. Instead, two semi-detached War Memorial Cottages were built in Flansham Lane for impoverished inhabitants, with preference given to applicants who fought in the Great War. In the shared porch the names of the fallen of Felpham and Middleton were inscribed on a memorial tablet. Practical local building expertise was mobilised; Thomas Richardson, landlord of the Fox Inn, was one of the bricklayers. The substantial sum of £737 13s 8d was raised, which covered building costs, the memorial tablet and provided a small endowment for maintenance.[702]

Ideas for a war memorial in Slinfold included secondary education scholarships, a parish cottage for a district nurse and a village club. The emphasis on amenities to serve the living arose from a tentative search for 'social betterment' in the countryside, especially where associational activity was stimulated by WIs and branches of Comrades of the Great War. Both these organisations blended deferential and democratic activism in rural counties in the immediate post-war years. The Comrades Memorial in front of the Reading Room at Slinfold was unveiled by Lord Leconfield in July 1921. This highly visible granite memorial with flagpost was described by local Comrades as our 'sixty pounder'. They expressed concern that the neighbouring Warnham Memorial Cross of Yorkshire stone, which had cost £300, was more conspicuous.[703] The Slinfold Memorial Stone exemplified the way in which a sectional group successfully implemented its own scheme, critically distant from the proceedings of the War Memorial Committee, which was insufficiently representative of returning soldiers. Fractured disputatious processes unfold in Slinfold's parochial records.

The **choices of memorial type and site, design, materials and craftsmanship** mattered in every locality, and were sometimes influenced by the cultural, historical and geological contexts of West Sussex. At Angmering the Revd George Gordon made the statement at the first public meeting, 'Our first duty, was to those who had made the supreme sacrifice, Our second, to those who came back, Our last, to ourselves'.[704] An 'outdoor' parish non-denominational memorial was in mind. Francis Tate, monumental mason and sculptor at the Carrara Marble Works in Worthing, received the contract for the cross, shaft and pedestal

Slinfold Comrades Memorial Stone, c. *1920. (WSCCLS, PC006717)*

of Portland stone for which £194 was paid. The meeting hoped that Sussex masons would carve Sussex stone and noted that the village was not in granite country. Francis Tate received at least eight commissions for local war memorials, including the marble tablet for Ashington church.[705]

Philip Johnston was invited to the Angmering War Memorial Committee meeting on 4 March 1919, where he was critical of all the designs for the stone cross and opposed the use of the village green to site the memorial. His antiquarian and architectural expertise was widely known in West Sussex. At Clayton in January 1921, where a lych-gate was under consideration, he was described as 'being "saturated" with the architecture of the ancient parish church'.[706] At Angmering he argued that the best site would be to use the churchyard and playground, so that the scene might incorporate the famous old yew tree. This recommendation led to a second public meeting which resolutely sustained the village's decision that the site would be the small shaded green, without fencing and near the sign-post.[707] The committee was 'thoroughly representative' of three religious organisations, two friendly societies and, unusually, relatives of the fallen. It secured a memorial site and service of dedication in which inhabitants of all denominations united, which expressly incorporated the schoolchildren.

War Memorial unveiling ceremony, Angmering. (WSCCLS, PC000311)

At Selsey, in January 1920, a public meeting was influenced by historic religious iconography. It wanted the churchyard war memorial cross, facing the High Street, to be of the type known to St Wilfrid. Surviving carved stones thought to be of the seventh-century cross were incorporated. On the panels at the base, fifty-five names are inscribed.[708] Eric Gill's war memorial cross of Portland stone in the churchyard of St Mary, Harting, completed in 1920, has sculptured panels of St George and St Richard and a draught of fishes.[709] The obelisk on Southwick Green, so characteristic of a coastal war memorial, was designed by Alfred Catt, Shoreham's Harbour Master, and constructed by Francis Tate. Public subscriptions raised £200 and concrete blocks from foundations of Admiralty huts on the Green were used in its construction.[710] Early in 1918 the arrival of 120 portable Nissen huts had 'entirely obliterated' the Green.[711] The unveiling of the War Memorial on 16 July 1922 restored the picturesque scene and found a way to incorporate evidence of naval buildings into the memorial landscape.

Eric Gill designed thirty-six Great War memorials, of which there are crosses at Angmering and Harting and stone tablets at West Wittering and Walberton. Fine examples of his lively italicised lower-case lettering may be found on these commissions. On the chancel wall at St Mary's church, Walberton, a Hopton-Wood stone tablet unveiled in 1917 commemorated the vicar, the Revd Philip Blakeway, who was chaplain in the London Mounted Brigade and died on active service at Ismailia on 16 June 1915.[712] Hopton-Wood stone from the Middleton quarries and mason's shop in Derbyshire was Gill's preferred sculpting medium for decorative interior work. The cross is gilded and the V-cut capital letters were highlighted in red and black. At St Peter and St Paul church, West Wittering, where his father was vicar, a Portland stone war memorial tablet has an epitaph in sloping italics, names in lower case and framing pilasters of different heights. His indoor stone tablets have an obvious integration with the contextual stones in places of worship, which reflected his instinctive awareness of distinctive localities and their memorial purpose. Few war memorials undertaken by Eric Gill were sculptured and lettered by him alone. They were the products of a remarkable outpouring of 'everyday' memorial inscriptions at his Guild workshop in Ditchling during the years 1907–24.[713]

If vernacular building stone was less readily available in West Sussex, the erection of **lych-gates** of timber posts, mostly without masonry pier-walls, point towards a unity of material, craft-working and sacred purpose in some parishes after the war. The idea of beautifying a churchyard entrance where coffin bearers might rest on sheltered benches in a picturesque ensemble had some resonance. New porch-like lych-gates at Bramber, Lyminster, Sompting, Sullington and Walberton suggest a vernacular mimicry of seventeenth-century examples at Pulborough and Rustington. Aymer Vallance argued after the war that lych-gates 'dignified beauty which the following of time hallowed precedent can impart'.[714]

In a much delayed debate at Itchingfield on the replacement of the decaying war shrine by an outdoor church memorial, Mr Weller 'proposed that funds be raised to build an Oak lych gate on stone supports made from Sussex oak as a most suitable memorial to Sussex men'.[715] The votes cast in the referendum in 1926 were: lych-gate (forty-six), stone cross (seventeen) and crucifix (seven) of 300 papers circulated in the parish. The rector was impressed by a lych-gate in Horsham which had only cost £65, but fear of spoiling the vista from Church Cottage was of greater concern. The proposal was indefinitely postponed and in 1932 the war shrine was repaired again.[716]

Evaluation of the war memorial movement in all its local diversity should not be confined to the immediate post-war years. Much research remains to be undertaken on the evolving significance of memorial sites in West Sussex in the **interwar years**. On St George's Day each year a civic, ecclesiastical and military procession connected the Roussillon Barracks, Council House and cathedral in homage to the war dead of the regiment. The soldiers wore roses and marched behind a Union flag which was used at the funerals of many men from the county regiment at the Sussex Cemetery, near Bray on the Somme.[717] On summer camp at Arundel, contingents from the regiment visited the chapel in the 1920s in memory of their fallen comrades at Gallipoli.[718] The Royal Sussex Calendar was rewritten in 1921 to incorporate many of its wartime exploits as a commemorative resource for the regiment. On the picturesque green at Chichester barracks trophies of the Great War were added to those of earlier wars.[719]

In Horsham the wartime colours of the 4th Battalion, RSR, was laid up at St Mary's church. A mosaic badge adorned the drill hall in Denne Road, Horsham, whose construction was privately funded by the battalion and opened in 1927.[720]

Some unit representatives journeyed to the old front lines to pay **homage to fallen comrades** and to provide news of the Imperial War Graves Commission's work at battalion reunions. In 1934 Colonel Godman and Dr Macarthur represented the 4th Battalion on a pilgrimage to the Dardanelles. They visited almost all the graves of the men and reassured relatives of the fallen that the cemeteries were beautifully sited, enclosed by stone walls and contained laburnum trees, iris and rosemary.[721] On the 21st anniversary of the landing at Suvla Bay, the battalion reunion in Horsham saw lantern slides which depicted a site of pilgrimage that most men would never revisit. More privately, the Western Front lived on in the memory of Edmund Blunden. He could not exorcise the spectre of war and in his preliminary to *Undertones of War* insisted, 'I must go over the ground again'.[722] In July 1929 he made the first of many pilgrimages to the Ypres salient to revisit the battlefields of 1917. The village pond at Thiepval was a site of remembrance where memories flooded back, but the vast coppice had 'fallen into the hands of the Memorial men'.[723] In search for vivid fragments to recollect past scenes, he found bathing places, dug outs and mine craters, where he honoured the memory of fallen comrades of 11th Southdown Battalion, shunning the Menin Gate.[724]

At Henfield, Arthur Mee reminded the enchanted traveller and seeker of lonely places of E.W. Hornung's troubled years of war, which included hut superintendent service on the Western Front in the search for his missing son. In Henfield churchyard this celebrated author wrote a poem which included the lines 'Go, live the wide world over, but when you come to die/A quiet English churchyard is the only place to lie'. This resting place was denied to his only son, who had 'the final honour of a simple wooden cross'.[725] Arthur Mee's New Domesday Survey, in the epic King's England series, *Sussex*, published in 1937, is a gazetteer of 'The Garden by the Sea' in the motor age. Insistently, he located monuments in the home landscape which conveyed the echo of battle from the Great War. For example, at Findon church a lancet window is a memorial to two brothers who died in the first two years of the war.[726]

The war memorials in West Sussex beautify the landscape in precisely planned ways, whether as monumental or amenity tributes. Plans for their purpose, location, design, materials and dedication expressed locally the relationships between deliverance and sacrifice, public and private, indoor and outdoor, parish and public, image and amenity, sacred and secular, ancient and modern, deferential and democratising. The coming of peace in 1919 did not lead to the erection of a peace cross on a Sussex hill, despite the extensive discussion of this proposal in local newspapers, as a marker of the county's sacrifice.[727] However, traditional moral language and signs were used to bring solace and comfort amid long historical continuities in visible, meditative and often therapeutic spaces. The beautiful churchyard cross at St John the Evangelist church, Bury, constructed from creamy brown Doulting Stone, from the Mendip hills, fittingly recalled the pre-Reformation countryside in a barely changed medieval landscape.[728] At Goodwood the tenantry presented ornate gates at the park entrance in memory of Lord Bernard Gordon Lennox, third son of the Duke of Richmond, who died at Ypres

War memorial, Eastergate, unveiled 19 December 1920; WSCCLS, CHPC0417

in 1914, and Lord Settrington, his eldest grandson, who died on active service in North Russia in 1919.[729] In the quest to become a war artist in 1942, Neville Lytton described his private commission to decorate Balcombe Victory Hall noting, 'it has become a place of Pilgrimage for the county of Sussex & neighbouring counties'.[730] Finally, for travellers to Bognor there is no mistaking the grey stone lion on a massive plinth at Eastergate, which demands that the passer-by might think about that community's loss on the village's little green.[731]

THOSE LEFT BEHIND – AND THOSE WHO RETURNED

By Emma White

Men returning from the war faced many problems, financial, mental and physical. This chapter examines these issues, specifically long-term mental and physical disability, employment and training, pensions, support groups and problems faced by bereaved families in the years directly after the war.

Long-Term Disability

For those men who returned with mental or physical wounds, life after the war was difficult. As with other ex-servicemen, there were issues of employment and supporting themselves and their families, but they had the added difficulty of coping with a disability in a society that was unused to such a large body of disabled men.

Some of the innovative institutions set up for recovery were reported in local newspapers, even though they were outside West Sussex, perhaps because local men were treated there and local residents helped to fund them. The wounded within military hospitals is covered in Chapter 8; here the emphasis is on the care and welfare of those who didn't return to the services and for whom life would be significantly changed by their injuries.

Regarding physical disabilities, the main institutions mentioned in local newspapers are Queen Mary Convalescent Auxiliary Hospital, Roehampton and the Chailey Heritage Craft Schools in East Sussex. There may have been other local examples, but these institutions were prominent in the press.

Men from Queen Mary's Hospital visited Horsham on a day trip in May 1916, thus raising awareness of the work done for disabled servicemen at the hospital.[732] In July 1917, a letter in the *West Sussex County Times,* written by Corporal Lee from Bosham who was at the hospital, waiting to be fitted with his artificial limb, thanked everyone who had subscribed to help the hospital.[733] Another soldier, Lance-Corporal Leonard Johnson of Haywards Heath, was, in April 1917, awaiting a place to become available so he could also go to Roehampton to receive his artificial leg.[734]

At the Heritage Craft Schools in Chailey, a new kind of convalescence was being undertaken. In August 1914 accommodation was offered as a hospital for wounded soldiers.[735] The soldiers undertook 'educative convalescence' which was described at a meeting of the Executive Council of the school board as 'the idea of utilising crippled children to assist crippled soldiers'.[736] At the same meeting it was stated that the appeal for funds for the military wards had been so successful that no charge to the school funds needed to be made for any part of its expenditure.[737]

Wounded Great War soldiers outside West Sussex Gazette *offices, Arundel High Street, 11 November 1918. (Arundel Museum, E117)*

Employment and Training

To promote volunteering, many employers, including West Sussex County Council (WSCC), promised to keep their employees' jobs open for their return.[738] In 1918 International Stores, an early supermarket chain, encouraged soldiers via newspaper advertisements to re-join the company.[739]

During the war there was some apprehension by employers about engaging ex-servicemen, fearing they could be conscripted again. A War Office announcement was printed in local newspapers in 1917, setting out discharge terms so that employers could be certain the employee would not be taken for further service in the army.[740]

Before the end of the war, local initiatives were taken to find employment for discharged and disabled servicemen in occupations which they could perform after a short amount of training.[741] These occupations included motor-vehicle drivers, lift clerks, gardeners, shop assistants and caretakers.[742]

However, many women who had taken men's jobs during the war were reluctant to give them up now that the men were returning. Major Jellicorse of Chichester wrote in the *West Sussex*

International Stores, High Street, Steyning, c. 1915. (Steyning Museum, 1992.74.1)

County Times: 'To keep a woman who has lost her main support owing to the War, one cannot altogether complain of, but many of them are young women who could be more usefully employed at other work, and more especially domestic work.'[743]

Nevertheless, disabled ex-servicemen did have opportunities for training and employment. These were mainly organised by the War Pensions Local Committees, which will be described in a later section. Information on similar schemes for able-bodied men is scarce. One scheme involved setting up smallholdings for use by ex-servicemen and their families. It was first mentioned at the WSCC Small Holdings and Allotments Committee meeting on 25 October 1917, after a letter from the Board of Agriculture and Fisheries asked WSCC how much land would be required after the war by discharged soldiers and sailors.[744] The cost of buying land and buildings, and adapting them for smallholding use, was over £122,000 (£6.95 million) as revealed in July 1919.[745] At that time WSCC had acquired 1,241 acres of land for smallholdings of which 790 acres had already been leased to ex-servicemen and the demand had not yet been satisfied.[746]

Horsham post office employed invalided soldiers.[747] Wounded soldiers were reinstated as police constables by WSCC after their discharge.[748] From the perspective of those involved in the placement of disabled men into training and/or employment, it was the employers of labour who needed to make themselves amenable to the plight of the ex-serviceman. In late 1917, meetings involving representatives of the West Sussex War Pension Committee attempted to get employers to consider training disabled servicemen.[749] The idea was to eliminate casual labour among disabled ex-servicemen, preventing them from taking blind-alley occupations and instead allowing them to learn a trade which would support them.[750] The YMCA pressed this same issue, for outdoor employment for those afflicted by poison gas and shell shock, with a newspaper campaign: 'They need fresh air and work – Pay your debt – Employ them.'[751]

Other forms of employment were set up by disabled servicemen themselves. Mr J.T. Tee, a disabled soldier from Lindfield, formed a band with other disabled soldiers which advertised for work in the local paper.[752] On a larger scale, the Middleton Orchestra, supported by the Middleton

*The Seal of Honour.
(Mid-Sussex
Times,
23 September 1919,
p. 7, col. c)*

Entertainment Club, was formed mainly from disabled soldiers to help them earn extra money and to use their musical skills.[753]

In 1919 a national scheme was started by the Ministry of Labour to help the employment and training of disabled servicemen by persuading employers to form at least 5 per cent of their work-force from disabled servicemen.[754] Participating employers would receive a certificate, be added to the National Roll and be able to proudly display the Seal of Honour.[755] By mid-October 1919 it was reported in the *Worthing Gazette* that over 5 per cent of Worthing Corporation employees were disabled ex-servicemen.[756]

The Lord Roberts Memorial Workshops in Brighton trained disabled servicemen in occupations that would support them in civilian life. West Sussex inhabitants would have benefitted from these workshops. They were designed to train disabled men in a particular trade adapted to their disability. There are numerous examples of fundraising for these workshops taking place in West Sussex. In Worthing, 'Forget Me Not Day' raised money for the workshops by selling artificial flowers made by disabled and orphaned children which raised over £74 (£4,218).[757] Fundraising for the workshops also took place in Bognor, where events and collection boxes helped fund the erection of the workshops which planned to train 500 men after they left hospital.[758]

As late as October 1917 West Sussex still had no training facilities for disabled servicemen within the county.[759] Men were being placed in training institutions outside the county, which often meant they did not return. This may have led to the Agricultural Education Committee's decision in December 1917 to devise a scheme to provide training for discharged and disabled servicemen in agricultural work.[760]

The training included dairy work, specifically feeding and attending cows, milking, butter making and rearing of calves. There was also work with horses, specifically feeding and grooming, ploughing and using horse-driven machinery. Shepherding work and farm engineering gave ex-servicemen the chance to work with steam engines, motor tractors and cars. Market gardening opportunities included working with bush and orchard fruit, vegetable cultivation, glasshouse work and raising seedlings. It was specified that the training should be for at least a year and not less than thirty hours a week. The aim was to 'enable the man to become specifically skilled in at least one branch of the work'.[761]

Pensions

A pension for many disabled and discharged men was the main form of income until employment or training could be found for them. For some it would be the only income they would ever receive again. The Naval and Military War Pensions Act 1915 provided for grants and allowances to be made on top of military pensions.[762] It also provided for the care, training and employment of disabled servicemen. The main body set up under the Act was the Statutory Committee, which was assisted by Local Committees who provided information on specific cases in their areas and could award additional grants or allowances. Each county and county borough was entitled to have a Local Committee, as well as urban districts with a population of over 50,000.[763] A Local Committee was set up for West Sussex as a whole, and one for Worthing Borough from August 1917.[764]

Before the Local War Pension Committees were in operation, cases were dealt with by local Boards of Guardians who granted poor relief, usually to those struggling on pensions or with nowhere to live. In 1915 the case of a Salvington soldier paralysed at the Battle of the Marne was considered by the East Preston Guardians. The nursing home where he was being cared for was closing and the Guardians were approached to take the man into the workhouse as his mother could not look after him.

George J. Atfield. (Reproduced by kind permission of Mr Owen Atfield)

The Guardians accommodated him in the meantime, but were concerned about setting a precedent.[765]

Around a quarter of the total of those who served in the war were entitled to a disability pension, of which two-thirds were granted for minor disabilities of 30 per cent disablement or less.[766] Wounds and amputation caused most cases of disability.[767]

Obtaining a pension was crucial for widows post-war. Between 1911 and 1921 the number of widows increased by 9,339 in East and West Sussex, of which 2,335 were in the 20–39 age group and therefore could be directly associated with the war.[768] It was not always easy for widows to attain a pension large enough to keep their families and many examples appear in newspapers.

A Durrington war widow's unjust pension was highlighted for many weeks in the local and national press. George J. Atfield (pictured left) of the Royal Sussex Regiment (RSR) was discharged in May 1918, owing to shrapnel wounds in his legs, arms and back.[769] On returning home from hospital he died four days later from influenza and pneumonia.[770] While alive, he had received a pension of £2 10s 5d (£143.64) a week for his wife and eight children.[771] After his death Mrs Atfield was reduced to a pension of 6s 10d (£19.38) a week as the cause of death of her husband was not attributed to his military service. The War Pension and Allowances Committee (Worthing) granted her an allowance which made up the difference while the award was being reviewed.[772] However, when this stopped, she was forced to apply for poor relief from the Guardians at East Preston Workhouse. The London papers had also taken an interest in the 'Durrington case' and the *Evening News* pressurised the Ministry of Pensions.[773] After all the publicity, plus representations from two local MPs, the Special Grants Committee of the Ministry of Pensions proposed a supplementary allowance of £1 10s (£85.50) a week, 10s for Mrs Atfield and 2s 6d for each of her eight of her children.[774] Eventually George's cause of death was reconsidered and ruled to have been caused by his war service. Mrs Atfield was finally awarded a total pension of £4 2d (£228.57) a week.[775] A ninth child, born to her after the death of her husband, was not provided for by this award.

Support Groups

Many families and individuals fell on hard times during the war and the end of hostilities did nothing to change their circumstances. For those who returned, a hero's welcome was not always what they received, which seems surprising given the great support for wartime fundraising and soldiers back from the front. Haywards Heath ex-servicemen describe scenes of disabled men being taunted in the street for not working or jeered at for claiming the out of work allowance.[776]

Organisations were set up to relieve the problems faced by ex-servicemen. In March 1919 Burgess Hill ex-servicemen, widows etc., who had a grievance, formed an organisation to help them present their problems to the right authorities.[777] The overriding ideal of the meeting was that 'justice must not be substituted by charity'.[778]

Other support groups were national, such as the Comrades of the Great War. The 'Comrades' were most active in Horsham, which opened a post on 5 November 1917, just weeks after the inaugural meeting of the movement in London.[779] Their aims were 'the welfare of the discharged men of all ranks, their wives and children, and the widows and dependents of those who had fallen'.[780] Horsham, uniquely in the county, set up a club where the Comrades could meet, which provided refreshments and even baths.[781] By March 1920 the branch had a membership of 563.[782] At the inaugural meeting of the Mid-Sussex post a request was made for members to submit, in their own handwriting, 'a record of their war services, so that future generations might see what had been done by the men in the district in [sic] their country's behalf.'[783]

At the inauguration of the Ardingly Comrades, Mr Franklyn, vice-commandant of the Sussex Division of the Comrades, relayed the importance of the veterans of previous wars, saying that after the South African war the Tommy had soon been forgotten, but that this was not to occur again.[784] The Comrades successfully campaigned nationally for the raising of pensions awarded to disabled veterans from previous wars to be brought up to the higher scale laid down for the Great War.[785] Locally they acted on behalf of many, including ex-soldiers waiting months for pay owed and war widows not receiving correct allowances.[786]

The Royal British Legion, which became the primary organisation caring for veterans and their dependents, was not created until 1921. The Legion was formed from four national societies which promoted the rights and welfare of ex-servicemen, widows and dependants, including the Comrades of the Great War.

Those Left Behind

Post-war the families of those who did not return had to face new challenges, particularly in the absence of the main breadwinner. These fall broadly into two categories: parents and widows.

For the parents of those who served in the forces, the fear of their death or serious injury must have been overwhelming and for those thousands of local families who did lose a relative, the loss they felt was sometimes unbearable. One such example was the case of John Johnson of Tilgate, Crawley, who had lost one son in the war, a second had been badly wounded and a third had just received notice he was to be conscripted.[787] The distressed father was heard to have said, 'This is the last blow, we have sacrificed two, and that ought to be enough'. Shortly afterwards he committed suicide.[788] This example illustrates the strain that many families would have been under, being left behind to continue life without their children. Another case, of a mother who attempted to drown herself in the sea, was heard at the County Bench in Chichester in May 1918. She had lost two sons in the war and another two had been seriously wounded.[789]

Training for war widows was available post-war through the Ministry of Labour, but only in professions which would lead to a reasonable prospect of support.[790] Training was not given in those professions which were deemed suitable for disabled servicemen, such as clock making, jewellery making and toy making. The roles which were specified as possibilities were midwifery, sick nursing, dress making and cookery.[791] Training for war widows as a District Nurse Midwife was highlighted by the West Sussex War Pensions Local Committee as a possible avenue for those war widows in need of an occupation to support themselves and their children.[792]

A happy ending did arrive for one Brighton war widow who, after her husband's death, had taken a job as a shop assistant. Whilst working there she saw a man in uniform pass the shop, who resembled her late husband. It was, in fact, her husband who had been suffering from memory loss following shell shock.[793] Although most widows were not as fortunate, it is important to highlight that some happy occasions did occur.

Spouses at home could find the pain of separation intolerable. A very sad case occurred at Worthing in May 1916 when a mother was charged with attempted suicide and the attempted murder of her youngest child, Winifred, by jumping into the sea.[794] She survived and when the suicide note was read, she had revealed the reason why she felt she had no option but to commit suicide:

> No one knows what I have suffered these last few weeks. Kindly see that Teddy is taken care of until his Dad comes home, if he ever does … to live without him is impossible. I have had twelve weary months waiting for his return, and I can hold out no longer.[795]

Post-War Deaths

Some servicemen returned from the war too ill to enjoy longevity. Perhaps some of the saddest cases are of those who came through such difficult times only to slip away quietly after the guns fell silent.

John Edward Lewis, of the 11th Battalion, RSR, joined up in August 1914 and was subsequently sent to France. He was wounded in 1916 and again in 1917 before being gassed in 1918. Owing to his injuries, he was no longer fit for service and was discharged in December 1918, when he returned to Balcombe. He died on Friday, 9 May 1919. His funeral, attended by a large group of villagers, included full military honours. The hearse was covered with the Union Jack and was preceded by men of the Royal Field Artillery.[796]

Apart from the physical disabilities which men carried home into their civilian lives, psychological problems left men just as scarred. Some found it difficult to readjust to civilian life and find purpose in their post-war existence. One case of a Horsham carpenter, Edward James Smith, who committed suicide after returning from France, illustrates the difficulty men had in returning to their pre-war lives. He had been in France building huts before he was sent home sick. He had been very depressed and had wanted to return to France, but his doctor had advised against it.[797] Another tragic story unfolded at Worthing Railway Station in February 1919 when Arthur Frankham, a young Artillery officer of 27, shot himself in the waiting room. The lieutenant had been gassed and had shell shock in France and had been recently injured by a lorry.[798]

Influenza

After the hardship suffered by residents and servicemen from West Sussex, another fight for survival was caused by the so-called Spanish influenza epidemic of 1918–19. The most virulent of these outbreaks was in the autumn of 1918, and unusually about half of the deaths occurred in the 25–45-year age group.[799] Some 200,000 deaths occurred in England and Wales[800] and West Sussex had 387 deaths in 1918, an increase of over 500 per cent on 1917.[801] These included seventy children under 16.[802]

Apart from the tragic multiple deaths in most localities in the county, there were further curtailments to inhabitants' lives. Many schools were closed, either due to influenza outbreaks as at Bognor, or as a precaution as at Ifield School, Crawley.[803] Children were also excluded from cinemas in an attempt to stop the spread of the disease.[804]

There are many cases described in local newspapers and several touching examples follow. Miss Mead had been headmistress of Bolney Schools since 1916 and was lieutenant of the village Girl Guides. At her funeral the Guides formed a guard of honour for her coffin to pass under and the path to the church was lined by the schoolchildren.[805] A memorial tablet in honour of Nurse Susan Ivy Wilson was installed in the Cuckfield Workhouse infirmary chapel.[806]

Bombardier Jack Smith from Horsham had been a pre-war regular soldier, was wounded in France and had his leg amputated.

He was training to become a hairdresser when he succumbed to double pneumonia following influenza.[807] The Comrades of the Horsham Branch and the Crawley Post, which also included the Horsham Town Band, marched to the departed's house. The inhabitants of Horsham also subscribed to a fund for the family which amounted to £20 7s 4d (£1,160.80).[808]

Some of the victims of the epidemic, as the figures above show, were very young. At Handcross the sorrowful story of the Pysing family was recorded in the *Mid-Sussex Times*. Private Pysing of the Royal Sussex Regiment survived his war service but, tragically, his 8-year-old daughter succumbed to influenza.[809]

In 1919 deaths from influenza receded but still remained high compared to pre-war figures.[810]

Conclusion

The challenges of life in post-war West Sussex for returned ex-servicemen and for the bereaved were many and complex. The principal need was to reintegrate veterans back into civilian life, to provide gainful employment and an income. Bereaved people and their families needed emotional and financial support. More research is needed in this area, but generally in West Sussex the financial challenges were met, governmental organisations helped with grants, allowances and job creation schemes, and some non-governmental organisations also played a key role.

POSTSCRIPT

Our county had a significant role in the war's conclusion. A meeting of the Imperial War Cabinet held at Danny House, Hurstpierpoint, on 13 October 1918 decided the terms of the Armistice which were then cabled to US President T. Woodrow Wilson. The house had been let to Lord Riddell for use by Prime Minister David Lloyd George from summer 1918. Among those Cabinet members present were Winston Churchill, A.J. Balfour and Bonar Law.[811] Lloyd George apparently signed off the document in the White Bedroom while ill in bed.[812]

An editorial in the *Mid-Sussex Times* at Christmas 1918 summarises well the county's contribution to the war, in domestic and military terms:

Another Christmas has come round again, and, thank God, it sees the war ended. If we at home are glad of that, doubly so must be the men who have been defending our country since the early days of the war. What they have endured only they, and their Maker, fully know. We cannot thank them enough, and we cannot do too much for them. When they return home from the battlefields we must let them see in a tangible manner that we are truly grateful to them for defending our hearths and homes and be prepared to pay whatever is necessary in the eyes of the State to enable them to enjoy some of the sweets of life. God and they secured for us a notable victory. All parents who sent sons to the war are entitled to our lasting respect, and should ever the time come when they, through no fault of their own, should be confronted with the demon of poverty, the nation must see to it that their needs are adequately met.

So far [Sussex] has behaved splendidly towards its fighting men. It has kept an open ear for their needs, and money has been given again and again to supply them with comforts. Women have worked with their needles, homes and gardens have been thrown open to wounded soldiers, entertainments have been arranged to cheer them up, books and papers....sent...to give them mental refreshment, and fruit and vegetables have also been supplied. There has been no blight, no mildew, on the giving. 'What can I do to help?' That has been the question which people of leisure have put to themselves and others, and they have deemed nothing too hard and too tiresome. Not being able to fight they did the next best thing – they gave! And this will ever redound to their credit. And as we write, our thoughts go out to the veterans and young men who left......Sussex early in the war......to serve their King and Country. All honour to them – the veterans – for 'playing the game' in spite of their years. On Christmas Day we shall think of them and drink to them and say – 'God bless them – the old and the young – and bring them safely back to the homes and loved ones they left behind in dear old England.'[813]

Finally, the best news for one grieving family, six weeks after the Armistice:

The anxious strain of Mr and Mrs J. King [John King, furniture seller[814]] of Church Avenue [Haywards Heath], since receiving ... an official intimation that their son, Private W. King, Northamptonshire Regt., was missing, was relieved on Christmas morning, when they received a postcard from him from Liege, stating he was a prisoner but in good health and expecting to be in 'Blighty' by Christmas.[815]

Notes

Prelude to War
    Mid-Sussex Times, 25 August 1914, p. 7a

Chapter 1
1   B. Gudmundsson, 'The Expansion of the British Army during World War I' in M. Strohn (ed.), *World War I Companion* (Osprey, 2013), pp. 47–8.
2   H. Miller, *'We Wunt be Druv': The Royal Sussex Regiment on the Western Front 1914–18* (Reveille Press, 2012), p. 3.
3   K. Grieves (ed.), *Sussex in the First World War* (Sussex Record Society, 2000), p. xvi.
4   Gudmundsson, 'Expansion of British Army', pp. 49–50.
5   P. Simkins, 'The Four Armies 1914–18' in D.G. Chandler and I. Beckett (eds), *The Oxford History of the British Army* (Oxford University Press, 1994), pp. 235–55.
6   Simkins, 'Four Armies', p. 235.
7   Gudmundsson, 'Expansion of the British Army', p. 50.
8   Grieves, *Sussex in the First World War*, p. xxi.
9   *Worthing Gazette*, 19 August 1914, p. 4, col. d.
10   *Chichester Observer*, 12 August 1914, p. 3, col. d.
11   Grieves, *Sussex in the First World War*, p. xvii.
12   *Chichester Observer*, 12 August 1914, p. 6, col. f.
13   *Littlehampton Observer*, 12 August 1914, p. 4, col. c.
14   *Ibid.*
15   Gudmundsson, 'Expansion of the British Army', pp. 47–60.
16   WSRO RSR MS 7/5, *A Call to Arms, 1914*
17   *Chichester Observer*, 19 August 1914, p. 5, col. c.
18   *Littlehampton Observer*, 26 August 1914, p. 3, col. a.
19   *Worthing Gazette*, 19 August 1914, p. 4, col. d.
20   *Littlehampton Observer*, 26 August 1014, p. 3, col. d.
21   *Chichester Observer*, 2 September 1914, p. 5. col. c.

22 WSRO Add Ms 1606 Letters written from the Western Front by Messrs Shippams' employees to Mr Ernest Shippam, chairman of Shippams (Chichester) Ltd.

23 K. Grieves, 'There are times when we would all prefer factory life: letters from the trenches to the Shippams works in Chichester during the First World War', *Family and Community History*, 6(1).

24 *West Sussex Gazette*, 10 September 1914, p. 2, col. f.

25 *Worthing Gazette*, 12 August 1914, p. 3, col. a; 2 September 1914, p. 6, cols a–g; 23 September 1914, p. 5, col. d.

26 *Worthing Gazette*, 16 September 1914, p. 2, cols c–e.

27 *Worthing Gazette*, 23 September 1914, p. 2, col. e.

28 *Chichester Observer*, 2 September 1914, p. 5, col. c; 23 September 1914, p. 2, cols a-d.

29 *Chichester Observer*, 9 September 1914, p. 2 cols e–f.

30 *West Sussex County Times*, 5 September 1914, p. 3, col. d.

31 *Mid-Sussex Times*, 18 August 1914, p. 2, col. c.

32 *West Sussex County Times*, 5 September 1914, p. 3, col. e.

33 *West Sussex County Times*, 12 September 1914, p. 8, col. c.

34 *West Sussex Gazette*, 3 September 1914, p. 2, col. b.

35 *Sussex and Surrey Courier*, 10 October 1914, p. 4, col. f.

36 *Sussex and Surrey Courier*, 19 December 1914, p. 5, col. e.

37 *Worthing Gazette*, 2 September 1914, p. 6, cols a–b.

38 Grieves, *Sussex in the First World War*, p. 13.

39 *West Sussex Gazette*, 10 September 1914, p. 2, col. f.

40 *Bognor Observer*, 9 September 1914, p. 4, col. d.

41 *West Sussex County Times*, 12 September 1914, p. 5, col. g.

42 Grieves, *Sussex in the First World War*, p. xx.

43 J. Godfrey, 'Landscapes of War and Peace: Sussex, the South Downs and the Western Front', *Sussex Archaeological Collections*, 152 (2014) (forthcoming).

44 *Sussex and Surrey Courier*, 17 October 1914, p. 2, col. b.

45 www.nationalarchives.go.uk/conscription_appeals/ Accessed 22 January 2014.

46 *Chichester Observer*, 8 March 1916, p. 3, cols b–d.

47 *Worthing Gazette*, 16 August 1916, p. 3, col. d.

48 *Worthing Gazette*, 20 September 1916, p. 2, col. b.

49 Notebook of W.J. Passmore, in possession of Mr C.W. Passmore, Applesham, Coombes, Lancing.

50 *West Sussex Gazette*, 1 June 1916, p. 7, col. d.

51 *Chichester Observer*, 13 September 1916, p. 3, col. e.

52 *Sussex and Surrey Courier*, 18 August 1917, p. 3 col. f.

53 *Mid-Sussex Times*, 14 March 1916, p. 3 cols e–f.

54 *Chichester Observer*, 5 July 1916, p. 5 col. d.

55 *Mid-Sussex Times,* 7 March 1916, p. 8 cols f–g.

56 Godfrey, 'Landscapes of War and Peace'.

Chapter 2

57   For a general history of the regiment in the Great War see
     G.D. Martineau, *A History of the Royal Sussex Regiment
     1701–1953* (Royal Sussex Regimental Association, 1955); for
     an in-depth study of the eleven battalions that served on the
     Western Front see H. Miller, *We Wunt be Druv: The Royal Sussex
     Regiment on the Western Front 1914–18* (Reveille Press, 2012).
58   *West Sussex Gazette*, 1 October 1914, p. 3, col. f.
59   WSRO RSR Ms. 2/59.
60   *Sussex and Surrey Courier*, 17 October 1914, p. 8, col. b.
61   *Ibid.*
62   *West Sussex Gazette*, 1 October 1914, p. 3, col. f.
63   Anon, *A Short History of the Royal Sussex Regiment* (Gale &
     Polden, 1927), pp. 34–5.
64   WSRO Acc 15,444. Diary of RSM W.F. Rainsford.
65   WSRO RSR Ms. 5/77.
66   *West Sussex Gazette*, 15 February 1917, p. 10, cols a–b.
67   *Sussex Daily News*, 21 May 1915, cutting in WSRO RSR Ms.
     5/65, pp. 59–60.
68   WSRO Acc.15,444
69   *Sussex and Surrey Courier*, 19 June 1915, p. 5, col. f.
70   See P.H. Liddle, *The Soldier's War 1914–1918* (Blandford Press, 1988), p. 53.
71   *Littlehampton Observer*, 27 October 1915, p. 8, col. f.
72   WSRO RSR Ms. 2/74.
73   *Mid-Sussex Times*, 12 October 1915, p. 5, col. g.
74   For a full history of the battalion's war see O. Rutter,
     *The History of the Seventh (Service) Battalion, the Royal Sussex
     Regiment, 1914–1919* (Times Publishing Co., 1934).
75   WSRO Add. Ms.25,001.
76   See J.A. Baines, *The Day Sussex Died: A History of Lowther's
     Lambs to the Boar's Head Massacre* (RSLHG, 2012).
77   P. Reed, *Forgotten Heroes* (privately printed, Rusper, 1986);
     Worthing Gazette, 16 August 1916, p. 6, cols c–e.
78   *Chichester Observer*, 26 July 1916, p. 5, col. c.
79   WSRO RSR Mss. 7/27–41.
80   WSRO RSR Museum Acc. 3179.
81   *Chichester Observer*, 23 August 1916, p. 3, col. c.
82   WSRO RSR Ms. 7/26.
83   *Mid-Sussex Times*, 26 September 1916, p. 1, col. f.
84   *Mid-Sussex Times*, 19 September 1916, p. 8, col. b.
85   WSRO Acc. 6813.
86   WSRO Add. Ms. 25,006.
87   RSR OH 25.
88   WSRO RSR Ms. Uncatalogued. Whitley papers.
89   *Ibid.*
90   WSRO RSR Ms. Uncatalogued. Banfield papers.
91   WSRO RSR Museum Acc. 3057.
92   'A Tribute from the Field', *The Blue*, magazine of Christ's
     Hospital, October 1917, Vol. XLV, No. 1, p. 11.

93 WSRO RSR Ms. Uncatalogued. Banfield papers.
94 *Worthing Gazette*, 17 April 1918, p. 2, col. d.
95 Martineau, *op. cit.*, p. 182.
96 WSRO RSR Ms. 2/57.
97 WSRO RSR Museum Acc. 3179.
98 WSRO Add. Ms. 1606. Letter from C. Tulett to Ernest Shippam, 12 November 1918.
99 WSRO RSR Ms. 2/57.
100 Martineau, *op. cit.*, p. 161.
101 *Chichester Observer*, 23 April 1919, p. 2, col. a.
102 WSRO RSR Mss. 2/64–65.
103 *Littlehampton Observer*, 29 September 1915, p. 8, col. e.
104 *Bognor Observer*, 1 September 1915, p. 5, col. c.
105 *Sussex Daily News*, 2 September 1915, p. 6, col. b.
106 *Mid-Sussex Times*, 14 September 1915, p. 7, col. f.
107 *Mid-Sussex Times*, 1 May 1917, p. 3, col. e.
108 H.I. Powell-Edwards, *The Sussex Yeomanry and 16th (Sussex Yeomanry) Battalion, Royal Sussex Regiment, 1914–1919* (Andrew Melrose Ltd, 1921), p. 106.
109 WSRO RSR PH 4/56.
110 H.V.F. Winstone, *Leachman: 'OC. Desert' The Life of Lieutenant-Colonel Gerard Leachman, DSO* (Quartet Books, 1982).
111 WSRO RSR Mss. 6/8, 10.
112 WSRO RSR PH 6/6-7; see *Kodak Trade Circular*, No. 136, Nov-Dec 1914.
113 WSRO RSR Ms. 6/8.
114 WSRO RSR Ms. 7/61.
115 WSRO Acc. 6813.
116 *Littlehampton Observer*, 11 November 1914, p. 6, col. f.
117 WSRO Par. 82/7/6.
118 WSRO RSR Museum Acc. 3179.
119 *Sussex and Surrey Courier*, 2 January 1915, p. 2, col. f.
120 WSRO RSR Ms. 7/27.
121 WSRO Add. Ms. 1606. Letter, 29 April 1917.
122 *Ibid.*
123 *Mid-Sussex Times*, 8 August 1916, p. 4, col. e.
124 WSRO Add. Ms. 25,001.
125 WSRO RSR Museum Acc. 3179.
126 *Bognor Observer*, 27 February 1918, p. 3, col. d.
127 *Worthing Gazette*, 11 April 1917, p. 6, col. d.
128 WSRO RSR Ms. 11/67.
129 WSRO Acc. 15,444.
130 *West Sussex County Times*, 22 May 1915, p. 5, col. f.
131 *Chichester Observer*, 31 October 1917, p. 4, col. e.
132 Birdsall & Son; WSRO RSR Library 5/21.
133 WSRO RSR Mss. 2/64–66.
134 *Bognor Observer*, 11 August 1915, p. 5, col. f.
135 A. Eyles, F. Gray, A. Readman, *Cinema West Sussex* (Phillimore, 1996), pp. 142–5.

136 WSRO RSR Ms. 7/45.
137 *Mid-Sussex Times*, 17 December 1918, p. 1, col. a.
138 See Richard Buckman, *The Royal Sussex Regiment. Military Honours & Awards 1864–1920* (J & KH Publishing, 2001).
139 *Chichester Observer*, 6 August 1924, p. 7, col. c-d.
140 E. Blunden, *Undertones of War* (Cobden-Sanderson, Revised Edition, 1930), p. 184.

Chapter 3
141 Shoreham-by-Sea History Portal website www.shorehambysea.com. Retrieved 31 January 2014.
142 G.I.S. Inglis, *The Kensington Battalion* (Pen & Sword, Barnsley, 2010), p. 30.
143 *Chichester Observer*, 5 September 1914.
144 T.M.A. Webb and Dennis L. Bird, *Shoreham Airport Sussex, The Story of Britain's Oldest Licensed Airfield* (Cirrus Associates, Gillingham, 1996), pp. 19–21.
145 Reginald Byron and David Coxon, *Tangmere, Famous Royal Air Force Fighter Station, An Authorised History* (Grub Street, London, 2013), pp. 15–16.
146 J. Green, *The American Aerodrome in Rustington* (J. Green & West Sussex CC Library Service, 2014) case study for the West Sussex & The Great War Project.
147 Mary Taylor, *This Was Rustington, No.3, In Times of War* (privately published, 1989), pp. 1–4.
148 John Goodwin, *The Military Defence of West Sussex, 500 Years of Fortification of the Coast between Brighton and Selsey* (Middleton Press, Midhurst, 1985), pp. 76–7.
149 Ian Evans, *The White and Thompson/Norman Thompson Flight Company Aircraft Factory in Middleton and Littlehampton (Hubert Williams)* (Ian Evans & West Sussex CC Library Service, 2014) case study for the West Sussex & The Great War Project.
150 *Chichester Observer*, 4 and 8 September 1914.
151 E. Gunston, 'Sussex Beneath the Sea', *Sussex County Magazine*, 28 (1954) p. 138.
152 Grehan, *Battles & Battlefields of Sussex*, p. 84.
153 Grieves, *Sussex in the First World War*, p. 244.
154 Gunston, 'Sussex Beneath the Sea', p. 138.
155 M. Snow, 'Mystery Towers' from www.mystery.adur.org.uk (22 March 2013).
156 Gunston, 'Sussex Beneath the Sea', p. 138 and Goodwin, *The Military Defence of West Sussex*, p. 80.
157 P. Longstaff-Tyrrell, *Tyrrell's List – an amalgam – The Artefacts of Two Great Wars in Sussex* (Gotehouse, 2002), p. 52.
158 John Grehan and Martin Mace, *Battleground Sussex, A Military History of Sussex from the Iron Age to the Present Day* (Pen & Sword, Barnsley, 2012), p. 115; D. Harries, *Maritime Sussex* (Seaford, 1997), pp. 105–6.

Chapter 4

159 K.W. Mitchinson, *Defending Albion – Britain's Home Army 1908–1919* (Palgrave Macmillan, 2005), p. 35 & p. 40. See also: D. Wragg, *Royal Navy Handbook 1914–1918* (Sutton, 2006), Chapter 4 – Guarding the North Sea.

160 Mitchinson, *Defending Albion*, p.6 & p.35. See also *Special Army Order (Para 1) 18 March 1908*.

161 The Long, Long Trail – The British Army in the Great War of 1914–1918, 2014. *The Royal Sussex Regiment* [online] available at: www.1914]1918.net/sussex.htm [Accessed 27 February 2014].

162 P. Kendall, *The Zeebrugge Raid 1918: The Finest Feat of Arms* (The History Press, 2009) p. 15.

163 As an example see 'Royal Sussex Regiment – 4th Battalion volunteers for foreign service', *Mid-Sussex Times*, 22 September 1914, p. 8, col. c. See also The Long, Long Trail – The British Army in the Great War of 1914–1918, 2014. *The Royal Sussex Regiment* [online] available at: www.1914]1918.net/sussex.htm [Accessed 27 February 2014].

164 J. Grehan, *Battleground Sussex: A Military History of Sussex from the Iron Age to the Present Day* (Pen & Sword, 2012), p. 114.

165 Grehan, *Battles & Battlefields of Sussex*, p. 83.

166 J. Goodwin, *The Military Defence of West Sussex* (Middleton Press, 1985), p. 75.

167 Friends of Shoreham Fort, 2014. *About Shoreham Fort 6* [online] available at: www.shorehamfort.co.uk/about/history/6/# [Accessed 28 February 2014]

168 'Good work by the Boy Scouts in Mid-Sussex', *Mid-Sussex Times*, 11 August 1914, p. 2, col. b.; 'The Local Civil Guard', *Worthing Gazette*, 19 August 1914, p. 4, col. e.

169 Mitchinson, *Defending Albion*, p. 68.

170 'Boy Scouts in War Time', *Sussex & Surrey Courier*, 29 August 1914, p. 2, cols e–f.

171 'The Boy Scouts', *Mid-Sussex Times*, 3 November 1914, p. 5, col. e; 'The Scout In War-Time – The Burgess Hill Troop Under The Red Ensign', *Mid-Sussex Times*, 17 November 1914, p. 3, col. g; 'Crawley Scout Boys', *Sussex & Surrey Courier*, 17/10/1914, p. 5, col. f.

172 'What the Sea Scouts are doing', *Worthing Gazette*, 1 May 1918, p. 3, col b.

173 C. Cole, E.F. Cheesman, *The Air Defence of Britain 1914–1918* (Putnam, 1984), p. 10.

174 Cole, Cheesman, *The Air Defence of Britain 1914–1918*, p. 36.

175 Cole, Cheesman, *The Air Defence of Britain 1914–1918*, p. 174.

176 E. Heron-Allen, *Journal of The Great War: From Sussex Shore to Flanders Fields* (Sussex Record Society, 2002), pp. 106–107.

177 MPI 1/612/2 Map of the coasts of Kent and Sussex and inland to Devizes (Wiltshire) illustrating an air raid 24–25 September 1917 at The National Archives.

178 J. Blackwell, 'The Selsey Sound Mirror', *Sussex Industrial Archaeology Society Newsletter* (144) (2009) pp. 6–7.

179 Heron-Allen, *Journal of The Great War*, p.207

180 'Dover Barrage' in S. Pope, E. Wheal (eds), *The Macmillan Dictionary of the First World War* (Macmillan, 1995), pp. 136–7.

181 'Aerial reconnaissance above and beyond the Sussex Shore' in K. Grieves (ed.), *Sussex in the First World War – Volume 84* (Sussex Record Society, 2004), pp. 152–62.

182 R. & B. Larn, 'Shipwreck Index of the British Isles – Volume 2' (Lloyds Register of Shipping, 1995), Section 3 *Sussex* (BC).

183 C. Butler, *West Sussex Under Attack: Anti-Invasion Sites 1500–1990* (Tempus, 2008), pp. 66–7.

184 R. Gunner, *World War One Airship Station*; slindonatwarmyblog.wordpress.com/ww1-airship-station/ (1 March 2014).

185 P. Abbott, *The British Airship at War 1914–1918* (Terence Dalton Limited, 1989), un-numbered page.

186 R. & B. Larn, Shipwreck Index of the British Isles – Volume 2 (Lloyds Register of Shipping, 1995), Section 3 – Sussex (BC).

187 'The Mayor's Appeal For A City Guard', *Chichester Observer*, 12 August 1914, p.5, col. d; 'Citizens' Protection Corps', *Worthing Gazette*, 12 August 1914, p. 6, col. d.

188 See G.T. Chesney, *The Battle for Dorking* (Blackwoods Magazine, 1871), E. Childers, *The Riddle of the Sands* (Smith, Elder & Co., 1903) and W. Le Queux, *The Invasion of 1910* (E. Nash, 1906). 31 'The Local Civil Guard', *Worthing Gazette*, 19 August 1914, p. 4, col. e.

189 I.F.W. Beckett 'Grenfell, William Henry, Baron Desborough (1855–1945)' Oxford Dictionary of National Biography, Oxford University Press, 2004; online edn Mary 2012 [www.oxforddnb.com/view/article/33566, accessed 1 March 2014].

190 'Home Defence – VTCs formed At East Grinstead', *Sussex and Surrey Courier*, 16 January 1915, p. 8, col. a and 'The Civil Guard', *Sussex and Surrey Courier*, 23 January 1915, p. 5, col. d.

191 'Ready for Home Defence', *Worthing Gazette*, 31 March 1915, p. 6, col. d.

192 J.P. Blake (ed.), *The Official Regulations for Volunteer Training Corps and for County Volunteer Organisations (England and Wales),* (The Central Association Volunteer Training Corps), 1916. pp. 76–124.

193 'The Volunteer Defence Corps', *Sussex and Surrey Courier*, 30 January 1915, p.5, col. b.

194 See: 'Motorists and the War', *Worthing Gazette*, 31 March 1915, p. 7, col. e; 'Volunteer Training Corps', *Sussex and Surrey Courier*, 29 May 1915, p. 2, cols e–f; 'Sussex Volunteers' Field Day', *Chichester Observer*, 7 July 1915, p. 8, cols e–f; 'Burgess Hill VTC – Victory at shooting', *Mid-Sussex Times*, 8 June 1915, p. 5 col. d. A.H. Gregory, *The Story of Burgess Hill* (Charles Clarke, 1933), pp. 98–99.

195 Mitchinson, *Defending Albion*, p. 150.

196 Mitchinson, *Defending Albion*, p. 86.
197 'A Funk Hole for Shirkers', *Chichester Observer*, 11 July 1917, p. 2, col. d.
198 Notes and comments, *Mid-Sussex Times*, 26 November 1918, p. 5, col. d.
199 Mitchinson, *Defending Albion*, p. 86 & pp. 226–7.
200 Add. Mss 51906 papers relating to emergency measures in the event of an invasion at WSRO.
201 'Small Shots', *Worthing Gazette*, 12 August 1914, p. 5, col. e.
202 POL.W/H/15/2 Memoranda on air raids and invasion at WSRO.
203 'Special Constables Enrolled', *Worthing Gazette*, 12 August 1914, p. 6, col. g.
204 N. Poulsom, M. Rumble and K. Smith, *Sussex Police Forces* (Middleton Press, 1987), plate 97.
205 'Chichester Special Constables – More Duties for Busy Men', *Chichester Observer*, 1 May 1918, p. 2.
206 Special Constables Act 1914 (4 & 5 Geo. c 61); See also: M. Barrett, *West Sussex Constabulary 110 Years of History – April 1857 – December 1967* (Malcolm Barrett, 2008), p. 83.
207 'The Local Civil Guard', *Worthing Gazette*, 19 April 1914, p. 4, col. e; 'Chichester's Special Constables Distribution of Badges', *Chichester Observer*, 27 January 1915, p. 2 col. b.
208 Miss Florence Ellis and Miss Emily Thorn, both relatives of servicing officers, were the first two Women Police Constables to serve with West Sussex Constabulary, albeit as Special Constables; 'Women Police', *Chichester Observer*, 13 February 1918, p. 1, col. d; 'Chichester's Special Constables Distribution of Badges', *Chichester Observer*, 27 January 1915, p. 2, col. b.
209 Add. Mss 51906 papers relating to emergency measures in the event of an invasion at WSRO.
210 P. Holden, *Brave Lads of Sunny Worthing: A Seaside Town During the Great War* (Beckett Features, 1991), p. 50; see also: N. Hanson, *First Blitz – The Secret German Plan to Raze London to the Ground in 1918* (Double Day 2008), Chapter 1, 'The First Blows'.
211 'Curtailed Lighting', *Worthing Gazette*, 7 October 1914, p. 5, col. g.
212 Heron-Allen, *Journal of The Great War*, pp. 64–5
213 V. Martin, 'The Great War in Findon' from www.findonvillage.com/0244_the_great_war_years.htm (02 March 2014)
214 'The Dangers of Darkened Streets', *Worthing Gazette*, 6 November 1918, p. 6, col. c.
215 Defence of the Realm Act 1914 (4 & 5 Geo.5 c. 29).
216 *Worthing Gazette*, 19 August 1914, p. 4, col. f.
217 *Chichester Observer*, 12 August 1914, p. 5, col. e.
218 *Mid-Sussex Times*, 18 August 1914, p. 6, col. b.
219 *Worthing Gazette*, 4 November 1914, p. 5, col. e.
220 *Worthing Gazette*, 12 August 1914, p. 5, col. c.
221 *Chichester Observer*, 26 August 1914, p. 3, col. f.

222 *Chichester Observer*, 12 August 1914, p. 3, col. e.
223 *Worthing Gazette*, 2 September 1914, p. 2, col. a.
224 *Chichester Observer*, 16 September 1914, p. 5, col. a.
225 *Worthing Gazette*, 16 September 1914, p. 6, cols d–e.
226 *Chichester Observer*, 4 November 1914, p. 5, col. b.
227 Holden, *Brave Lads of Sunny Worthing*, pp. 22–3.
228 *Worthing Gazette*, 10 March 1915, p. 3, cols c–d.
229 'The Night of the Zeppelin Raid', *Chichester Observer*,
     18 October 1916, p. 4, cols c–d.
230 *Worthing Gazette*, 26 August 1914, p. 7, col. a.
231 B.W. Harvey & C. Fitzgerald, *Edward Heron-Allen's Journal of
     the Great War, From Sussex Shore to Flanders Field* SRS Volume
     86 (Sussex Record Society, 2002), pp. 15 on & 54 on.
232 *West Sussex Gazette*, 11 and 26 August 1915, p. 5, col. c & p. 8, col. g.
233 *Littlehampton Observer*, 19 May 1915, p. 8, col. d.
234 *Chichester Observer*, 28 October 1914, p. 5 col. d.
235 *Worthing Gazette*, 16 September 1914, p. 5, col. e.

Chapter 5

236 *Chichester Observer*, 19 August 1914, p. 2.
237 *Chichester Observer*, 19 August 1914, p. 2.
238 *Horsham Times*, 5 September 1914, p. 8.
239 *Chichester Observer*, 7 October 1914, p. 8.
240 *West Sussex Gazette*, 21 January 1915, p. 7.
241 *West Sussex County Times*, 29 August 1914, p. 5.
242 *Chichester Observer*, 14 October 1914, p. 5.
243 *West Sussex Gazette*, 11 February 1915, p. 12.
244 *Mid-Sussex Times*, 11 August 1914, p. 2, cols a–b.
245 *Mid-Sussex Times*, 15 September 1914, p. 8.
246 *Worthing Gazette*, 12 August 1914, p. 6.
247 *Worthing Gazette*, 26 August 1914, p. 5.
248 *Worthing Gazette*, 16 September 1914, p. 6.
249 *Worthing Gazette*, 20 January 1915, p. 6.
250 *Horsham Times*, 22 August 1914, p. 2.
251 *Horsham Times*, 22 August 1914, p. 8.
252 *Horsham Times*, 29 August 1914, p. 5.
253 *Sussex & Surrey Courier*, 24 October 1914, p. 5.
254 *Horsham Times*, 15 August 1914, p. 5.
255 *Horsham Times*, 22 August 1914, p. 2.
256 *Sussex & Surrey Courier*, 19 December 1914, p. 5.
257 *Chichester Observer*, 19 July 1916, p. 5.
258 *Chichester Observer*, 26 July 1916, p. 8.
259 *West Sussex Gazette*, 27 June 1918, p. 7.
260 *West Sussex Gazette*, 27 June 1918, p. 8.
261 *Worthing Gazette*, 28 August 1918, p. 6.
262 *Mid-Sussex Times*, 12 September 1916, p. 2, cols d–f.
263 T. Johnston *The Financiers and the Nation* (Methuen, 1934), pp. 45–52
264 *Worthing Gazette*, 14 July 1915, p. 5.
265 *Worthing Gazette*, 9 August 1916, p. 7.

266 *West Sussex County Times*, 16 June 1917, p. 3.
267 *Worthing Gazette*, 19 September 1917, p. 6.
268 *Chichester Observer*, 31 January 1917, p. 2.
269 *West Sussex Gazette*, 29 November 1917, p. 3.
270 *Bognor Observer*, 6 March 1918, pp. 1 & 4.
271 J. Paxman, *Great Britain's Great War* (Viking/Penguin, Kindle edition, 2013), pp. 207–8.
272 *West Sussex Gazette*, 14 March 1918, p. 8.
273 *Kelly's Directory of Sussex*, 1915 edition (Kelly's Directories Ltd, 1915), pp. 381–2.
274 *West Sussex Gazette*, 13 June 1918, p. 3 & 27 June, p. 7.
275 *Worthing Gazette*, 18 October 1916, p. 6.
276 *Chichester Observer*, 23 December 1914, p. 5.
277 *Mid-Sussex Times*, 18 May 1915, p. 7.
278 *West Sussex Gazette*, 2 November 1916, p. 6.
279 *Mid-Sussex Times*, 8 May 1917, p. 1.
280 *West Sussex County Times*, 1 April 1916, p. 3.
281 *Bognor Observer*, 18 August 1915, p. 3 col. c.
282 *Chichester Observer*, 5 May 1915, p. 8 col. d.
283 *Chichester Observer*, 30 June 1915, p. 4, col. e.
284 *Mid-Sussex Times*, 2 July 1918, p. 1, col. d.
285 *Mid-Sussex Times*, 8 September 1914, p. 8, col. g.
286 *Chichester Observer*, 19 May 1915, p. 4, cols a–b.
287 *Bognor Observer*, 22 & 29 September 1915, p. 5 col. c & p. 8, col. e.
288 *West Sussex County Times*, 17 March 1917, p. 4, col. a.
289 *West Sussex County Times*, 13 July 1918, p. 2, col. a.
290 *West Sussex County Times,* 6 April 1918, p. 2, col. f.
291 *Ibid.*
292 *West Sussex County Times*, 10 August 1918, p. 4, col. a.
293 *Sussex & Surrey Courier*, 1 April 1916, p. 8, col. d.
294 *Bognor Observer*, 13 March 1918, p. 1, col. f.
295 *Mid-Sussex Times*, 1 September 1914, p. 5.
296 Lytton Leonard Boyd Medal Rolls Index Card 1914–20, The National Archives.
297 *Kelly's Directory of Sussex*, 1915 edition (Kelly's Directories Ltd, 1915), p. 468.
298 *Chichester Observer*, 21 October 1914, p. 2.
299 *Ibid.*
300 *Chichester Observer*, 23 August 1916, p. 2.
301 *Mid-Sussex Times*, 22 August 1916, p. 3, cols d–f.
302 *West Sussex County Times*, 17 February 1917, p. 2.
303 *West Sussex Gazette*, 11 May 1916, p. 3.
304 *Littlehampton Observer*, 30 December 1914, p. 2, col. c.
305 *Mid-Sussex Times*, 30 May 1916, p. 6, col. b.
306 *Sussex & Surrey Courier*, 21 & 28 September 1918, p. 4, col. c; p. 2, col. e & p. 4, col. b.
307 West Sussex Federation of WIs *West Sussex Within Living Memory* (Countryside Books/WSFWI, 1993), pp. 172.

308 *Chichester Observer*, 28 October 1914, p. 8.
309 *Chichester Observer*, 23 December 1914, p. 5.
310 *West Sussex Gazette*, 22 October 1914, p. 3.
311 *Worthing Gazette*, 6 January 1915, p. 4, col. g.
312 *Worthing Gazette*, 17 March 1915, p. 6.
313 *Worthing Gazette*, 20 March 1918, p. 3, col. c.
314 *Worthing Gazette*, 17 July 1918, p. 5, col. d.
315 *West Sussex County Times*, 19 September 1914, p. 8, col. b.
316 *West Sussex County Times*, 26 September 1914, p. 5, col. e.
317 *West Sussex County Times*, 3 October 1914, p. 8.
318 *West Sussex CountyTimes*, 2 January 1915, p. 5, col. c.
319 *West Sussex County Times,* 1 April 1916, p. 6.
320 *West Sussex County Times*, 24 February 1917, p. 4.
321 *West Sussex County Times*, 25 May 1918, p. 3.
322 *Chichester Observer*, 23 September 1914, p. 5.
323 *Chichester Observer*, 7 October 1914, p. 3, col. f.
324 *Chichester Observer*, 14 October 1914, p. 2.
325 *West Sussex Gazette*, 22 October 1914, p. 3.
326 *Horsham Times*, 19 September 1914, p. 5, col. a.
327 *Sussex &Surrey Courier*, 10 October 1914, p. 2, col. c.
328 *Sussex & Surrey Courier*, 10 October, p. 8, col. b &
     17 October 1914, p. 5, col. b.
329 *Worthing Gazette*, 14 April 1915, p. 7, col. f.
330 *Bognor Observer*, 6 January 1915, p. 4, col. d.
331 *Chichester Observer*, 21 October 1914, p. 3, col. f.
332 *Worthing Gazette*, 14 April 1915, p. 7, col. f.
333 *Mid-Sussex Times*, 3 November 1914, p. 7, col. e.
334 *West Sussex Gazette*, 1 October 1914, p. 12, col. e.
335 *Chichester Observer*, 16 September 1914, p. 5, col. c.
336 *West Sussex Gazette*, 1 October 1914, p.4, col. g.
337 *West Sussex Gazette*, 22 October 1914, p. 3, col. d.
338 *Sussex & Surrey Courier*, 24 October 1914, p. 5, col. f.
339 *West Sussex Gazette*, 26 August 1915, p. 7, cols g–h.
340 *West Sussex Gazette*, 1 March 1917, p. 1, col. f.
341 *Mid-Sussex Times*, 15 February 1916, p. 1, col. f.
342 P. Doyle, *First World War Britain* (Shire Publications Ltd, 2012),
     pp. 63–5.
343 A. Eyles, F. Gray & A. Readman, *Cinema West Sussex: The First
     Hundred Years* (Phillimore & WSCC, 1996).
344 *Worthing Gazette*, 5 August 1914, p. 6, cols c–d.
345 A. Eyles *et al.*, *Cinema West Sussex: the First Hundred Years*
     (Phillimore, 1996), pp. 189–98
346 *Ibid.*, pp. 65–75.
347 *Mid-Sussex Times*, 15 September 1914, p. 8, col. f.
348 *Chichester Observer*, 23 June 1915, p. 4, cols e–f.
349 *Worthing Gazette*, 19 August 1914, p. 5, cols c–e.
350 A. Eyles *et al.*, *Cinema West Sussex: the First Hundred Years*
     (Phillimore, 1996), p.119.
351 *Ibid.*, p140.

352 www.nationalarchives.gov.uk/pathways/firstworldwar/britain/
     espionage.htm.
353 *Worthing Gazette*, 9 September 1914, p. 3, col. c.
354 *Worthing Gazette*, 12 January 1916, p. 5, col. e.
355 *Worthing Gazette*, 20 September 1916, p. 6, col. f.
356 *Littlehampton Observer*, 28 March 1917, p. 8, col. a.
357 *Worthing Gazette*, 5 & 12 August 1914, p. 7, col. d & p. 7, cols
     c–d.
358 *Worthing Gazette*, 25 July 1917, p. 3, col. d.
359 *Worthing Gazette*, 5 September 1917, p. 3, col. e & p. 6, col. a.
360 P. Doyle, *First World War Britain* (Shire Publications Ltd, 2012),
     pp.66–7.
361 Spencer C. Tucker, *The Encyclopedia of World War I: A Political,
     Social, and Military History*, vol. 2, pp. 341–2.
362 www.europeanbeerguide.net/ukstats.htm.
363 www.westernfrontassociation.com/component/content/
     article/160-life-on-the-home-front/1591-lloyd-georges-beer-or-
     when-it-was-illegal-to-buy-your-round.html.
364 *Chichester Observer*, 9 December 1914, p. 7, col. e.
365 *Worthing Gazette*, 27 January 1915, p. 7, col. c.
366 *Worthing Gazette*, 10 March 1915, p. 3, col. b.
367 *West Sussex Gazette*, 8 June 1916, p. 8, col. g.
368 *West Sussex Gazette*, 14 February 1918, p. 8, col. f.
369 *Mid-Sussex Times*, 22 August 1916, p. 5, col. e.
370 *West Sussex Gazette*, 25 May 1916, p. 3.
371 *West Sussex Gazette*, 23 May 1918, p. 2, cols f–g.
372 *Chichester Observer*, 9 August 1916, p. 8, col. e.
373 *Mid-Sussex Times*, 12 November 1918, p. 2, col. c.
374 *Worthing Gazette*, 30 September 1914, p. 5, col. f.
375 *Sussex and Surrey Courier*, 26 December 1914, p. 3, col. a.
376 *Mid-Sussex Times*, 12 June 1917, p. 3, col. b.
377 *West Sussex County Times*, 5 June 1915, p. 5, col. d.
378 *Chichester Observer*, 26 May 1915, p. 3, col. c.
379 *Chichester Observer*, 20 September 1916, p. 4, col. c.
380 *Bognor Observer*, 19 May 1915, p. 4, col. c.
381 *Worthing Gazette*, 5 June 1918, p. 7, col. d & 11 September 1918,
     p. 6, col c.

Chapter 6
382 P. Doyle, *First World War Britain* (Shire Publications Ltd, 2012),
     p. 21.
383 The National Archives Web Archive http://webarchive.nation-
     alarchives.gov.uk/+/www.hmrc.gov.uk/history/taxhis4.htm.
384 www.measuringworth.com/index.php.
385 *Worthing Gazette*, 19 August 1914, p. 4.
386 P. Holden, *Brave Lads of Sunny Worthing* (Beckett
     Features, 1991), pp. 58–9.
387 *Bognor Observer*, 13 February 1918, p. 3 col. f.
388 *Bognor Observer*, 22 September 1915, p. 4, col. f.

389 *Worthing Gazette*, 30 September 1914, p. 5, col. e.

390 *Chichester Observer*, 30 June 1915, p. 4, col. d.

391 *Chichester Observer*, 26 August, p. 4, col. f & 2 September 1914, p. 8, cols a–b.

392 *Worthing Gazette*, 12 August 1914, p. 7, col. c.

393 *Worthing Gazette*, 31 March 1915, p. 7, col. c.

394 *West Sussex County Times*, 14 October 1916, p. 3, col. c.

395 *West Sussex Gazette*, 2 May 1918, p. 3, col. d.

396 *West Sussex Gazette*, 13 April 1916, p. 2, col. c.

397 *House of Commons Parliamentary Papers* Geo V Year 8, cc 921–1056. 23 July 1917. Corn production. A bill for encouraging the production of corn, and for purposes connected therewith (including provision as to agricultural wages and rents).

398 *West Sussex Gazette*, 17 February 1916, p. 3, col. c.

399 *West Sussex County Times*, 17 August 1918, p. 3, col. d.

400 *West Sussex Gazette*, 9 March 1916, p. 12, col. a.

401 *Bognor Observer*, 31 March 1915, p. 5, col. b.

402 *Mid-Sussex Times*, 26 October 1915, p. 2, col. e.

403 *Mid-Sussex Times*, 22 August 1916, p. 8, col. b.

404 *Worthing Gazette*, 3 March 1915, p. 5, col. a.

405 *Chichester Observer*, 30 June 1915, p. 4, col. d.

406 *Bognor Observer*, 28 July 1915, p. 4, col. d.

407 *Mid-Sussex Times*, 22 August 1916, p. 5, col. e.

408 *Mid-Sussex Times*, 22 August 1916, p. 4, col. f.

409 *Worthing Gazette*, 26 August 1914, p. 6, col. c.

410 *Worthing Gazette*, 8 November 1916, p. 6, col. e.

411 *Worthing Gazette*, 13 February 1918, p. 6, col. c.

412 *Worthing Gazette*, 17 March 1915, p. 5, col. d.

413 *Chichester Observer*, 23 February 1916, p. 2, col. f.

414 *Chichester Observer*, 2 June 1915, p. 4, col. f.

415 J.H. Farrant, *Mid-Victorian Littlehampton: The Railway and the Cross-Channel Steamers* (Littlehampton UDC, 1972), p.23.

416 *Sussex and Surrey Courier*, 5 February 1916, p. 6, col. d.

417 J. Godfrey et al., *A Very Special County: West Sussex County Council, the First 100 Years* (WSCC, 1988), p.36.

418 *Horsham Times*, 22 August 1914, p. 6, col. b.

419 *West Sussex County Council Summary of Proceedings of Quarterly Meeting Held on the 20th November 1914* (WSCC, 1914).

420 *Chichester Observer*, 28 April 1915, p. 2, col. e.

421 *Chichester Observer*, 9 June 1915, p. 3, col. b.

422 J. Godfrey et al., *A Very Special County: West Sussex County Council, the First 100 Years* (WSCC, 1988), p. 41.

423 *Chichester Observer*, 22 November 1916, p. 2, col. b.

424 *Littlehampton Observer*, 17 January 1917, p. 4, col. e.

425 *Littlehampton Observer*, 8 December 1915, p. 8, col. e.

426 *Bognor Observer*, 18 August 1915, p. 6, col. a.

427 *Worthing Gazette*, 11 July 1917, p. 3, col. a.

428 *Sussex & Surrey Courier*, 16 February 1918, p. 4, col. f.

429 *Worthing Gazette*, 16 January 1918, p. 6, col. b.
430 *West Sussex County Times*, 2 February 1918, p. 3, col. a.
431 *Worthing Gazette*, 3 April 1918, p. 3, col. a.
432 *West Sussex Gazette*, 28 February 1918, p. 7, col. c.
433 *Worthing Gazette*, 24 April 1918, p. 4, cols a–b.
434 *Worthing Gazette*, 15 May 1918, p. 7, col. d.
435 *Worthing Gazette*, 25 September 1918, p. 2, col. e.
436 *West Sussex County Times*, 27 July 1918, p. 2, col. g.
437 *West Sussex County Times*, 27 July 1918, p. 2, col. g.
438 *Worthing Gazette*, 6 November 1918, p. 6, col. d.
439 *Worthing Gazette*, 23 September 1914, p. 4, cols d–e.
440 *Bognor Observer*, 31 March 1915, p. 5, col. f.
441 *Chichester Observer*, 7 April 1915, p. 7, col. c.
442 *Mid-Sussex Times*, 5 & 19 September 1916, p. 5, col. a & p. 1, col. f.
443 *Chichester Observer*, 24 May 1916, p. 4, col. e.
444 *Mid-Sussex Times*, 1 August 1916, p. 5, col. f.
445 *Mid-Sussex Times*, 25 October 1914, p. 8, col. b.
446 *Worthing Gazette*, 17 March 1915, p. 7, col. e.
447 *Worthing Gazette*, 24 November 1915, p. 6, col. d.
448 *Worthing Gazette*, 29 August 1917, p. 5, col. a & p. 5, col. d.
449 *Mid-Sussex Times*, 22 August 1916, p. 2, col. e.
450 *Sussex and Surrey Courier*, 2 March 1918, p. 8, cols a–b.
451 *Chichester Observer*, 24 April 1918, p. 4, col. a.
452 *Chichester Observer*, 14 August 1918, p. 3, col. e.
453 *Mid-Sussex Times*, 8 October 1918, p. 3, col. c.
454 *West Sussex Gazette*, 6 June 1918, p. 7, col. f.
455 *West Sussex Gazette*, 18 November 1915, p. 11, col. g.
456 *Horsham Times*, 22 August 1914, p. 2 & p. 8.
457 *Sussex and Surrey Courier*, 1 January 1916, p. 3, col. c.
458 *Worthing Gazette*, 5 & 12 August 1914, p. 7, col. d & p. 7, cols c–d.
459 *Worthing Gazette*, 25 July 1917, p. 3, col. d.
460 *Littlehampton Observer*, 10 November 1915, p. 7, col. f.
461 *Littlehampton Observer*, 26 May 1915, p. 7, col. b.
462 *Sussex and Surrey Courier*, 15 January 1916, p. 8, col. a.
463 *Worthing Gazette*, 17 March 1915, p. 6, col. b.
464 *West Sussex County Times*, 3 March 1917, p. 3, cols e–g.
465 B.W. Harvey & C. Fitzgerald *Edward Heron-Allen's Journal of the Great War, From Sussex Shore to Flanders Field* SRS Volume 86 (Sussex Record Society, 2002), pp. 98–9.
466 *Ibid.*, pp. 51–3.
467 *Mid-Sussex Times*, 15 October 1918, p. 1.
468 J. Paxman, *Great Britain's Great War* (Viking/Penguin, Kindle edition, 2013), pp. 211–17.
469 *Bognor Observer*, 13 February 1918, p. 3, col. f.
470 West Sussex Federation of WIs, *West Sussex Within Living Memory* (Countryside Books/WSFWI, 1993), pp. 171.
471 *Ibid.*
472 *Chichester Observer*, 23 June 1915, p. 3, col. b.

Chapter 7

473 *Mid-Sussex Times*, 8 September 1914, p. 1, col. a.

474 *Worthing Gazette*, 20 January 1915, p. 2, col. a.

475 *Worthing Gazette*, 21 July 1915, p. 7, col. c.

476 *Chichester Observer*, 28 April 1915, p. 7, col. d.

477 *Chichester Observer*, 10 November 1915, p. 7, col. f.

478 *West Sussex County Times*, 19 May 1917, p. 4, col. a.

479 *West Sussex within Living Memory* compiled by the West Sussex Federation of WIs (Countryside Books, 1993), p. 172

480 *West Sussex Gazette*, 30 May 1918, p. 8, col. g.

481 *Mid-Sussex Times*, 26 November 1918, p. 3, col. b.

482 *Mid-Sussex Times*, 4 July 1916, p. 3, col. d.

483 *Chichester Observer*, 11 November 1914, p. 6, col. d.

484 *West Sussex Gazette*, 13 August 1914, p. 1.

485 *Littlehampton Observer*, 12 August 1914, p. 5.

486 *Bognor Observer*, 22 September 1915, p. 4, col. f.

487 *Worthing Gazette*, 3 January 1917, p. 6, col. e.

488 *Mid-Sussex Times*, 12 October 1915, p. 4, cols f–g.

489 *Bognor Observer*, 10 March 1915, p. 5, col. c.

490 *Sussex and Surrey Courier*, 12 December 1914, p. 6, col. a.

491 *Chichester Observer*, 12 August 1914, p. 5, col. e.

492 *Bognor Observer*, 11 November 1914, p. 5, col. c.

493 *Chichester Observer*, 14 October 1914, p.2, col. c.

494 *Chichester Observer*, 26 May 1915, p. 7, col. d.

495 *Chichester Observer*, 7 October 1914, p. 8, col. d.

496 *Bognor Observer*, 11 November 1914, p. 5, col. c.

497 *Worthing Gazette*, 19 January 1916, p. 6, col. f.

498 *West Sussex Gazette*, 4 January 1917, p. 7, col. d.

499 *Mid-Sussex Times*, 1 August 1916, p. 3, col. c.

500 *Ibid.*

501 *West Sussex Gazette*, 25 April 1918, p. 7, col. e.

502 *Chichester Observer*, 5 August 1914, p. 5, col. e.

503 *Chichester Observer*, 7 June 1916, p. 4, col. c.

504 *Ibid.*

505 *Chichester Observer*, 16 June 1915, p. 4, col. a.

506 *West Sussex County Times*, 4 December 1915, p. 5, col. d.

507 *West Sussex County Times*, 1 May 1915, p. 5, col. a.

508 *West Sussex County Times*, 15 May 1915, p. 8, col. d.

509 *West Sussex County Times*, 10 July 1915, p. 8, col. c.

510 *Sussex and Surrey Courier*, 7 August 1915, p. 5, col. c.

511 *Sussex and Surrey Courier*, 25 December 1915, p. 8, col. e.

512 *West Sussex County Times*, 2 December 1916, p. 4, col. a.

513 *West Sussex County Times*, 6 January 1917, p. 3, col. b.

514 *West Sussex County Times*, 20 May 1916, p. 5, col. e.

515 *West Sussex County Times*, 7 April 1917, p. 4, col. d.

516 *West Sussex County Times*, 20 January 1917 p. 4, col. a & 17 February 1917, p. 3, col. g.

517 *Chichester Observer*, 30 June 1915, p. 5, col. a.

518 *West Sussex Gazette*, 4 May 1916, p. 8, col. d.

519 *Chichester Observer*, 1 December 1915, p. 3, col. f.
520 *Worthing Gazette*, 21 June1916, p. 6, col. a.
521 *Worthing Gazette*, 9 December 1914, p. 7, col. b.
522 *West Sussex County Times*, 17 April 1915, p. 5, col. f.
523 *Worthing Gazette*, 9 December 1914, p. 7, col. b.
524 *Worthing Gazette*, 23 September 1914, p. 5, col. e.
525 *West Sussex County Times*, 5 September 1914, p. 8, col. d.
526 *Worthing Gazette*, 16 September 1914, p. 5, col. f.
527 *Chichester Observer*, 21 April 1915, p. 5, cols c–d.
528 *Chichester Observer*, 28 April 1915, p. 4, col. b.
529 *Littlehampton Observer*, 2 June 1915, p. 3, col. b.
530 *Worthing Gazette*, 14 June 1916, p. 3, col. b.
531 *Worthing Gazette*, 21 July 1915, p. 3, col. d.
532 *Mid-Sussex Times*, 1 August 1916, p. 8, col. b.
533 *West Sussex Gazette*, 16 December 1915, p. 2, col. d.
534 *Mid-Sussex Times*, 18 July 1916, p. 2, col. e.
535 *Mid-Sussex Times*, 15 August 1916, p. 7, col. c.
536 *Worthing Gazette*, 7 June 1916, p. 5, col. d.
537 *Worthing Gazette*, 4 July 1917, p. 5, col. c.
538 *Worthing Gazette*, 8 August 1917, p. 7, col. c.
539 *Chichester Observer*, 14 & 21 November 1917, p. 3, col. d & p. 3, col. a.
540 *West Sussex County Times*, 13 October 1917, p. 3, col. f.
541 *West Sussex Gazette*, 15 November 1917, p. 3, col. d.
542 *Sussex and Surrey Courier*, 3 August 1918, p. 4, col. e.
543 *Worthing Gazette*, 18 April 1917, p. 6, col. c.
544 www.thewi.org.uk/about-the-wi & www.bbc.co.uk/programmes/p01s2n61.
545 *Mid-Sussex Times*, 8 May 1917, p. 6, col. a.
546 J. Robinson, *A Force To Be Reckoned With, A History of the Women's Institute* (Virago, 2011), p. 56.
547 J. Robinson, *A Force To Be Reckoned With*, p. 57.
548 *West Sussex Gazette*, 6 June 1918, p. 3, col. c.
549 *Mid-Sussex Times*, 11 September 1917, p. 5, col. e.
550 *Mid-Sussex Times*, 11 September 1917, p. 5, col. d.
551 *Mid-Sussex Times*, 11 September 1917, p. 5, col. e.
552 www.thewi.org.uk/about-the-wi.
553 *Mid-Sussex Times*, 17 December 1918, p. 4, col. c.
554 *Mid-Sussex Times*, 11 September 1917, p. 5, col. e.
555 *Mid-Sussex Times*, 16 March 1915, p. 4, col. g.
556 *Mid-Sussex Times*, 16 March 1915, p. 4, col. g.
557 *Worthing Gazette*, 7 July 1915, p. 6, col. e.
558 *West Sussex Gazette*, 8 July 1915, p. 11, col. f.
559 *Sussex and Surrey Courier*, 29 April 1916, p. 2, col. d.
560 *Worthing Gazette*, 7 July 1915, p. 6, col. e.
561 *Worthing Gazette*, 7 July 1915, p. 6, col. d.
562 *Sussex and Surrey Courier*, 29 April 1916, p. 2, col. d.
563 *Sussex and Surrey Courier*, 3 June 1916, p. 5, col. d.
564 *Chichester Observer*, 19 April 1916, p. 4, col. e.

565 *Chichester Observer*, 19 July 1916, p. 2, col. b.
566 *Mid-Sussex Times*, 3 April 1917, p. 5, col. a.
567 *Ibid.*
568 *West Sussex Gazette*, 25 April 1918, p. 2, col. d.
569 *Ibid.*
570 *Mid-Sussex Times*, 26 June 1917, p. 3, col. c.
571 *Sussex and Surrey Courier*, 28 April 1917, p. 2, col. c.
572 *West Sussex Gazette*, 17 October 1918, p. 2, col. c.

Chapter 8

573 *Mid-Sussex Times*, 17 August 1915, p. 7.
574 WSRO HCGR/2/1 Graylingwell Hospital 23rd annual report, 1920. For more detailed information about Graylingwell, see: K. Slay, *Graylingwell War Hospital, 1915–1919*, New Chichester Papers no.5, 2013, available from WSRO.
575 *Worthing Gazette*, 1 May 1918, p. 6.
576 *West Sussex Gazette*, 9 November 1916, p. 2.
577 *Chichester Observer*, 4 November 1914, p. 6.
578 These eyewitness reports on each missing man were compiled from many sources, and some can be seen on the internet. For example, www.awm.gov.au/research/people/wounded_and_missing To see one that Violet Lady Beaumont (V. Beaumont) had written, enter Egan (name) and 1671 (service number).
579 *Mid-Sussex Times*, 14 March 1916, p. 4.
580 *Mid-Sussex Times*, 22 February 1916, p. 3; 27 February 1917, p. 6; 5 February 1918, p. 4.
581 *West Sussex Gazette*, 31 May 1917, p. 8.
582 *Bognor Observer*, 30 January 1918, p. 2.
583 *Worthing Gazette*, 5 June 1918, p. 2.
584 *Worthing Gazette*, 1 December 1915, p. 5; *West Sussex County Times*, 4 May 1918, p. 4.
585 *West Sussex Gazette*, 26 October 1916, p. 9.
586 *Worthing Gazette*, 26 June 1918, p. 7.
587 *West Sussex County Times*, 6 November 1915, p. 8.
588 *Mid-Sussex Times*, 2 January 1917, p. 5.
589 *Sussex and Surrey Courier*, 16 November 1918, p. 3.

Chapter 9

590 *BBC History Magazine*, January 2014, pp. 28–30.
591 Wilkinson, A., *The Church of England and the First World War* (London, SCM Press Ltd, 1978, 1996), p. 57.
592 Wilkinson, p. 9.
593 *Chichester Observer,* 12 August 1914, p. 6, col. f – CO1914JultoSep036.doc.
594 *West Sussex County Times,* 29 August 1914, p. 7, col. f – WSCT1914JultoSep00107.
595 *West Sussex Gazette*, 16 September 1914, p. 2, cols e–f – WSG1914OcttoDec020.

596 *Littlehampton Observer*, 25 November 1914, p. 8, col. d –
LO1914OcttoDec203.

597 MacCulloch, D., *A History of Christianity* (London, Penguin, 2010),
p. 917.

598 *West Sussex County Times,* 8 August 1914, p. 5, col. g –
WSCT1914JultoSep13.

599 *Worthing Gazette*, 23 September 1914, p. 2, col. c –
WG1914JultoSep107.

600 *Chichester Observer,* 4 August 1915, p. 5, cols a–b –
CO1915JulytoSept041.

601 *Chichester Observer*, 9 September 1914, p. 5, col. d –
CO1914JultoSep115.doc.

602 *Chichester Observer*, 4 and 11 November 1914, p. 5,
col. b in each case – CO1914OcttoDec05.7.doc and
CO1914OcttoDec072.doc.

603 *Mid-Sussex Times*, 1 August 1914, p. 3, cols a–b –
MST1914JulytoSept055.

604 *Chichester Observer,* 4 August 1914, p. 5, cols a–b –
CO1915JulytoSept041.

605 *Worthing Gazette*, 29 July 1914, p. 7, col. c –
WG1914JultoSep025.

606 *West Sussex Gazette*, 12 September 1914, p. 5, cols b–c –
WSG1914JultoSep57.

607 *West Sussex Gazette*, 13 June 1918, p. 7, col. e –
WSG1918AprtoJune151.

608 Wilkinson, p. 319. The Archbishop was only supported by a
minority of clergy, although he had the official support of the
Free Church Council.

609 Grieves, K., *Sussex in the First World War* (Lewes: *SRS* vol. 84,
2000), p. 246.

610 Fernhurst parish magazines WSRO, Par 82/7.

611 Fernhurst parish magazine, Jan 1917 WSRO, Par 82/7/10.

612 News on Andrew Warden-Morris in Fernhurst parish magazine,
April 1917, WSRO, Par 82/7/10.

613 Fernhurst parish magazine, November 1917 WSRO, Par 82/7.

614 As an epitaph to wartime Fernhurst, it is interesting to note the
census figures for 1911 and 1921. In 1911 there were 654 men and
650 women – about equal numbers. Ten years later, the village
had not grown significantly: from 1304 to 1397. However, there
were 799 women, and only 598 men – the effect of the war on
the population of Fernhurst, and particularly that of its young
men had been critical. *Census of England and Wales, 1911:
County of Sussex* WSRO, Lib no. 15502; and *Census of England
and Wales, 1921: County of Sussex* WSRO, Lib no. 15501.

615 Fernhurst parish magazine, April 1917 WSRO, Par 82/7/10.

Chapter 10

616 R.E. Prothero, president of the Board of Agriculture,
December 1916, cited in J. Sheail, 'The role of the war

agricultural and executive committees in the food production campaign of 1915–1918 in England and Wales' *Agricultural administration,* 1 (1974), p. 144.

617 E. Whetham, *The Agrarian History of England and Wales 1914–1939* , Vol. 8 (Cambridge University Press, 1978), p. 70.

618 *West Sussex County Times*, 5 September 1914, p. 6, col. d.

619 *Chichester Observer*, 9 September 1914, p. 2, cols c–d.

620 K. Grieves, *Sussex in the First World War* (Sussex Record Society, 2004), pp. 58–69.

621 *Chichester Observer*, 25 August 1915, p. 6, col. c.

622 *Littlehampton Observer*, 15 May 1915, p. 7, cols d–e.

623 *Worthing Gazette*, 24 November 1915, p. 3, col. d; J. Chapman and S. Seeliger, 'The influence of the Agricultural Executive committees in the First World War: Some Evidence from West Sussex' *Southern History,* 13 (1991), pp. 105–22.

624 P.E. Dewey, *British Agriculture in the First World War* (Routledge 1989).

625 *Chichester Observer*, 5 July 1916, p. 5, col. c.

626 *Worthing Gazette*, 27 September 1916, p. 6, col. d; *West Sussex Gazette* 5 October 1916, p. 12, col. c and 9 November 1916, p. 12, col. f.

627 *British Parliamentary Papers* (*BPP*), 8 February 1916: Departmental committee on the settlement and employment of sailors and soldiers on the land. W.J. Passmore (Member of the West Sussex Farmers' Union) evidence, para 6414. And also Royal Commission on Agriculture 1920 [cmd. 665], Vol. V, evidence on 5 November 1919, p. 32.

628 *Sussex and Surrey Courier*, 18 March 1916, p. 2, col. f; 25 March 1916, p. 5, col. f.

629 *West Sussex Gazette*, 4 April 1918, p. 2, col. e.

630 *Chichester Observer*, 21 October 1914, p. 2, col. f; 18 November 1914, p. 3, col. c; *West Sussex Gazette*, 21 October 1915, p. 3, cols c–d.

631 Dewey, *British Agriculture in the First World War*, p. 47, citing WSRO, WOC/CM82/1/1 *22 January 1917 – 19 November 1917.*

632 *West Sussex Gazette*, 18 January 1917, p. 3, col. d; R.W. Standing, *East Preston and Kingston in the Great War: Two Villages and Parishes in West Sussex a Century Ago* (privately printed, 2013), p. 27.

633 The National Archives, MAF 42. Board of Agriculture and Fisheries, Food Production Department Correspondence and Papers 1915–1920.

634 *BPP* Geo V Year 8, cc 921–1056. 23 July 1917. Corn production. A bill [as amended in committee] for encouraging the production of corn, and for purposes connected therewith (including provision as to agricultural wages and rents).

635 A.F. Cooper, *British Agricultural Policy, 1912–36: A Study in Conservative Politics* (Manchester University Press 1989), p. 41.

And *BPP*, evidence to the Royal Commission on Agriculture 1920 [cmd. 665], Vol. V, evidence on 15 and 19 January 1920, pp. 54–63, 91–100.

636 Lord Ernle [R.E. Prothero], *English Farming Past and Present* (6th edn Heinemann and Frank Cass 1961 [1920]), p. 401.

637 T. Middleton, *Food Production in War* (Clarendon, 1923), p. 174; P. Horn, *Rural Life in England in the First World War* (Gill and Macmillan, 1984), p. 51.

638 Sheail, 'The role of the war agricultural and executive committees', p. 147.

639 *Chichester Observer*, 17 January 1917, p. 8, cols d–e.

640 Grieves, *Sussex in the First World War,* p. 219; WSRO, Blunt Mss Box 64, W.S. Blunt to Lady Anne Blunt, 18 August 1917.

641 *Sussex and Surrey Courier*, 16 June 1917, p. 2, col. f.

642 Dewey, *British Agriculture in the First World War* pp. 172–4 and 180. The Coolhurst survey was reported in the West Sussex Executive Committee report on the land survey 1917, pp. 6–7.

643 *Chichester Observer*, 9 August 1916, p. 5, col. e.

644 *West Sussex County Times*, 9 February 1918, p. 3, col. d.

645 P. Dewey, *'Iron Harvests of the Field': The Making of Farm Machinery in Britain Since 1800* (Carnegie 2008), p. 173.

646 Dewey, *British Agriculture in the First World War,* pp. 60–2.

647 Chapman and Seeliger, 'The influence of the Agricultural Executive committees', p. 116.

648 *West Sussex County Times*, 31 March 1917, p. 4, col. d.

649 Whetham, *The Agrarian History of England and Wales*, p. 112.

650 J.A. Venn, *The foundations of agricultural economics together with an economic history of British agriculture during and after the Great War* (Cambridge University Press, 2nd edn 1933 [1923]), pp. 488–92; Dewey, *British agriculture in the First World War,* pp. 206–7.

651 R.H.B. Jesse, *A Survey of the Agriculture of Sussex* (Royal Agricultural Society of England, 1960), pp. 100–4.

652 *West Sussex County Times*, 13 January 1917, p. 2, col. g; *Chichester Observer* 17 January 1917, pp. 2, cols c–d, p. 7, cols a–b.

653 *West Sussex Gazette*, 18 April 1918, p. 7, col. g.

654 *Chichester Observer*, 7 February 1917, p. 6, cols c–d.

655 Dewey, *British Agriculture in the First World War*, p. 193.

656 L. Acton, 'Allotment Gardens: A Reflection of History, Heritage, Community and Self' *Papers from the Institute of Archaeology* 21 (2011), pp. 46–58.

657 *Chichester Observer*, 12 August 1914, p. 5, col. c; B.W. Harvey and C. Fitzgerald, *Edward Heron-Allen's Journal of the Great War* (Sussex Record Society, 2002), pp. 6–7, 28–9, 181.

658 *Worthing Gazette*, 23 June 1915, p. 7, col. c.

659 *West Sussex County Times*, 31 March 1917, p. 3, col. e.

660 *Bognor Observer*, 6 March 1918, p. 2, cols b–e.

661 Grieves, *Sussex in the First World War,* pp. 223–9;

Worthing Gazette, 22 August 1917, p. 5, col. e; *Chichester Observer*, 19 September 1917, p. 1, col. e.

662 I. Beckett, *Home Front 1914–1918: How Britain Survived the Great War* (National Archives, 2006), pp. 114–21.

663 Harvey and Fitzgerald, *Edward Heron-Allen's Journal*, p. 139.

664 W. Wood, *A Sussex Farmer* (Jonathan Cape 1938), p. 128.

665 *BPP* 1919, 51, Agricultural Statistics 1918, p. 6.

666 W.J. Passmore evidence to Royal Commission on Agriculture 1920, p. 40.

667 A. Offer, *The First World War: an Agrarian Interpretation* (Clarendon Press, 1989), pp. 81, 221.

Chapter 11

668 For discussion of Blighty as differentiated places see K. Grieves, 'The Propinquity of Place: Home, Landscape and Soldier Poets of the First World War' in J. Meyer (ed.) *British Popular Culture and the First World War* (Brill, 2008), pp. 21–46.

669 Personal observation 20 July 1997; PAR 14/4/19 Faculty for War Memorial Tablet 14 June 1920 (WSRO).

670 Personal observation, 13 July 1997.

671 PAR 29/7/13 Broadwater Roll of Honour, undated (WSRO); PAR 234/7/6 Balcombe, Incumbent's list of men killed in the First World War, undated (WSRO).

672 G.D. Sheffield and G.I.S. Inglis (eds), *From Vimy Ridge to the Rhine. The Great War Letters of Christopher Stone DSO MC* (The Crowood Press, 1989); Letter dated 28 July 1916, p. 63; P. Reed 'Rusper and the Two World Wars' in *The Men Who Marched Away*. Rusper War Memorial (Averys Press, 1991) p. 4; See also Lady Maxse, *The Story of Fittleworth* (National Review, 1935), p. 97 for a returned soldier's perspective on the local list of names of those who joined the army.

673 PAR 27/12/1 Boxgrove, annual vestry meeting, 13 Apr 1915 (WSRO).

674 PAR 27/12/1 Boxgrove, special vestry meeting, 12 October 1915 (WSRO).

675 PAR 202/7/24 Walberton parish magazine, August 1918 (WSRO).

676 B.W. Harvey and C. Fitzgerald (eds), *Edward Heron-Allen's Journal of the Great War. From Sussex Shore to Flanders Fields* (Sussex Record Society, 2002), p. 276.

677 PAR 223/7/9 *St Paul's Church Magazine*, Worthing, vicar's column, September 1918, p. 34 and June 1919, p. 24 (WSRO).

678 N. Divers, 'Southwick Men in the Great War', *West Sussex History* 61 (April 1998), p. 5.

679 *West Sussex County Times*, 26 July 1919, p. 5.

680 *West Sussex County Times*, 29 November 1919, p. 6.

681 *West Sussex County Times*, 8 March 1919, p. 5.

682 PAR 183/7/3 Steyning War Memorial Committee, note of proceedings, 1919 (WSRO).

683 PAR 122/4/10 West Lavington war memorial account book, undated [1922] (WSRO).

684 PAR197/12/3, Tillington vestry minute book (WSRO).

685 PAR 197/4/3 Tillington, minutes of vestry meeting, 14 May 1920 and Faculty dated 13 August 1920 (WSRO).

686 RSR MS 11/8 Order of Service on the Feast of St George, 23 April 1919 (WSRO); *Sussex Daily News*, 23 December 1919, p. 5, 27 March 1919, p. 5, 29 April 1919, p. 5.

687 RSR MS 11/7 programme, choral commemoration of the heroic deeds of the first seven divisions, Mons to Ypres 1914, Royal Albert Hall, 15 December 1917 (WSRO).

688 RSR MS 11/9 Order of Service, Chapel of St George restored by the RSR as a thank-offering memorial to all ranks who fell in the war, 11 November 1921 (WSRO); G. Pass 'The Royal Sussex Regiment in the First World War', *Sussex County Magazine* 18(4) (April 1944) pp. 128–132; A. Mee, *Sussex* (Hodder and Stoughton, 1937, 1964 edn), p. 44; *Sussex Daily News*, 11 November 1921, p. 5, 12 November 1921, p. 5; S.P.B. Mais, *Sussex* (Richards, undated), p. 30.

689 RSR MS 11/14 St George's Chapel Fund, Col. W.S. Osborn to Lt-Col V. Dashwood, 24 May 1934 (WSRO).

690 PAR 27/12/1 Boxgrove, minutes of vestry meeting, 4 August 1919 (WSRO).

691 PAR 122/4/10 West Lavington, invoice, undated [September 1922] (WSRO).

692 PAR 223/7/9 *St Paul's Church Parish Magazine*, Worthing, September 1918, p. 34 (WSRO).

693 PAR 176/4/9 Slinfold war memorial, letters, suggestions for war memorials, July 1919 (WSRO).

694 *West Sussex County Times*, 24 May 1919, p. 6; 18 October 1919 p. 5; 25 October 1919 p. 6; 1 November 1919 p. 5; 22 February 1920 p. 5; 28 February 1920, p. 5.

695 W.F. Sellens, 'Sussex War Memorials "Pro rege et patria"', *Sussex County Magazine*, 8 (11) (November 1934), p. 694.

696 *Sussex Daily News*, 10 July 1919, p. 5.

697 *Sussex Daily News*, 22 January 1920, p. 5.

698 *Sussex Daily News*, 20 January 1919 p. 5.

699 Knebworth MSS Q.201204, Neville Lytton to Lord Lytton, 12 September 1925 (Knebworth House); *The Times*, 12 November 1923; N. Lytton, *English Country Gentleman* (Hurst and Blackett, 1924), p. 163.

700 Goodwood Ms 1370, Thomas Webb-Roley to the Duke of Richmond, 16 January 1919 (WSRO).

701 Goodwood Ms 1318, Guy Woodman to the Duke of Richmond, Lavant War Memorial Hall draft conveyance, 20 October 1921.

702 Mr R.H. Brooks, letter to the author, 2 October 2000, enclosing typescript copy of an article by Gerard Young, *The Bognor Post*, 14 November 1970.

703 PAR 176/43/4 Slinfold war memorial, letter by J.H. Dobbie, 6 October 1920 (WSRO).
704 PAR 6/7/7 Angmering war memorial, minutes of public meeting, 14 January 1919 (WSRO); *Sussex Daily News*, 16 January 1919, p. 6.
705 PAR 9/12/1 Ashington minutes of special vestry meeting, 3 November 1919 (WSRO).
706 PAR 6/7/7 Angmering war memorial, minutes of war memorial committee meeting, 4 March 1919 (WSRO); *Sussex Daily News*, 22 January 1918 p. 3; 'Obituaries Philip M. Johnston', *Sussex Notes and Queries*, 6(5) (February 1937), pp. 152–3.
707 PAR 6/7/7 Angmering war memorial, minutes of second public meeting, 1 April 1919 (WSRO); *Sussex Daily News*, 28 May 1920, p. 2.
708 F. Mee, *A History of Selsey* (Phillimore, 1988), p. 99.
709 D. Peace, *Eric Gill. The Inscriptions: A Descriptive Catalogue* (The Herbert Press, 1994), p. 92.
710 N. Divers, 'Southwick Men in the Great War', *West Sussex History*, 61 (April 1998), p. 3.
711 *Sussex Daily News*, 14 November 1919, p. 2.
712 PAR 202/7/24 *Walberton Parish Magazine*, March 1918 (WSRO).
713 D. Peace, *Eric Gill*, pp. 18, 89, 96; T.J. McCann 'Eric Gill's Inscriptional Work in Ditchling' in P. Holliday (ed.), *Eric Gill in Ditchling. Four Essays* (Oak Knoll Press, 2002), pp. 29–50.
714 A. Vallance, *Old Crosses and Lychgates* (Batsford, 1920), p. vii; PAR 177/4/9 Sompting, Faculty for war memorial lychgate, 1920; PAR 190/4/8 Sullington, Faculty for the erection of a lych-gate, 27 October 1931.
715 PAR 113/14/1 Itchingfield, minutes of meetings of Parochial Church Council, 2 November 1926 and 21 February 1927 (WSRO).
716 PAR 113/14/1 Itchingfield, minutes of meetings of Parochial Church Council, 27 July and 12 December 1932 (WSRO). The reredos at St Nicholas' church is a thank-offering for victory and peace in the 1914–1918 war.
717 Bishop Southwell, 'St George's Day', *The Roussillon Gazette*, 18(1) (May 1930) pp. 27–8 (WSRO); *Sussex Daily News*, 24 April 1925, p. 5; 24 April 1928, p. 5; 24 April 1930, p. 5; 24 April 1939, p. 4.
718 RSR MS 4/107 account of the 4th Battalion, (TA) 1908–40, J.F. Ainsworth, undated (WSRO).
719 *A Short History of the Royal Sussex Regiment* 1701–1926 (Gale and Polden, 1927) p.viii, 80, 97.
720 RSR MS 11/18 *Memorials, Colours, Standards and Badges, Royal Sussex Regiment* (WSRO); A. Windrum, *Horsham: A Historical Survey* (Phillimore, 1978), p. 111.
721 RSR MS 4/93 scrapbook of newspaper cuttings, letter C.R.B. Godman, 6 June [1934] untitled newspaper (WSRO); *West Sussex County Times*, 14 August 1936, p. 5; *HMSO Soldiers Died in the Great War: Part 40 The Royal Sussex*

Regiment (HMSO, 1921); D.W. Lloyd Battlefield, *Tourism, Pilgrimage and the Commemoration of the Great War in Britain, Australia and Canada 1919–1939* (Berg, 1998), p. 100.

722 E. Blunden, 'Preliminary' to his *Undertones of War* (Penguin, 1982 edn), p. 8.

723 E. Blunden, *We'll Shift Our Ground or Two on a Tour: Almost a Novel* (Cobden-Sanderson, 1933) pp. 180–2.

724 E. Blunden, 'We went to Ypres' in his *The Mind's Eye* (Jonathan Cape, 1934), pp. 47–9; B. Webb Edmund, *Blunden. A Biography* (Yale University Press, 1990), pp. 98, 101.

725 A. Mee, *Sussex*, pp. 201–2.

726 A. Mee, *Sussex*, pp. 154–5.

727 *Sussex Daily News*, 10 March 1919 letter by H. Linfold Beale, dated 7 March 1919; *Sussex Daily News*, 10 July 1919, letter by 'Sussex Man' dated 10 July 1919.

728 PAR 33/4/4 Bury vestry meeting 17 May 1921, invoices and Faculty, 1 July 1921 (WSRO).

729 *Kelly's Directory of Sussex* (Kelly's, 1924), p. 76.

730 IWM 252/6 N. Lytton to the Director, Imperial War Museum, 27 October 1942 (Imperial War Museum).

731 A. Mee, *Sussex*, p. 133.

Chapter 12

732 *West Sussex County Times*, 6 May 1916, p. 5 col. d.

733 *Ibid.*

734 *Mid-Sussex Times*, 10 April 1917, p. 8, col. a.

735 *Horsham Times*, 22 August 1914, p. 3, col. d.

736 Meeting of the Executive Council of the Heritage Craft Schools, Chailey, Tuesday 15 June 1915 HB/22/1/121 (East Sussex Record Office).

737 Meeting of the Executive Council of the Heritage Craft Schools, Chailey, Tuesday 15 June 1915 HB/22/1/121 (East Sussex Record Office).

738 *Littlehampton Observer*, 19 August 1914, 2e.

739 *West Sussex Gazette*, 12 December 1918, 2ab.

740 *Worthing Gazette*, 1 August 1917, 6c.

741 *Worthing Gazette*, 18 September 1918, p. 5, col. c.

742 *Ibid.*

743 *West Sussex County Times*, 5 July 1919, p. 3, col. g.

744 Small Holdings and Allotments Committee 25 October 1917, West Sussex County Council Minutes and Agendas.

745 *West Sussex Gazette*, 31 July 1919, p. 2, col. c.

746 *West Sussex Gazette*, 31 July 1919, p. 2, col. c.

747 *West Sussex County Times*, 30 December 1916, p. 3, col. e.

748 *West Sussex Gazette*, 23 May 1918, p. 3, col. b.

749 *Chichester Observer*, 5 December 1917, p. 4, col. g.

750 *Ibid.*

751 *West Sussex Gazette*, 3 October 1918, p. 6, cols a–b.

752 *Mid-Sussex Times*, 12 August 1919, p. 3, col. a.

753 *Chichester Observer*, 7 August 1918, p. 1, col. e.
754 *Mid-Sussex Times*, 23 September 1919, p. 7, col. c.
755 *Ibid.*
756 *Worthing Gazette*, 15 October 1919, p. 7, col. c.
757 *Worthing Gazette*, 10 May 1916, p. 6, col. e.
758 *Bognor Observer*, 24 April 1918, p. 2, col. d.
759 *Chichester Observer*, 31 October 1917, p. 2, col. e.
760 Agricultural Education Committee, 31 December 1917, West Sussex County Council Minutes and Agendas.
761 Agricultural Education Committee, 8 April 1918, West Sussex County Council Minutes and Agendas.
762 Finance, Legal and Parliamentary Committee, Worthing Borough Council, 4 February 1916.
763 Finance, Legal and Parliamentary Committee, Worthing Borough Council, 4 February 1916.
764 Finance, Legal and Parliamentary Committee, Worthing Borough, 21 September 1917.
765 *Chichester Observer*, 27 October 1915, p. 8, cols e–f & *Worthing Gazette*, 27 October 1915, p. 7, col. b.
766 J. Winter, *The Great War and the British People* (Palgrave Macmillan, 2003[1985]), pp. 273–4.
767 J. Winter, *The Great War and the British People* (Palgrave Macmillan, 2003[1985]), pp. 273–4.
768 Census of England & Wales 1921: County of Sussex, (HMSO, London, 1923), p. xxiv.
769 *Worthing Gazette*, 3 September 1919, p. 5, col. f.
770 *Ibid.*
771 *Ibid.*
772 *Ibid.*
773 *Worthing Gazette*, 10 September 1919, p. 7, col. c, & *The Times*, 3 September 1919 & 2 October 1919.
774 *Worthing Gazette*, 8 October 1919, p. 7, col. c.
775 *Worthing Gazette*, 29 October 1919, p. 6, col. d.
776 *Mid-Sussex Times Supplement*, 27 May 1919.
777 *Mid-Sussex Times*, 18 March 1919, p. 7, cols a–b.
778 *Mid-Sussex Times*, 18 March 1919, p. 7, cols a–b.
779 *West Sussex County Times*, 20 September 1919, p. 5, col. e & *West Sussex County Times*, 24 November 1917, p. 3, col. d.
780 *Worthing Gazette*, 2 April 1919, p. 6, col. c.
781 *West Sussex Gazette*, 18 April 1918, p. 7, col. c.
782 *West Sussex County Times*, 13 March 1920, p. 5, col. e.
783 *Mid-Sussex Times*, 1 April 1919, p. 2, cols a–b.
784 *Mid-Sussex Times*, 18 May 1920, p. 7, cols c–d.
785 *West Sussex County Times*, 13 March 1920, p. 5, col. e.
786 *West Sussex County Times*, 20 September 1919, p. 5, col. e.
787 *Sussex and Surrey Courier*, 25 March 1916, p. 8, cols e–f.
788 *Ibid.*
789 *West Sussex Gazette*, 30 May 1918, p. 3, col. d.
790 *Mid-Sussex Times*, 30 September 1919, p. 7, col. d.

791 *Ibid.*

792 *West Sussex County Times*, 19 January 1918, p. 4, col. d.

793 *Mid-Sussex Times*, 30 September 1919, p. 2, col. c.

794 *Worthing Gazette*, 5 July 1916, p. 5, col. c.

795 *Ibid.*

796 *Mid-Sussex Times*, 20 May 1919, p. 2, col. d.

797 *West Sussex County Times*, 1 June 1918, p. 4, col. a &
     West Sussex Gazette, 6 June 1918, p. 7, col. e.

798 *Worthing Gazette*, 19 February 1919, p. 6, col. e.

799 W.I.B. Beveridge, *Influenza: The Last Great Plague* (Heineman
     Educational Books Ltd, 1977), p. 31.

800 W.I.B. Beveridge, *Influenza: The Last Great Plague* (Heineman
     Educational Books Ltd, 1977), p. 31.

801 West Sussex Annual Health Reports for 1917 & 1918, WSRO
     WDC/HE2/1/2.

802 West Sussex Annual Health Reports for 1917 & 1918, WSRO
     WDC/HE2/1/2.

803 *Chichester Observer*, 30 October 1918, p. 3, col. e & *Sussex and
     Surrey Courier*, 2 November 1918, p. 4, col. f.

804 *Worthing Gazette*, 5 March 1919, p. 2, col. d.

805 *Mid-Sussex Times*, 26 November 1918, p. 1, col. d.

806 *Mid-Sussex Times*, 18 November 1919, p. 7, col. d.

807 *West Sussex County Times*, 15 February 1919, p. 4, col. c.

808 *Ibid.*

809 *Mid-Sussex Times*, 10 December 1918, p. 8, col. c.

810 West Sussex Annual Health Reports for 1919, WSRO WDC/
     HE2/1/2.

Postscript

811 L.F. Salzman (ed.), *Victoria History of the County of Sussex*,
     Vol. 7; *The Rape of Lewes* (Oxford University Press/University
     of London Institute of Historical Research, 1940), p. 173.

812 *Sussex County Magazine*, Vol. VIII No.4, April 1934, p. 274.

813 *Mid-Sussex Times*, 24 December 1918, p. 5.

814 *Clarke's Mid-Sussex Directory* (Clarke's Ltd, 1914), p. 286.

815 *Mid-Sussex Times*, 31 December 1918, p. 8.

FURTHER RESEARCH

West Sussex Record Office and West Sussex County Council Library Service have substantial collections on the First World War, useful for general, military, local and family history research. Free comprehensive research guides, listing books, records, websites and how to access them, may be downloaded from the Great War West Sussex 1914–18 website: www.westsussexpast.org.uk.

This website has over 90 original pieces of research on soldiers and topics, over 200 newspaper articles, indexes to nearly 10,000 events and 14,000 servicemen and other people, educational resources for schools, RSR battalion war diaries and research advice.

For research on individual soldiers, who served in the First World War, see the campaign medal cards, service papers and pension papers at The National Archives and now online on the Ancestry subscription website (available at WSRO and Worthing, Crawley and Horsham libraries).

Digitised Local Newspapers

Some ten local newspapers, 1914 to 1925, were digitised as part of the Great War project and all are now available at WSRO, Crawley and Worthing libraries, plus each relevant town library. They are keyword searchable pdf files, meaning that you can look for individual names, topics or any word in the text recognised by the OCR (Optical Character Recognition) software:

Bognor Observer	*Mid-Sussex Times*
Chichester Observer	*Sussex & Surrey Courier*
East Grinstead Observer	*West Sussex County Times*
Littlehampton Observer	*West Sussex Gazette*
Horsham Times	*Worthing Gazette*

Royal Sussex Regimental Archive

This archive at WSRO, deposited by The Royal Sussex Regiment Museum Trust, is one the finest collections on a county regiment in the UK and is particularly rich in Great War material.

The archive consists of some 200 boxes of documents, 40,000 photographs, 1,250 printed books and periodicals, and 50 films. These are derived from both official and private sources covering the history of the regiment from its establishment in 1701 as the 35th Regiment of Foot to its amalgamation in The Queen's Regiment in 1966.

First World War records include:

Nominal rolls
Casualty lists
Unit war diaries
Battalion orders
Regimental and battalion journals
Newspaper cuttings albums
Personal papers, letters and diaries, and photographs of officers
    and other ranks

Contacts

West Sussex County Council website: www.westsussex.gov.uk. Libraries and Record Office are listed under 'Leisure'.

BIBLIOGRAPHY

Books and Articles

P. Abbott, *The British Airship at War 1914–1918* (Terence Dalton Ltd, 1989).

K. Adie, *Fighting on the Home Front: The Legacy of Women in World War One* (Hodder & Stoughton, 2013).

Anon., *A Short History of The Royal Sussex Regiment 1701–1926* (Gale & Polden, 1927).

Anon., 'Work in Great Britain: notes on military hospitals', *Nursing Times*, 12 June 1915, p. 728.

J.A. Baines, *The Day Sussex Died: A History of Lowther's Lambs to the Boar's Head Massacre* (Royal Sussex Living History Group, 2012).

M. Barrett., *West Sussex Constabulary 110 Years of History: April 1857 – December 1967* (Malcolm Barrett, 2008).

BBC History Magazine, January 2014.

I. Beckett, *Home Front 1914–1918: How Britain Survived the Great War* (National Archives, 2006).

W.I.B. Beveridge, *Influenza: The Last Great Plague* (Heineman Educational Books Ltd, 1977).

J. Blackwell, 'The Selsey Sound Mirror', *Sussex Industrial Archaeology Society Newsletter* (144) (2009).

J.P. Blake (ed.), *The Official Regulations for Volunteer Training Corps and for County Volunteer Organisations (England and Wales),* (Central Association Volunteer Training Corps, 1916).

E. Blunden, 'Preliminary' to his *Undertones of War* (Penguin, 1982 edn).

E. Blunden, *The Mind's Eye* (Jonathan Cape, 1934).

E. Blunden, *Undertones of War* (Cobden-Sanderson, Revised Edition, 1930).

E. Blunden, *We'll Shift Our Ground or Two on a Tour: Almost a Novel* (Cobden-Sanderson, 1933).

T. Bowser, *The Story of British VAD Work in the Great War* (Andrew Melrose Ltd, 1917).

Richard Buckman, *The Royal Sussex Regiment. Military Honours & Awards 1864–1920* (J & KH Publishing, 2001).

C. Butler, *West Sussex Under Attack: Anti-Invasion Sites 1500–1990* (Tempus, 2008).

R. Byron and D. Coxon, *Tangmere, Famous Royal Air Force Fighter Station, An Authorised History* (Grub Street, London, 2013).

J. Chapman and S. Seeliger, 'The influence of the Agricultural Executive committees in the First World War: some evidence from West Sussex', *Southern History*, 13 (1991), pp. 105–22.

G.T. Chesney, *The Battle for Dorking* (Blackwoods Magazine, 1871).

E. Childers, *The Riddle of the Sands* (Smith, Elder & Co., 1903).

C. Cole, E.F. Cheesman, *The Air Defence of Britain 1914–1918* (Putnam, 1984).

D. Collett Wadge (ed.), *Women in Uniform* (Sampson Low, Marston & Co. Ltd, 1946).

P.E. Dewey, *British Agriculture in the First World War* (Routledge, 1989).

P.E. Dewey, *'Iron Harvests of the field': The Making of Farm Machinery in Britain Since 1800* (Carnegie, 2008).

N. Divers, 'Southwick Men in the Great War' in *West Sussex History*, 61 (April 1998).

P. Doyle, *First World War Britain; Shire Living Histories* (Shire Publications Ltd, 2012).

J.H. Dumbrell, *A Short History of the Second Battalion, The Royal Sussex Regiment* (C.A. Ribeiro, 1925).

Lord [R.E. Prothero] Ernle, *English Farming Past and Present* (6th edn Heinemann and Frank Cass 1961 [1920]).

I. Evans, *The White and Thompson/Norman Thompson Flight Company Aircraft Factory in Middleton and Littlehampton (Hubert Williams)* (Ian Evans & WSCC Library Service, 2014) case study for the West Sussex & the Great War Project – www.westsussexpast.org.uk.

A. Eyles, F. Gray & A. Readman, *Cinema West Sussex: The First Hundred Years* (Phillimore & WSCC, 1996).

H. Farrant, *Mid-Victorian Littlehampton: The Railway and the Cross-Channel Steamers* (Littlehampton UDC, 1972).

E.A.C. Fazan, *Cinque Ports Battalion. The Story of the 5th (Cinque Ports) Battalion, The Royal Sussex Regiment* (Royal Sussex Regimental Association, 1971).

'Field Officer', *A Soldier's Sonnets. Verses Grave and Gay* (Birdsall & Son, 1916).

L. German, *How a Century of War Changed the Lives of Women* (Pluto Press, 2013).

J. Godfrey, 'Landscapes of War and Peace: Sussex, the South Downs and the Western Front 1914–18', *Sussex Archaeological Collections*, Vol. 152, Lewes, 2014.

J. Godfrey et al., *A Very Special County: West Sussex County Council, the First 100 Years* (WSCC, 1988).

J. Goodwin, *The Military Defence of West Sussex* (Middleton Press, 1985).

S.R. Grayzel, *Women and the First World War* (Pearson Education Ltd, 2002).

J. Green, *The American Aerodrome in Rustington* (J. Green & WSCC Library Service, 2014) case study for the West Sussex & the Great War Project – www.westsussexpast.org.uk.

J. Grehan, *Battles & Battlefields of Sussex: A Military History of Sussex from the Iron Age to the Second World War* (Historic Military Press, 2001).

J. Grehan & M. Mace, *Battleground Sussex: A Military History of Sussex from the Iron Age to the Present Day* (Pen & Sword, 2012).

K. Grieves, *Sussex in the First World War* (Sussex Record Society, Vol. 84, 2004).

K. Grieves, 'The Propinquity of Place: Home, Landscape and Soldier Poets of the First World War' in J. Meyer (ed.), *British Popular Culture and the First World War* (Brill, 2008).

B. Gudmundsson, 'The Expansion of the British Army During World War I' in M. Strohn (ed.) , *World War I Companion* (Osprey, 2013).

E. Gunston, 'Sussex Beneath the Sea', in *Sussex County Magazine*, 28 (1954).

N. Hanson, *First Blitz – The Secret German Plan to Raze London to the Ground in 1918* (Double Day 2008).

W.E. Harker, *Sussex: At Peace and War* (Southern Publishing, 1918).

D. Harries, *Maritime Sussex* (Seaford, 1997).

B.W. Harvey & C. Fitzgerald, *Edward Heron-Allen's Journal of the Great War, From Sussex Shore to Flanders Field* SRS Vol. 86 (Sussex Record Society, 2002).

P. Holden, *Brave Lads of Sunny Worthing: A Seaside Town During the Great War* (Beckett Features, 1991).

P. Horn, *Rural Life in England in the First World War* (Gill and Macmillan, 1984).

G.I.S. Inglis, *The Kensington Battalion* (Pen & Sword, 2010).

R.H.B. Jesse, *A Survey of the Agriculture of Sussex* (Royal Agricultural Society of England, 1960).

T. Johnston, *The Financiers and the Nation* (Methuen, 1934).

P. Kendall, *The Zeebrugge Raid 1918: The Finest Feat of Arms* (History Press, 2009).

R & B. Larn, *Shipwreck Index of the British Isles – Volume 2* (Lloyds Register of Shipping, 1995).

W. Le Queux, *The Invasion of 1910* (E. Nash, 1906).

K.C. Leslie, *The Great War, Illustrated by Documents from the West Sussex Record Office* (WSCC, 1989).

Oxford Dictionary of National Biography (Oxford University Press, 2004).

D.W. Lloyd, *Battlefield Tourism. Pilgrimage and the Commemoration of the Great War in Britain, Australia and Canada 1919–1939* (Berg, 1998).

P. Longstaff-Tyrrell, *Tyrrell's List – an amalgam – The Artefacts of Two Great Wars in Sussex* (Gotehouse, 2002).

L. Macdonald, *The Roses of No Man's Land* (Papermac, 1980).

G.D. Martineau, *A History of The Royal Sussex Regiment 1701–1953* (Royal Sussex Regimental Association, 1955).

A. Marwick, *Women at War* (Croom Helm, 1977).

Lady Maxse, *The Story of Fittleworth* (National Review, 1935).

T.J. McCann, 'Eric Gill's Inscriptional Work in Ditchling' in P. Holliday (ed.) *Eric Gill in Ditchling: Four Essays* (Oak Knoll Press, 2002).

F. Mee, *A History of Selsey* (Phillimore, 1988).

A. Mee, *Sussex* (Hodder and Stoughton, 2nd edn 1964).

T. Middleton, *Food Production in War* (Clarendon, 1923).

H. Miller, *We Wunt be Druv: The Royal Sussex Regiment on the Western Front 1914–18* (Reveille Press, 2012).

K.W. Mitchinson, *Defending Albion – Britain's Home Army 1908–1919* (Palgrave Macmillan, 2005).

D. Peace, *Eric Gill. The Inscriptions: A Descriptive Catalogue* (The Herbert Press, 1994).

J. Paxman, *Great Britain's Great War* (Viking/Penguin, 2013).

S. Pope, E. Wheal (eds), *The Macmillan Dictionary of the First World War* (Macmillan, 1995).

N. Poulsom, M. Rumble and K. Smith, *Sussex Police Forces* (Middleton Press, 1987).

H.I. Powell-Edwards, *The Sussex Yeomanry and 16th (Sussex Yeomanry) Battalion, Royal Sussex Regiment, 1914–1919* (Andrew Melrose, 1921).

P. Reed, *Forgotten Heroes* (privately printed, Rusper, 1986).

P. Reed, *The Men who Marched Away, Rusper War Memorial* (Averys Press, 1991).

J. Robinson, *A Force To Be Reckoned With, A History of the Women's Institute* (Virago Press, 2012).

O. Rutter, *The History of the Seventh (Service) Battalion, The Royal Sussex Regiment, 1914–1919* (Times Publishing Co., 1934).

W.F. Sellens 'Sussex War Memorials "Pro rege et patria"' in *Sussex County Magazine*, vol. 8 (November 1934).

J. Sheail, 'The role of the war agricultural and executive committees in the food production campaign of 1915–1918 in England and Wales', *Agricultural Administration*, 1 (1974).

G.D. Sheffield and G.I.S. Inglis (eds), *From Vimy Ridge to the Rhine. The Great War Letters of Christopher Stone DSO MC* (The Crowood Press, 1989).

P. Simkins, 'The Four Armies 1914–18' in D. Chandler and I. Beckett (eds), *The Oxford History of the British Army* (Oxford University Press, 1994).

K. Slay, *Graylingwell War Hospital, 1915–1919*, New Chichester Papers no.5 (Chichester Local History Society, 2013).

Soldiers Died in the Great War: Part 40 The Royal Sussex Regiment (HMSO, 1921) [also online via Ancestry, Find My Past and Forces War Records websites].

Bishop Southwell, 'St George's Day' in *The Roussillon Gazette*, 18(1) (May 1930).

N.R. Storey & M. Housego, *Women in the First World War* (Shire Publications, 2010).

M. Taylor, *This Was Rustington, No.3, In Times of War* (privately published, 1989).

G. Thomas, *Life on All Fronts: Women in the First World War* (Cambridge University Press, 1995).

S.C. Tucker, *The Encyclopedia of World War I: A Political, Social, and Military History* (ABC-CLIO Ltd, 2005).

T. Travers, 'The Army and the Challenge of War 1914–18' in D. Chandler and I. Beckett (eds), *The Oxford History of the British Army* (Oxford University Press, 1994).

A. Vallance, *Old Crosses and Lychgates* (Batsford, 1920).

B. Webb, *Edmund Blunden: A Biography* (Yale University Press, 1990).

T.M.A. Webb and D.L. Bird, *Shoreham Airport Sussex, The Story of Britain's Oldest Licensed Airfield* (Cirrus Associates, 1996).

West Sussex Federation of WIs *West Sussex Within Living Memory* (Countryside Books/WSFWI, 1993).

E. Whetham, *The Agrarian History of England and Wales 1914–1939*, vol. 8 (Cambridge university Press, 1978).

A. Wilkinson, *The Church of England and the First World War* (SCM Press Ltd, 1978, 1996).

A. Windrum, *Horsham: A Historical Survey* (Phillimore, 1978).

J. Winter, *The Great War and the British People*, (Palgrave Macmillan, 2003[1985]).

E. Wood, *The Red Cross Story: a pictorial history of 125 years of the British Red Cross* (Dorling Kindersley, 1995).

W. Wood, *A Sussex Farmer* (Jonathan Cape, 1938).

D. Wragg, *Royal Navy Handbook 1914–1918* (Sutton, 2006).

Websites

BBC: www.bbc.co.uk/ww1

Findon Village: www.findonvillage.com

Friends of Shoreham Fort: www.shorehamfort.co.uk

Horsham (Museum) Posters: www.horshamposters.com

Imperial War Museum: www.iwm.org.uk

Long, Long Trail. Royal Sussex Regiment: www.1914–1918.net

Measuring Worth: www.measuringworth.com

National Archives: www.nationalarchives.gov.uk

Royal Sussex Living History Group: www.royalsussex.org.uk.

Royal Sussex Regimental Museum: www.eastbournemuseums.co.uk

Scarletfinders [twentieth-century British military nursing] www.scarletfinders.co.uk

Shoreham By Sea History Portal website: www.shorehambysea.com
Slindon at War: Rodney Gunner: slindonatwarmyblog.wordpress.com
Southdown Battalions: royalsussex-southdowns.co.uk
Sussex War Memorials & Rolls of Honour: www.roll-of-honour.com
Western Front Association: www.westernfrontassociation.com
Women's Institute: www.thewi.org.uk
WSCC Library Service catalogue: www.westsussex.gov.uk
WSRO: Royal Sussex Regiment: www.westsussex.gov.uk

Primary Sources

British Parliamentary Papers 8 February 1916: Departmental committee on the settlement and employment of sailors and soldiers on the land. W.J. Passmore (Member of the West Sussex Farmers' Union) evidence, para 6414.

British Parliamentary Papers 1919, 51, Agricultural Statistics 1918.

British Parliamentary Papers Royal Commission on Agriculture 1920 [cmd. 665], Vol. V, evidence on 5 November 1919 and 15–19 January 1920.

British Parliamentary Papers Geo V Year 8, cc 921–1056. 23 July 1917. Corn production. A bill [as amended in committee] for encouraging the production of corn, and for purposes connected therewith (including provision as to agricultural wages and rents).

British Red Cross RCB/2/5/174/4-7 Annual reports of the Sussex Branch of the British Red Cross Society, Aug 1914–Dec 1915, 1916, 1917, 1918.

Census of England and Wales, 1911: County of Sussex.

Census of England and Wales, 1921: County of Sussex.

Defence of the Realm Act 1914, (4 & 5 Geo.5 c. 29).

Emergency measures in the event of an invasion at WSRO, Add. Mss 51906.

Fernhurst Parish magazines, WSRO, Par 82/7.

Kelly's Directory of Sussex 1913, 1915 & 1918 editions (Kelly's Directories Ltd, 1913–18).

Map of the coasts of Kent and Sussex etc. (air raid, 24–25 September 1917); at The National Archives, MPI 1/612/2.

Medal Rolls Index Cards 1914–20, The National Archives (also online at www.ancestry.co.uk).

Memoranda on air raids and invasion; at WSRO, POL.W/H/15/2.

Minutes of Executive Council of Heritage Craft Schools, Chailey, from 1915, East Sussex Record Office HB122/1/121/1/1 onwards.

National Archives, MAF 42.

Parish Council minutes, parish magazines and other parish records at WSRO.

Special Constables Act 1914 (4 & 5 Geo. c 61).

West Sussex Annual Health Reports, 1917–19 and other years.

West Sussex County Council Minutes and Agendas: Agricultural Education Committee and Small Holdings and Allotments Committee, 1914–18.

West Sussex County Council Summary of Proceedings of Quarterly Meeting (WSCC minutes 1914–18).

Worthing Borough Council minutes: Finance, Legal and Parliamentary Committee 1916 onwards.

WSRO HCGR 2/1 Graylingwell Hospital 23rd annual report, 1920.

WSRO HCRW/30 Annual reports of the Royal West Sussex Hospital, Chichester.

WSRO, WOC/CM82/1/1 *22 January 1917 – 19 November 1917.*

WSRO, Blunt Mss Box 64, W.S. Blunt to Lady Anne Blunt, 18 August 1917.

Detailed lists of Royal Sussex Regiment archives are accessible via these three sources:

A.E. Readman, *The Royal Sussex Regiment. A Catalogue of Records* (West Sussex County Council, 1985).

WSRO Search Online: www.westsussexpast.org.uk/searchonline.

The National Archives: Access to Archives:
www.nationalarchives.gov.uk/a2a/records.aspx?cat=182-rsr&cid=-1#-1

INDEX

Visit our website and discover many other First World War books.

www.thehistorypress.co.uk/first_world_war

The History Press